THE RELATIONSHIP BETWEEN ARTIFICIAL OXYTOCIN (PITOCIN) USE AT BIRTH FOR LABOR INDUCTION OR AUGMENTATION AND THE PSYCHOSOCIAL FUNCTIONING OF 3-YEAR-OLDS

A Dissertation Submitted in Partial Fulfillment of the Requirements for the Degree of Doctor of Philosophy in Clinical Psychology Specialty in Prenatal and Perinatal Psychology

by

Claire Lilian Winstone

Santa Barbara Graduate Institute

December 2008

This is to certify that the dissertation entitled

THE RELATIONSHIP BETWEEN ARTIFICIAL OXYTOCIN (PITOCIN) USE AT BIRTH FOR LABOR INDUCTION OR AUGMENTATION AND THE PSYCHOSOCIAL FUNCTIONING OF 3-YEAR-OLDS

by

Claire Lilian Winstone

is approved in partial fulfillment of the requirements for the degree of Doctor of Philosophy in Clinical Psychology (Speciality in Prenatal and Perinatal Psychology).

Approved by:

David C. Gardner, PhD, Chairperson   August 20, 2008
                                            Date

Joely Gardner, PhD, Committee Member   August 20, 2008
                                              Date

Bobbi Jo Lyman, PhD, Committee Member   December 10, 2008
                                               Date

Jane R. W. Fisher, PhD, External Examiner   1st August 2008
                                                   Date

Abstract

The Relationship Between Artificial Oxytocin (Pitocin) Use at Birth for Labor Induction or

Augmentation and the Psychosocial Functioning of 3-Year-Olds

Claire Lilian Winstone

2008

The use of artificial oxytocin (Pitocin) at birth to initiate or augment labor has become commonplace in a vast number of American hospitals, where 99% of women give birth, yet little research to date has explored the possibility of enduring effects of such an intervention on children born with the use of this medication. This study attempted to answer the question, "What is the relationship between the use of artificial oxytocin at birth and the psychosocial functioning of the children at age 3?" It was hypothesized that artificial oxytocin use at birth contributes to an enduring imprint, revealed in the psychosocial functioning of young children. The sample comprised 514 mothers of vaginally-born 3-year-olds who were exposed (N = 231) or not exposed (N = 267) to artificial oxytocin at birth. Mothers responded to an online self-report survey about the hospital birth of these children, their development, and their current psychosocial functioning. Responses from mothers who received Pitocin at birth were compared to those of mothers who gave birth without Pitocin. Pitocin use raised scores on a group of eight items pertaining to mothers' recollections of giving birth, suggesting a more difficult experience, reduced time spent together by mother and infant in the first hour postpartum, and a reduced number of infants fed exclusively at the breast in the first 6 months.

Two factors were found via principal component analysis and analyses of variance to distinguish children born with Pitocin use and those born without. They were interpreted as Assertiveness and Need to Control Environment. S. W. Porges' (1995) Polyvagal Theory served to provide an understanding of these factors, interpreted as (a) Assertiveness (exemplifying social engagement) and (b) Need to Control Environment (exemplifying sympathetic nervous system activation). Both factors appeared to portray internally dysregulated responses to outside-in influences. The study's findings appear to support the concept of hormonal imprinting (G. Csaba, 2008), in that Pitocin use at birth seems to result in enduring faulty oxytocin systems in mother, infant, or both, apparently affecting internal regulation and mother-child attunement.

Acknowledgments

Dissertation-writing is, much of the time, a very solitary process, yet bringing it to completion would be impossible without a very significant "cast of supporting characters."

I must begin by expressing my deep gratitude to Drs. Marti Glenn, Wendy McCarty, Judyth Weaver, and Ken Bruer, who were inspired to create a graduate school dedicated to scholarship and research in the fields of Prenatal and Perinatal Psychology and Somatic Psychology. Without their dedication, unstinting hard work, and hundreds of post-it notes, there would have been no Santa Barbara Graduate Institute and I would not have had the opportunity to pursue my desire to deepen and broaden my understanding of my field in order to bring that knowledge to others.

It may be that without Drs. David Chamberlain and Thomas Verny, there would be no field of prenatal and perinatal psychology, and no organization to support and further its knowledge and I will be eternally grateful for their persistence, humor and dedication in the creation of APPPAH (Association for Prenatal and Perinatal Psychology and Health) and the Journal of Prenatal and Perinatal Psychology and Health.

I was honored to receive the help and support of those who were so generous with their time and energy in helping me with the hard and tedious work of paring down and refining my research instrument, particularly Deborah Kinninger, Stephanie Foster and her mother, Ellen Bavaro. Drs. Wendy McCarty, William Emerson, and Ray Castellino, and Jennifer Absey, Karlton Terry and Jean Weitensteiner, the six clinicians I interviewed for the preliminary study, not only donated their valuable time to meet with me, but also voluntarily participated further in the development of the survey and gave generously of their wisdom and clinical experience such that their contributions greatly enhanced my interpretations of the research findings.

I wish to express my gratitude to Dr. William Emerson, in particular, whose empathy, compassion and mastery provided the original inspiration for my passion for birth psychology and my research topic in particular, and for helping me to heal my own birth trauma sufficiently to take the leap of faith of moving 1,200 miles to another country to pursue that passion as a scholar.

The members of my dissertation support group, Kristi Foster, Carol Landsberg, and Grant Ramey, were with me on a monthly basis throughout this challenging and amazing journey and shared my struggles and frustrations, tears and laughter with an empathy only others on the dissertation journey can offer. Others from whom I drew strength and who offered enthusiastic support and faith in my ability to complete this project when my own faith wavered include my SBGI classmates, my colleagues at Children's Bureau, assistants and fellow trainees in the Castellino Foundation training, and doulas, doctors, midwives, labor/delivery nurses, family and friends scattered around the world.

While many people participated in the dissemination of the invitation to participate in my research survey, Connie Lillas, Stephanie and Jim Foster, Shelley Cox, Jeanne Ohm, president of the International Chiropractic Pediatric Association and Peggy O'Mara, publisher and editor of *Mothering* magazine and the Mothering.com Web site, in particular, are owed special thanks for placing the invitation on their Web sites and in their e-mail bulletins, which served to recruit a magnificent number of respondents. I am also very grateful indeed to the mothers who gave their time, experience and enthusiasm to complete the survey and to the significant number of mothers who took the trouble to send e-mails checking to see if they met the criteria for participation, or acknowledging that they didn't, but wanted to offer their support anyway.

I am particularly grateful to master statistician, Rich Harang, who went far and above his obligation not only to guide me to the most appropriate analyses of my data, but to explain them patiently, sometimes more than once, until I understood them well enough to describe them with confidence. Without his help I could not have uncovered the richness and significance of the data I gathered from the survey respondents.

Drs. Sarah Buckley, Sue Carter and Carol Sakala all provided not only superb data from their own research and publications, but also abundant guidance and encouragement—I am deeply indebted to them all.

John Chitty was cheerfully willing to engage with me in debate about symptoms of sympathetic nervous system activation and provided a valuable illustration for my discussion chapter. Drs. Judith Jacobson, Martha Welch, and classmate Dr. Susan Highsmith all generously shared their wisdom and experience and provided much needed encouragement and cheerleading.

Dr. Jane Thompson, Dr. Anna Schwartz, Claudia Handler, Julian Lee and Janet Miller all provided valuable consultation from their unique areas of expertise and with that encouraged and inspired me when they were most needed. To Dr. John Whitaker I owe a double debt of gratitude: first, for making the offer of employment that made it possible to support myself in California for the duration of my Ph.D. program and supporting the application of my clinical studies to my work with very young clients, and second, for introducing me to two of my committee members.

I want especially to express my admiration and gratitude to my committee: Dr. Wendy McCarty, who, as a subject matter expert, sensitively shepherded the development of the survey in its early stages to ensure that it would be comprehensible to the mothers who would ultimately respond to it before handing over the reins to Dr. Lyman, and Drs. David and Joely Gardner and Dr. Bobbi Jo (BJ) Lyman, who patiently guided, educated, encouraged, and mentored me through the years of this dissertation's completion. I know without a doubt I could not have accomplished this research project without the constant support of these inspiring, rigorous and dedicated scholars. Finally, as the external reader, Dr. Jane R. W. Fisher's painstaking review contributed astute observations and wise suggestions that not only improved the quality of the dissertation but will serve as guidance towards eventual publication of the research.

Dedication

This dissertation is dedicated to the late Robert Oliver, M.D., an obstetrician who was exquisitely conscious of the needs of both mothers and babies during labor and birth and constantly sought ways to minimize the need for intervention and to make even those births necessitating the use of interventions and technology respectful and healing experiences for both mother and child. His willingness to share his wisdom, experience and unique perspective, his playfulness and his constant encouragement to pursue my research interests taught and inspired me time and again throughout this dissertation journey.

Table of Contents

List of Tables

List of Figures

Chapter 1. Introduction

Since 1990, the rate of induction of labor has risen more than 200% to an average variously reported at 20.5% (Simpson & Atterbury, 2003), 22.3% in 2005 (Martin et al., 2007), and up to 41%, as reported in the Listening to Mothers II survey (Declercq, Sakala, Corry, & Applebaum, 2006). Some hospitals have induction rates of over 50% (Zhang, Yancey, & Henderson, 2002). Of these inductions, two-thirds are for nonmedical indications (Ramsey, Ramin, & Ramin, 2000) and the rate of these is rising faster than the rate for medically indicated inductions (Zhang et al., 2002). According to Simpson and Atterbury (2003), the American College of Obstetricians and Gynecologists (ACOG) "lists 'psychosocial indications' as an accepted reason for induction of labor. A psychosocial indication has become the catch-all indication for elective induction in the U.S., however" (p. 768).

At the same time, increasing numbers of children are being diagnosed with attachment disorders, autism spectrum disorders, attention deficit and hyperactivity disorders, sensory processing disorders, learning disabilities, and other regulatory, socioemotional, and behavioral problems that affect their ability to develop social competencies and achieve academically; therefore, it becomes vital to identify factors contributing to these increases in childhood dysfunctions. Clinical perinatologist, perinatal epidemiologist, and former director of Women's and Children's Health at the World Health Organization, Marsden Wagner (2001), wrote:

> Although obstetric care is gradually becoming more evidence based, there is a tendency not to evaluate obstetric interventions for their subtle and/or long term risks. For example, evidence suggests an increasing incidence of certain neurological problems such as attention deficit disorder, dyslexia, and autism. While attempts are being made to find causes for these problems, I know of no attempt to determine any correlations with simultaneously increasing obstetric interventions such as prenatal ultrasound scanning, pharmacological labour induction, epidural block for normal labour pain, elective [cesarean section]. (¶ 21)

Statement of the Problem

Although it is unlikely that any single event can be held responsible for each of the various problems described above, it is essential that all events and experiences that may play a role in their genesis be identified and addressed. If, as prenatal and perinatal psychology theorists propose, how we are born serves as a powerful template for our future lives, then researchers in our field have an obligation to explore the extent of birth's influence and how each event and intervention of birth contributes to the socioemotional and neurobiological development and functional and relational style of the individual. There appears to be a significant gap in our understanding of the pronounced increase in the prevalence of a variety of disorders being diagnosed in young children, and although research into the genetic bases of physical and psychological disorders is increasingly popular, widespread, and well funded, there seems to be a paucity of research into the possible influences of the perinatal period on the functioning of infants and young children.

Despite the fact that the use of a number of obstetrical interventions has moved from the exceptional to the commonplace during the past 20 or 30 years, and from use strictly based on medical indications to much more frequent "elective" use, remarkably few studies to date have explored the possible effects of these interventions on children beyond the immediate postpartum period, or on adolescents or adults. Of the studies that do exist, most have clustered birth interventions with birth complications when seeking associations between these and the development of serious disorders such as drug addiction, autism, or schizophrenia. Very few have narrowed their focus to a specific birth intervention and how it may affect the babies in mother-baby dyads with whom such an intervention was employed.

Among studies specifically investigating the possible effects of labor induction and augmentation using artificial oxytocin (Pitocin or Syntocinon), most either (a) examined newborns during the postpartum hospital stay, typically using standardized instruments such as measures of physical, behavioral, and neurological functioning; or (b) evaluated children at a later stage, using measures of learning ability, intelligence, or motor functioning. Overall, the findings of these researchers have been conflicting or inconclusive and extremely few have been replicated. Almost no study to date appears to have begun by observing the child's functioning or the child-parent relationship, or by exploring a parent's observations of the child, in order to identify any relationship between the child's functioning and Pitocin use at birth.

Theoretical Basis and Rationale for the Study

Obstetrical Interventions

It is a tenet of the field of prenatal and perinatal psychology that babies are conscious, aware, and communicating meaningfully from the beginning of life (McCarty, 2002a), a stance supported by the evident awareness and differential responses to varied stimuli of babies born prematurely. Further, prenatal and perinatal psychology posits that "our earliest experiences in the womb, at birth, and during infancy establish a foundational blueprint for life. This blueprint becomes the infrastructure from which we grow and experience life physically, emotionally, mentally, relationally, and spiritually" (McCarty, 2002b, p. 11). It follows, then, that a baby's experience of the journey from womb to world represents a highly significant event at a time when the structure of the brain is still forming and neurons are multiplying with amazing rapidity.

As far back as 1929, Otto Rank (1929) asserted in *The Trauma of Birth* that all neurotic anxiety was a repetition of the physiological phenomenon of birth, which he considered to be a traumatic experience for babies. In the 1970s, Frédérick LeBoyer (1975) advocated "gentle birth" (soft lights, quiet, late cord clamping, and a warm bath following delivery) as an antidote for this same perceived trauma.

Salk, Lipsitt, Sturner, Reilly, and Levat (1985) demonstrated a statistically significant relationship between maternal and perinatal conditions and adolescent suicide—the perinatal risk factor being respiratory distress for more than 1 hour at birth—and showed that each risk factor occurred alone in 81% of the suicide cases. This study suggested that a traumatic perinatal event could be associated with suicide years later.

A series of studies conducted by researchers of the Karolinska Institute in Stockholm, Sweden, demonstrated relationships between pain medications used at birth and adult amphetamine addiction (Jacobson, Nyberg, Eklund, Bygdeman, & Rydberg, 1988), between opiates and barbiturates used at birth and later opiate addiction (Jacobson et al., 1990), and between types of birth trauma and means of suicide (Jacobson et al., 1987).

Together, these studies suggest that aspects of the birth process, specifically certain obstetrical interventions, may leave on the child an enduring imprint that has the power to affect behavior much later in life. More recently, Raine, Brennan, and Mednick (1994), in a study of male subjects born in Copenhagen, Denmark, found a strong relationship between birth complications, coupled with maternal rejection of the infant in the first year (characterized by the pregnancy being unwanted, an attempt to abort the fetus, and placing the infant in an institution for a period of not less than 4 months during the first year of life), and violent crime by age 18. In a subsequent study, Raine, Brennan, and Mednick (1997) extended the follow-up period for violent offending from 18 years to 34 years to increase the sample of violent offenders and permit a more detailed analysis. This study emphasized that the biosocial interaction effect best applies to early-onset, severe forms of violence (robbery, rape, and murder) and ruled out maternal psychiatric illness in accounting for the interaction between birth complications, maternal rejection, and violence outcome.

Although there is considerable doubt that birth is universally traumatic for babies (Arms, 1997; Davis-Floyd, 1992; Panthuraamphorn, 1994), the combined findings of these studies appear to support prenatal and perinatal psychologists' premise that events at birth form imprints that have significant and enduring effects, especially if these events are accompanied by subsequent reinforcing events, and lend credibility to the clinical experience of those in the field who work with babies, children, and adults to resolve issues arising from prenatal and perinatal events. The present study was designed to add to the small but persuasive body of research investigating the effects of birth events by exploring the relationship between a commonplace obstetrical intervention and the functioning of 3-year-olds exposed to it at birth, in comparison to those who were not exposed.

Selection of the Age Range of the Sample to Be Studied

The rationale for selecting 3-year-olds was partly based on anecdotal evidence of Pitocin's effects. Prenatal and perinatal clinician colleagues suggested that children's psychosocial functioning becomes more apparent around this age because more demands are made upon children to comply with social norms, both in their families and as they enter more structured environments outside the home. As detailed in a preliminary interview study with 6 such clinicians, these observations formed the basis of the survey used in this study and are discussed in greater detail in chapter 3.

In addition, the preschool age group is of great interest to educators because what emerges at this age has significance for how children will function upon entering school. This age also was chosen because it bears predictive value for older children. A National Institute of Child Health and Human Development (2004) study found that children in affect-dysregulated mother-child dyads at 24 and 36 months had more problematic cognitive, social, and behavioral outcomes at 54 months, during kindergarten, and in first grade.

A further reason for studying the effects on 3-year-olds is that by age 3 the brain is essentially fully developed—with all major fiber tracts identifiable (Matsuzawa et al., 2001). According to Schore (2005), "The cellular architecture of the cerebral cortex is sculpted by input from the social environment embedded in the early attachment relationships" (p. 205). With the early maturing of the right hemisphere of the brain, which for the first 3 years after birth is "dominant for the emotional and corporeal self" over the later-developing verbal left brain, "the social experience–dependent maturation of the right brain in human infancy is equated with the early development of the self" (p. 205). How the self develops, Schore reports, is through repeated episodes of "affect synchrony" between mother and infant: "Psychobiological attunement and the interactive mutual entrainment of physiologic rhythms are fundamental processes that mediate attachment" (p. 207), and "the spontaneous emotional communication that occurs within the attachment relationship has been described as 'a conversation between limbic systems'" (p. 208).

Although there is a substantial body of scientific literature addressing the broader issues of labor induction—including clinical indications, appropriate conditions (such as favorable cervix or term pregnancy), methods of induction, side effects, risks and possible consequences, and other topics— relatively little research to date has examined whether there are any long-term physiological or psychological effects on the neonate. This is partly due to the way birth is typically managed: An obstetrician prescribes artificial oxytocin for induction or augmentation of labor and has responsibility for the mother's postpartum care; however, the infant is the responsibility of a pediatrician who was not present until the mother is close to delivery. Furthermore, the pediatrician present to care for the newborn following the birth is, more often than not, a different pediatrician from the one selected by the parents for ongoing care of the infant. Thus, no association is generally made between birth events and outcomes for the child, particularly after the child is discharged from the hospital.

Neonatal outcomes, when studied, typically address predominantly physiological measures, such as Apgar scores, umbilical artery pH, seizures, admission to the neonatal intensive care unit, and perinatal mortality (Alexander, McIntire, & Leveno, 2000). A few studies have employed neurological screening tools (Eishima, 1992) or infant behavioral measures like the Brazelton Neonatal Behavior Assessment Scale (Als, Tronick, Lester, & Brazelton, 1977; Brazelton, 1984), whereas others have contemplated a link between obstetrical interventions, perinatal complications, and severe disorders such as autism (Gale, Ozonoff, & Lainhart, 2003; Hollander, 1996; Wahl, 2004), schizophrenia (O'Dwyer, 1997), or attention-deficit/hyperactivity disorder (ADHD) (Claycomb, Ryan, Miller, & Schnakenberg-Ott, 2004; Zappitelli, Pinto, & Grizenko, 2001).

To date, the findings of such studies typically have been inconclusive. Studies indicating links have not been replicated or, at best, suggest a more complex relationship between birth events and the disorders examined than the methodology employed was able to delineate. As a result, little is known about any enduring effects on children of artificial oxytocin use at birth, especially when such effects may be too subtle or too diffuse to result in a diagnosis such as autism, schizophrenia, or ADHD.

Purpose of the Study

The primary purpose of this study was to explore mothers' perceptions of the effects of the use of artificial oxytocin (Pitocin) for induction or augmentation of labor on their children's psychosocial functioning at age 3. The investigation was intended to extend the theoretical perspective of prenatal and perinatal psychology by addressing Pitocin use as a commonplace intervention that is a component of many births.

Research Questions

The research questions were initially addressed in a preliminary interview study conducted with 6 expert prenatal and perinatal clinicians who described their observations of 3-year-olds who had been born with the use of Pitocin. Hypotheses to be tested in the present study, and the pilot survey employed to do so, were both derived from the findings of this preliminary study.

The main independent variable examined in the study was the use of artificial oxytocin at birth, with the dependent variable being the psychosocial functioning of 3-year-old children as described by their mothers' survey responses. Operational definitions of the independent and dependent variables are located in Appendix A.

The underlying premise of this study was that although it is the mother's body into which the artificial oxytocin is delivered intravenously, the infant is simultaneously exposed to the drug via the maternal bloodstream, through the umbilical cord. It was hypothesized that the use of artificial oxytocin at birth has effects upon the infant that endure beyond the immediate postpartum period in ways that can be perceived by the mothers of those children at age 3, and that can be differentiated from what is perceived by mothers of children who did not receive artificial oxytocin at birth. It was further hypothesized that mothers' responses to the survey would substantiate the observations of the expert clinicians interviewed in the preliminary study.

Clearly, it is not possible, using a survey in a retrospective study, to establish a cause-and-effect relationship between Pitocin and later functioning; however, it was expected that a significant relationship might be found between artificial oxytocin use at birth (independent variable) and certain aspects of psychosocial functioning in 3-year-olds (dependent variables) that could be described by their mothers and that differentiated these children from those not exposed to artificial oxytocin at birth. Because the measure used was a pilot survey completed by mothers of 3-year-old children, all hypothesis testing was based upon the mothers' perceptions of their children's functioning or their own experiences.

The research questions are as follows:

Research Question 1: Is there a relationship between Pitocin use at birth and the psychosocial functioning of children at age 3?

Research Question 2: Is there a relationship between when Pitocin was administered and how children move through sequences in daily life?

Research Question 3: Is the overall context of the child's birth—the mother's experience of pregnancy, her support system, her relationship with the baby's father, her experience of the birth itself and of those attending her delivery, and postpartum events—affected by the use of Pitocin, and is there a relationship between a context thus affected and the child's psychosocial functioning at age 3?

Research Question 4: Is there an interaction between the sex of the child, or the age or education level of either parent, and psychosocial functioning at age 3, that is significantly related to Pitocin use at birth?

Significance of the Study

The present research is timely in that the attention of educators, epidemiologists, and psychologists currently is focused on children about to enter preschool, because early moderate-to-severe regulatory disorders are predictive of emotional/behavioral difficulties during the preschool years (DeGangi, Breinbauer, Doussard-Roosevelt, Porges, & Greenspan, 2000) and because children's functioning in the preschool environment is highly predictive of their ability to function in the classroom, both socially and academically (National Institute of Child Health and Human Development, 2004). If there is a relationship between the use of artificial oxytocin at birth and the psychosocial functioning of 3-year-olds, we would be wise to give careful consideration to the prevalent use of artificial oxytocin for the induction or augmentation of labor, because the current view of its use as a benign and merely short-term intervention would require further study and perhaps would need to be reconsidered.

It also is important for the relatively new field of prenatal and perinatal psychology to develop a solid foundation of research that substantiates its theories. Although studies in a variety of disciplines form a significant basis for the new field, those studying in and focused on prenatal and perinatal psychology bear a duty to their discipline, and to the prenates, infants, and families they serve, to examine with scholarly rigor the premises upon which our field is based.

In summary, this study explored the psychosocial effects of one portion of the larger picture of obstetrical birth, namely the use of artificial oxytocin for induction or augmentation of labor. The premise discussed is that birth has enduring effects in shaping the beliefs, personality, and psychosocial functioning of individuals. This premise is examined by investigating the possible impacts of a specific obstetrical intervention (the use of artificial oxytocin to induce or augment labor) on children at age 3.

Chapter 2 examines the research relevant to this study's investigation. Chapter 3 and Chapter 4 outline the design of the research study. Chapter 5 details the results of the study, and Chapter 6 provides a discussion of the findings and the implications of these for theory, practice, and future research.

Chapter 2. Review of the Literature

This literature review is arranged to provide a contextual summary as well as a review of the literature pertinent to the dissertation research. Computer-assisted searches of Medline, CINAHL, the Cochrane Library, and the PsycINFO and PsycARTICLES databases were performed to identify studies of outcomes of obstetrical care and procedures; perinatal risk factors; and the functions, use, and effects of oxytocin. Initial keywords searched included *labor, induced, oxytocin, Pitocin, perinatal, newborn, neonate, infant, child, psychosocial,* and *effects.* Searches also were conducted to identify studies examining the relationship of labor induction with oxytocin to later-diagnosed disorders such as schizophrenia, autism, and attention-deficit/hyperactivity disorder, and to identify studies pertinent to some of the findings and the potentially confounding variables such as, for example, the effects of fathering on child development. A glossary of terms used throughout the dissertation is provided in Appendix B.

The review begins by briefly addressing the reasons obstetrics has failed to ground itself in evidence-based approaches, and how that affects modern obstetrical curricula and practice. The focus then shifts to a brief overview and history of labor induction and augmentation, introducing the concept that such interventions may affect perinatal events and produce enduring effects on young children. Studies summarily reviewed include those comparing oxytocin with other induction agents; studies examining the short-term outcomes of oxytocin administration; and studies considering possible relationships between oxytocin use at birth and certain disorders, such as autism, schizophrenia, and ADHD, and other possible long-term associations between birth events and circumstances of later life. Closer attention is then paid to a series of studies exploring an apparent association between obstetrical interventions and later drug addiction and suicide.

The relevant research on oxytocin functions in mammals is outlined, and the focus then turns to reviewing in greater depth research into the behavioral, cognitive, neurological, and psychosocial problems in human offspring that may have been associated with the use of Pitocin. Finally summarized are studies from the field of prenatal and perinatal psychology that suggest the possibility of an imprinting effect of birth events/experiences.

Perspectives on Birth in the United States

The Use of Interventions in Contemporary Obstetric Practice

The research study documented in this dissertation is founded on two broad hypotheses: (a) that the use of artificial oxytocin to induce or augment labor in the United States appears to be significantly out of proportion with the medical need for labors to be so induced or augmented, without adequate consideration of the risk/benefit ratios under these circumstances or the potential effects on individuals personally affected by its prevalence; and (b) that the use of artificial oxytocin at birth has enduring effects on babies born with its use.

In the 1970s, electronic fetal monitors replaced intermittent listening to a baby's heartbeat. Continuous monitoring, using a machine that recorded the pattern on a graph, eventually permitted the monitoring of several labors simultaneously from a nursing station rather than individually at the mother's bedside. Intravenous infusions of fluids for hydration and a drip of artificial oxytocin to stimulate or augment uterine contractions permitted further active management of labor. The use of these technologies restricted mothers' mobility in labor, preventing them from moving instinctively to alleviate pain and discomfort and to facilitate their efforts, and limiting the aid of gravity in the descent of the baby through the birth canal.

By the end of the 20th century, the typical large maternity unit had developed a standardization of procedures, applying hospital protocols to vaginal as well as surgical deliveries. "Normal birth" in a North American hospital was described in the Listening to Mothers survey (Corry, 2004; Declercq, Sakala, Corry, Applebaum, & Risher, 2002), the first national United States survey designed to examine women's attitudes, feelings, and knowledge about their maternity care and childbearing experiences. This survey also quantified the typical birth experience of these mothers, reporting that a majority of mothers surveyed experienced a number of labor and birth interventions, including "electronic fetal monitoring (93%), intravenous drip (86%), epidural analgesia (63%), artificial rupture of membranes (55%), artificial oxytocin to strengthen contractions (53%), bladder catheterization (52%), and stitching to repair an episiotomy or a tear (52%)" (Corry, 2004, p. 62). A significant minority of women reported experiencing other interventions: 44% had an attempted labor induction, 35% of the women who birthed vaginally were given an episiotomy, and 24% of respondents had a cesarean delivery.

Figures in the later Listening to Mothers II survey (Declercq et al., 2006), in which 1,573 women participated, were similar. Marsden Wagner (1994) described the proliferation of birth technology in the United States in his book *Pursuing the Birth Machine,* and later publications by obstetrician and researcher Michel Odent, *The Scientification of Love* (1999) and *The Farmer and the Obstetrician* (2002), and by Harvard Medical School professor, surgeon, and author Atul Gawande (2006) drew similar conclusions: that in the service of reliability, the process of childbirth has become "industrialized," with the mother no longer a participant but a passive patient.

Obstetrics and Evidence-Based Practice

Why is current obstetrical practice so frequently perceived, not only by midwifery proponents but also by physicians and many obstetricians themselves, to be failing to ground itself in the evidence of current research? Why, in fact, is there relatively little research to verify the safety and value of the technologies now accompanying the majority of births?

Wagner (1994) reported that in many countries there is neither regulation nor oversight of the manufacture or administration of new drugs and technology. In the United States, drugs, devices, procedures, and systems require approval from the Food and Drug Administration, but these efforts have been inconsistent at best: the law demands that new products be "efficacious and safe," but neither term is clearly defined or easy to demonstrate. How safe is safe enough? The Food and Drug Administration typically relies heavily on the data gathered by manufacturers, and although a code provides guidelines for what can be considered acceptable scientific evidence, it still permits enormous latitude in how products are studied. Products are sometimes released and then later withdrawn as information comes to light about risks and side effects that may have been initially withheld.

Wagner (1994) offered examples of situations in which, as new technologies are developed, physicians work closely with manufacturers, resulting in frequent economic and professional conflicts of interest. Horror stories about harm to or death of individual mothers or babies may be used either to promote the use of a technology—by claiming that a life might have been saved or a harm prevented with the use of a new technology, had it been available—or to argue against such technology by citing the harm it caused to an individual mother or baby. Naturally, employing such anecdotal accounts is far from appropriate in making decisions regarding suitable technologies for an entire community.

Wagner (1994) offered three reasons that doctors promote and use technology:

1. The obstetrical profession's desire for technical expertise, credibility, and success is one of the driving forces behind the development and implementation of new technologies, as opposed to relying (as was the case through the 19th and much of the 20th centuries) on a woman's own knowledge and ability to assess, for example, where she is in her pregnancy, or on a midwife's estimate. Hence the profession's insistence on the reliability of, first, X-rays and then ultrasound to date a pregnancy, despite a complete absence of evidence in support of the superiority of such technologies. In the case of the now almost ubiquitous use of continuous electronic fetal monitoring, the monitoring equipment itself impairs labor by reducing a mother's ability to assume positions that reduce pain and facilitate the descent of the fetus (Wagner, 1994). Studies have overwhelmingly demonstrated that continuous monitoring does nothing to improve outcomes and may increase the rate of surgical deliveries (Alfirevic, Devane, & Gyte, 2006; Graham, Petersen, Christo, & Fox, 2006).

2. Now that new technologies permit the monitoring of the fetus, the mandate of obstetrics has been redefined: the child is viewed as a patient in need of medical care, therefore requiring observation, diagnosis, and sometimes treatment prior to birth, which thus requires additional new technologies (Wagner, 1994).

3. Who controls and uses specific technologies depends on the relative use by women of services provided by obstetricians, midwives and family physicians. Because midwives typically use less technology, and because only physicians are permitted to employ some procedures, the number of practicing midwives and their degree of independence dictates the prevalence of technology in each country (Wagner, 1994).

With obstetricians providing all but a tiny proportion of perinatal care in the United States, and the attendant dictates of health maintenance organizations, malpractice insurers, and hospital administrations, it is hardly surprising that technology is a large component of the vast majority of North American births. However, because no single individual or body is assigned to track evidence of the safety and efficacy of technologies, practitioners have to depend on their own ability to evaluate emerging research. Practitioners are vulnerable to the claims made in manufacturers' advertising, to which they are extensively exposed during conferences, on the Internet, and by manufacturers' sales representatives offering samples and other incentives.

Recently, articles reviewing specific procedures are increasingly appearing in professional journals. On all levels, funding priorities influence the availability of different technologies, whereas health policies are influenced by the concerns of each state or province—such as promoting larger families (e.g., in Quebec, Canada) or providing prenatal care to more women—which in turn influence the development of birth technologies, and pharmaceutical and other industries wield powerful lobbies in support of the continuing use of their products. Individuals and committees in each hospital and clinic determine which technologies are to be purchased and from whom, and then how to implement the new technologies to optimize their value (Wagner, 1994).

Such research as takes place is typically biased in favor of commercial interests, according to Wagner (1994), because solutions that rely on people, as opposed to those that are technology-intensive, are rarely profitable. Private-sector research and development typically is conducted without public accountability, and assessment procedures are developed by manufacturers and conducted by doctors connected to the manufacturers in some way, although such relationships and potential conflicts of interests are frequently not disclosed in related journal publications. This results in a tendency in the medical literature to review capital-intensive, as opposed to labor-intensive, approaches to problems of birth.

Both Wagner (1994, 2006) and Gawande (2006) noted that much of the innovation in obstetrics is not the result of extensive and high-quality research into the reliability and efficacy of something new but of experimentation and word of mouth, with any study being conducted after the fact. Gawande likened the approach of obstetrics in adopting new techniques to that of the factory floor. He questioned whether medicine is a craft or an industry. If a craft, he said, the focus should be on teaching obstetricians a set of "artisanal skills," different maneuvers for different problems (e.g., a stuck shoulder, a breech presentation, a large head, or malpresentation), and on researching new techniques, accepting "that things will not always work out in everyone's hands" (p. 8).

If medicine is an industry, however, with some 42,000 obstetricians in the United States responsible for the safe delivery of millions of babies per year, then by factory-floor reasoning both obstetricians and liability insurers will prefer the relative reliability and predictability of the cesarean surgery. Gawande (2006) noted that a professor emeritus interviewed about teaching the use of forceps to aid deliveries is "a virtuoso of a difficult instrument" (p. 9) who observed regretfully that it has become unwise to instruct residents in the use of forceps because of the risk that some would apply them inexpertly. Thus, the cesarean section has become the procedure of choice for resolving the various complications formerly addressed with forceps, as well as for a variety of other complications and risks.

In the foreword to Henci Goer's (1995) book *Obstetric Myths Versus Research Realities: A Guide to the Medical Literature,* obstetrician and professor Don Creevy described how doctors are trained to practice as they do, drifting gradually from their medical-school training in the scientific method to implementing practical techniques passed from doctor to doctor and modeled by their clinical mentors. These techniques have the appearance of being effective and are promoted as scientifically valid yet lack adequate support in the peer-reviewed literature. In addition, obstetrics residents rarely witness spontaneous, noninterventive births and are trained to intervene medically or surgically; they learn to distrust nature and to put their faith in technology.

Women's Contribution to the Current Way of Birthing in the United States

Women have been giving birth to babies naturally since the dawn of humanity. How has birthing become so medicalized? In 2006, 30.3% of American women giving birth had a cesarean section, an increase of over 46% since 1996 (Hamilton, Martin, & Ventura, 2007). According to the findings of the Listening to Mothers II survey (Declercq et al., 2006), the mobility during labor of most women giving birth in the United States today will be impeded: 93% will have electronic fetal monitor belts; 80% will have an IV line. Labor will be artificially induced by a uterine stimulant to initiate or augment labor (41% and 55%, respectively). Labor is further medicalized by giving women epidural anesthesia (66%) and a bladder catheter (43%). As a result, 92% of women give birth in less than physiologically optimal positions.

In a two-part round-table discussion in the journal *Birth* entitled "Why Do Women Go Along With This Stuff?" (Kitzinger et al., 2006; Klein et al., 2006), a group of maternity care professionals and advocates shared their individual responses to this provocative question. The titles of some contributions are self-explanatory: "Birth Is Managed in a Climate of Fear," "They Trust Their Caregivers," "Man Can Improve on Nature," "Modern Medicine Knows Better," and "Women Want to Avoid Regret" (Kitzinger et al., 2006).

One writer, Dr. Carol Sakala, director of programs at Childbirth Connection (formerly the Maternity Center Association), began her contribution with the statement, "Women don't know what they don't know" (Klein et al., 2006, p. 246) and attributed the current state of birth in the United States to the following: Technological birth has become the cultural norm even for healthy, low-risk women, who are generally unaware of their capacity to give birth without intervention and are socialized to believe that even practices that are not evidence-based are justified, and when these practices result in a cascade of interventions, that the failure is with the mother's body. In addition, pregnant and birthing women, as well as physicians and hospitals, are the targets of a powerful and lucrative industry that markets equipment, tests, medications, infant formula, and the concept of hospital birth as the best and safest option. The low-technology alternatives, even when more evidence-based, may be more challenging to access or implement.

Sakala (Klein et al., 2006) pointed out that elevated oxytocin levels around the time of birth may contribute to women trusting in, and assuming that their best interests are central to, caregivers and settings they have taken a limited role in selecting. The majority of pregnant women are not highly proactive in learning about their rights and ensuring that they have been fully informed of the risks and benefits of routine care and practices. Fear of problems with their babies or of elements of labor and delivery such as labor pain tends to result in compliance with whatever they have been told will ensure a controlled delivery and a healthy baby. Sakala suspects that both the use of medications and the birth setting itself tend to influence the mother while she is at her most vulnerable.

Finally, Sakala (Klein et al., 2006) noted that most women give birth only once or twice. On the first occasion, the mother may not be in a position to make sense of what took place. On the other hand, women with previous children are better informed and may be more selective about caregivers and settings but have little time to advocate for themselves or their babies because of competing responsibilities.

Although many mothers may be concerned about the possible effects on their babies of birth or interventions, research has not yet substantiated the assertion of prenatal and perinatal psychology that the shared experience of birth may leave enduring imprints not only on the mother but also on the child and on their relationship.

The Effects of "Industrialized" Childbirth

According to a report by Save the Children (2006), the United States has the second worst newborn mortality rate in the modern world (much as it did in the 1920s and 1930s). U.S. babies are three times more likely than babies born in Japan to die within the first month postpartum, and the U.S. newborn mortality rate is 2.5 times higher than in Finland, Iceland, or Norway. "The United States has more neonatologists and neonatal intensive care beds per person than Australia, Canada, and the United Kingdom, but its newborn mortality rate is higher than any of those countries" (p. 38).

According to the World Health Organization (2005), the United States is listed as 32nd out of 33 industrialized nations in newborn mortality (Figure 2.1), and only Latvia has a higher rate (Save the Children, 2006). The U.S. Department of Health and Human Services publication *Child Health USA 2007* reports a rate of 4.5 neonatal deaths per 1,000 live births, although for non-Hispanic Blacks, the rate is 9.4 deaths per 1,000 live births.

In the 1970s and 1980s the pendulum of birth trends swung in the direction of women reclaiming control over their births, including the establishment of freestanding birthing centers, the resurrection of midwifery, and the emergence and naming of the *doula,* from the Greek word for "servant," a professional labor support person (the vast majority of whom are female), which implied that a specific servant knowledgeable in childbirth should attend the deliveries of the women of the household. These changes were accompanied by a substantial increase in vaginal births after cesareans (VBACs).

The pendulum swing reversed again in the late 1990s and into the new century, as ACOG (2004) declared that "because uterine rupture may be catastrophic, VBAC should be attempted in institutions equipped to respond to emergencies, with physicians immediately available to provide emergency care" (p. 6), leading to a precipitous decline in the availability of the procedure.

At the beginning of the 21st century, as in the 1970s and 1980s, the entrenchment of available birth technology into hospital protocols and expanded efforts to avoid costly litigation have again spurred a countermovement among women disillusioned with the medical model of birth, who seek more control over their birth experiences, and a return to trusting the process of birth when it is allowed to progress without interventions—or at least with fewer than are typically employed, and those only with genuinely informed consent.

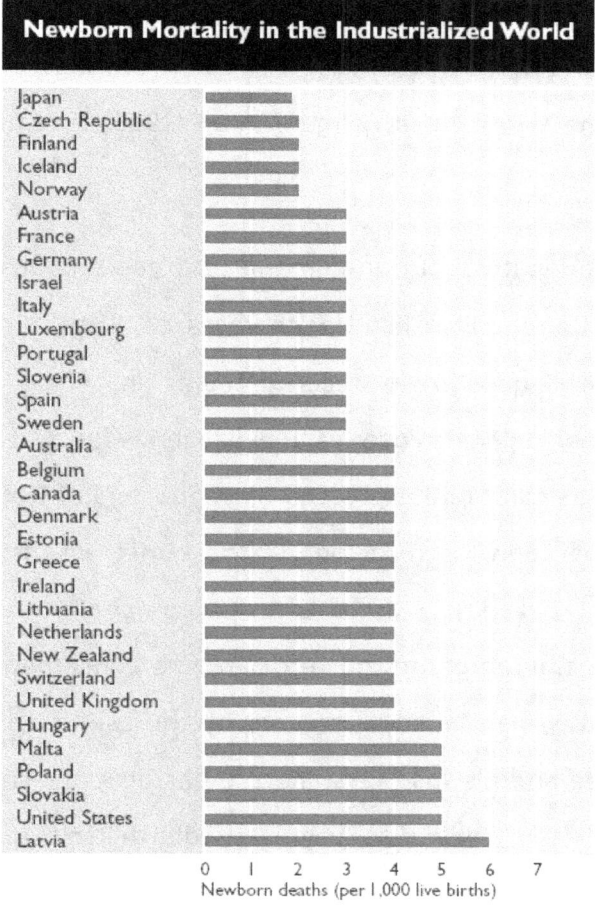

Figure 2.1. Newborn mortality in the industrialized world.

Note. From State of the World's Mothers 2006: Saving the Lives of Mothers and Newborns, Retrieved December 3, 2006, from www.savethechildren.org/publications/mothers/2006/SOWM_2006_final.pdf. ©2006 by Save the Children. Reprinted with permission of the author.

An additional, growing group of women advocating against the increased use of technology and liability-driven restrictions on birthing options are those who have had cesarean deliveries and wish to have a subsequent vaginal birth. Spurred by a recent dramatic drop in the number of hospitals willing to support VBAC attempts and the subsequent large increase in repeat cesarean deliveries, women are demonstrating outside hospitals for the option of VBACs and the opportunity to make their own informed decisions about labor and delivery (Cassidy, 2006a).

As a consequence of the ACOG (2004) guidelines, the peak rate of 28.3% VBAC deliveries in 1996 fell by 67%, to 9.2%, by 2004. Concurrently, the likelihood of a primary cesarean being followed by a repeat cesarean rose to approximately 90% (Martin et al., 2007). During virtually the same period of increased birth interventions, total cesarean birth rates rose by 46%, from 20.7% in 1996 to 30.3% in 2005, a record high for the nation. The World Health Organization (1985) recommends a cesarean rate of no more than 10% to 15%.

In a review of the current debate about on-demand cesarean sections, Michael Klein (2004), senior scientist emeritus, Centre for Community Child Health Research, British Columbia Research Institute for Children's & Women's Health, questioned recent studies in which obstetricians declared their preferences for elective cesarean deliveries over vaginal deliveries for themselves or their loved ones. He compared this preference to a similar one expressed by supporters of DeLee's (1921) famous paper on "The Prophylactic Forceps Operation," and for one of the same reasons: the protection of the pelvic floor. Klein (2004) noted that DeLee saw the use of forceps and the subsequent surgical repair as protective of the pelvic floor. Contemporary obstetricians are concerned about damage to the pelvic floor by forceps, a situation they had failed to prevent by the use of episiotomy, as they had hoped. According to Klein, both DeLee and his followers and the obstetricians choosing elective cesareans for themselves thus appear to view the problem as "vaginal childbirth itself" (p. 162), the solution now being the cesarean section.

Klein (2004) noted that many of the obstetricians surveyed on this question practice in countries where they see only difficult and complicated cases; thus, their view of vaginal birth would be distorted. Klein called for pregnant women and their doctors to discuss fully the complexities of birth alternatives. Klein acknowledged that the person who typically would provide such counseling often experiences a conflict of interest because elective cesarean surgery is clearly an easier choice for the obstetrician. He observed that, because obstetrics is a surgical specialty, birth is rarely viewed as a natural process but as one that requires intervention.

Like Sakala (2006), Klein (2004) suggested that the children of the women who fought the battles for family-centered childbirth now have other priorities in a changed cultural context and a time of increased consumerism. As a family physician, possibly representing a variety of perspectives from the middle ground between obstetrics and midwifery, Klein observed:

Absent from the conventional obstetrical literature on birth, perhaps considered "soft" or "unscientific," were the personal and spiritual issues of power, control, depression and other psychological trauma, self-esteem, feelings of confidence and competence, breastfeeding, or the maturational and growth-promoting features of vaginal birth. Discussing these issues had even become unfashionable: the domain of the social and behavioral scientist, midwifery, nursing, doulas, and family practice. (p. 163)

Sheila Kitzinger's (2006) recently published *Birth Crisis* delineated these issues, noting that recent studies found that 1 in 20 new mothers is diagnosed with traumatic stress after childbirth.

Like Klein (2004) and Leboyer (1975), surgeon, obstetrician, home birth midwife, and researcher Michel Odent (2001) sees birth in the context of society, and like Leboyer he expressed concern about the kind of society our current way of birth and caring for our infants may engender:

We are at a turning point in the history of childbirth. Until recently, in order to have a baby, a woman was obliged to release a complex cocktail of hormones that play a key role in the initiation of lactation. Today, in many industrialised countries, for the first time in the history of mankind, most women give birth without releasing such hormones. Either they rely on substitutes for natural hormones (drip of synthetic oxytocin plus epidural anaesthesia) or they give birth by caesarean section. The issue of breastfeeding cannot be dissociated from the issue of childbirth. (pp. 5-6)

In a technical report for Childbirth Connection, family physician, author, and mother of four children born at home, Sarah Buckley (2007), emphasized that research in humans and other mammals supports the understanding that the success of reproductive processes—birth, mother-child attachment, and breast-feeding—depend on "an elaborate orchestration of hormonal release for both mother and offspring" (p. 4) and that these same hormones continue to play a significant role in social relationships among mammals. She suggested that disruption of these hormonal systems in the perinatal period may have repercussions in later life in terms of effects on social and reproductive behavior, and she found substantial and growing support in the research for such a theory.

Although Gawande's (2006) article drew criticism from the midwifery community as a vehicle promoting the "obstetrical package," he noted the possibility that much may be lost if natural birth is entirely superseded by the industrialized version:

And yet there's something disquieting about the fact that childbirth is becoming so readily surgical. Some hospitals are already doing cesarean sections in more than half of child deliveries. It is not mere nostalgia to find this disturbing. We are losing our connection to yet another natural process of life. And we are seeing the waning of the art of childbirth. The skill required to bring a child in trouble safely through a vaginal delivery, however unevenly distributed, has been nurtured over centuries. In the medical mainstream, it will soon be lost. (p. 4)

These writers appear to be asserting that there is value both in the experience of natural childbirth and in individualized care, which is forfeited in the interests of the predictability and reliability required by a model of medicine (and thereby obstetrics) as an industry that currently dominates North American birthing practices. The meaning of the experience of childbirth may be lost to women who, as Sakala suggested, "don't know what they don't know" (Klein et al., 2006, p. 246)—sometimes until it is too late to turn back the clock.

To date, the meaning of birth to the infant has rarely been contemplated by writers debating the increasing use of cesareans. Like cesareans, the use of increasingly early labor inductions, resulting in increasing numbers of late preterm deliveries (Martin et al., 2007), is still the subject of much debate among birth professionals. Nonetheless, the practice continues and is increasing in prevalence, even though its effects beyond the immediate postpartum period are still virtually unknown.

A Brief History and Overview of Labor Induction

Methods of labor induction have existed since time immemorial. Midwives gave women agents such as ergot or herbs and advocated (as they still do) the use of walking, nipple stimulation, intercourse, and orgasm to attempt to start or accelerate labor.

In 1906, physiologist Sir Henry H. Dale discovered that extract of the human postpituitary gland stimulated uterine contractions in a pregnant cat. He named the substance oxytocin, using the Greek words for "fast" (oxy) and "birth" (tocos). The posterior pituitary extract of cattle was subsequently harvested by slaughterhouses and sold to physicians as Pituitrin. Administered by injection, it was initially used to treat postpartum hemorrhage and later was used for starting labor or hastening a slow labor. It was found to be more reliable than its antecedent, ergot, but it still presented problems because, once administered, if anything went wrong nothing could be done; the Pituitrin simply had to wear off, sometimes resulting in complications that included maternal and fetal deaths (Block, 2007).

Artificial oxytocin was first synthesized in 1953 by biochemist Vincent du Vigneaud. By 1974, a bioidentical form with fewer side effects, known as Pitocin (or Syntocinon), was widely available for use in a dilute IV solution for the induction and augmentation of labor. Elective use of Pitocin was already commonplace in the 1950s.

As a result of a simplistic interpretation of Emmanuel Friedman's (1955) study of the length of the phases of labor, what became known as the Friedman curve became the standard for labor's progress, at an expected rate of 1 cm of cervical dilatation per hour. What became known as the Dublin protocol was established by O'Driscoll, Jackson, and Gallagher (1969) at the National Maternity Hospital in Dublin, Ireland, in an article that described trials conducted with 200,000 women over 25 years. The protocol was designed for the first-time mother, who was not admitted to the hospital until she met the criteria for "active labor." Upon admission, her waters were broken and she was assigned to a midwife who remained with her throughout labor and delivery. If her labor pattern failed to comply with the Friedman curve, the mother received artificial oxytocin by IV and dosage was increased until she attained an acceptable frequency of contractions. Women participating in this protocol were assured that their labors would not last more than 12 hours. Under this protocol, 40% of women received artificial oxytocin, cesarean rates gradually increased (from 4% to 9%), and epidural anesthesia use increased 12-fold to over 50% of women, suggesting that oxytocin-induced/augmented labors were significantly more painful (O'Herlihy, 1993).

Translated to the United States by the 1980s with a goal of reducing the cesarean rate, the protocol lost what may well have been two of its most vital elements: the admission of women only when they were already in active labor (others were encouraged to take a walk to facilitate progress to active labor) and the presence of continuous, one-on-one midwifery care by women experienced in the support of normal birth (Block, 2007). Expectations that women conform to the Friedman curve continue, even though large numbers of women now receive epidural anesthesia, which is known to alter the course of labor and in some cases to slow it down. In a systematic review of studies, Lieberman and O'Donoghue (2002) concluded that epidural use "is associated with a lower rate of spontaneous vaginal delivery, a higher rate of instrumental vaginal delivery, and longer labors, particularly in nulliparous women" (p.

S31). In addition, women receiving an epidural are more likely to have intrapartum fever, and their infants are more likely to be evaluated and treated for suspected sepsis.

A clinical trial (Bloom et al., 2006) of 5,341 low-risk first-time mothers delivering at large teaching hospitals, which investigated whether knowledge of fetal oxygen saturation was associated with a reduction in the rate of cesarean delivery or with any improvement in the condition of the newborn, reported that 40% of the mothers studied underwent induced labor and 70% received Pitocin at some point during labor. Research by cultural anthropologist Davis-Floyd (1992) found that 81% of women giving birth in U.S. hospitals received Pitocin (or Syntocinon) to induce or augment their labors, and 80% of the inductions reported in the Listening to Mothers II survey (Declercq et al., 2006) involved the use of Pitocin.

Clearly, we cannot conclude that more than two-thirds of American women have faulty uteri that are incapable either of initiating labor spontaneously or of maintaining it to delivery without help, nor that equally as many American babies have faulty endocrine systems that lack the capacity to secrete the hormones that initiate labor. Wagner (2006) suggested that the rate of medical indications for using drugs for induction should be 10%, this being the actual rate of induction in most industrialized countries before 1990.

A study by Glantz (2003), using a birth database from an area of upstate New York that included over 30,000 deliveries from 1998 through 1999 to determine the degree of variation of labor induction rates among hospitals and practitioners, found that total induction rates among hospitals varied from 10% to 39%, and that the percentage of those that were elective was between 12% and 55%, whereas the rates for individual practitioners for total inductions varied from 7% to 48% and the percentage that were elective ranged from 3% to 76%. If these ranges typify those of other hospitals and practitioners, it might be considered that up to three-quarters of all inductions may needlessly put both mother and baby at risk. Glantz concluded that practitioners' decisions to induce labor are far more likely to be subjective than evidence-based.

In the Listening to Mothers II survey (Declercq et al., 2006), 19% of mothers cited wanting "to get the pregnancy over with" (p. 30) as a factor in their medical induction, raising the question of whether the consent given for the procedure is fully informed. Were these mothers made aware that the risks might outweigh the benefits of induction? In fact, Buckley (2007) suggested that our acceptance, both cultural and medical, of induction for either minor or elective reasons occurs despite our lack of understanding of the complexity and benefits of physiological initiation of labor and despite our ignorance of the possible short- and long-term implications of scheduling birth.

ACOG (1999) stated, "Induction of labor is indicated when the benefits of expeditious delivery outweigh the risks of continuing the pregnancy" (¶ 5). Medical indications for inducing labor may include, but are not limited to, the following conditions:

1. Abruptio placentae
2. Chorioamnionitis
3. Fetal demise
4. Pregnancy-induced hypertension
5. Premature rupture of membranes
6. Postterm pregnancy
7. Maternal medical conditions (e.g., diabetes mellitus, renal disease, chronic pulmonary disease, chronic hypertension)
8. Fetal compromise (e.g., severe fetal growth restriction, isoimmunization)
9. Preeclampsia, eclampsia. (ACOG, 1999, p. 4)

If these conditions and related ones are present in only approximately 10% of cases of induction of labor (Wagner, 2006), it is clear that what is taking place in this epidemic of induced and augmented labors is some form of cultural phenomenon. The United States, perhaps more than any other culture in the world, historically has both advanced and embraced technological developments in the field of obstetrics. In the last century, as birth moved from the care of midwives in the home to that of obstetricians in the hospital, some writers consider this movement toward medicalization to be propelled by the fear of the unpredictable or unknown that is birth; disconnection from an earlier familiarity with the normal physiology of birth; or "professional mistrust of the female body, hope for a pain-free experience, and wishful thinking that technology can produce perfect babies and assume total responsibility for the outcome" (Chamberlain,1999, p. 97). In her book *Pushed*, Block (2007) added the opinion that what is taking place in most hospitals today is that birth is being "stabilized . . . and the ability to stabilize, to bring the chaos of labor under control, is a relatively recent development in human history made possible by synthetic oxytocin, brand name Pitocin" (p. 5).

This is what the president of the American Foundation for Maternal-Child Health, Doris Haire (1972), called the "cultural warping" of childbirth. With the development of the present methods of intravenous delivery of artificial oxytocin—"from simple, manually adjusted, gravity-fed systems, through mechanically or electronically controlled infusion pumps, to fully automated closed-loop feedback systems in which the dose of oxytocin is regulated by the intensity of uterine contractions" (Enkin et al., 2000, p. 387)—came the advent of "daylight obstetrics"—the practice of scheduling inductions of labor (and elective cesarean sections) at times convenient to the doctor, hospital staff, the family, or all of these.

A commentary by obstetrical researchers Rayburn and Zhang in the journal of the American College of Obstetricians and Gynecologists described the causes of the rapid increase in inductions of labor as "complex and multifactorial" (2002, p. 165), specifically citing the availability of cervical ripeners, increasingly accepting attitudes toward marginal or elective inductions, concerns about medical liability in a more expectant management paradigm, pressures from patients wanting control over their delivery date, and financial gains for providers. The authors noted that advocates of induction believe that elective inductions permit improved planning of deliveries during the daytime, when mothers are presumably less fatigued and more perinatal caregivers are available.

Illustrating this trend, Block (2007) cited birth statistics from the National Vital Statistics Reports for 2004, which reported an average of 12,000 babies born daily between Monday and Friday, with the numbers falling to around 8,000 on weekends. Sakala (2006) posited, "The fixed global fee payment mechanism for maternity services penalizes practitioners who patiently support physiologic labor, which involves unpredictable onset and generally requires more time with no increase in reimbursement" (p. 333). Sakala also noted the "greater scope for profit" (p. 333) for hospitals from cesarean as opposed to vaginal deliveries. However, Rayburn and Zhang (2002) also perceived cost increases resulting from induction of labor, which can lead to longer predelivery stays to allow time for cervical ripening, more frequent requests for epidural anesthesia, an increased risk of cesarean deliveries, and costs associated with increased maternal morbidity. Based on interviews for her book *Pushed,* in which Block (2007) described the pressures on obstetricians to practice defensively and to schedule inductions in order to manage the multiple demands of their practices, hospitals, insurers, and personal lives, Block noted, "Physiological birth doesn't look good in court; getting the baby out earlier, faster, and with as many medical interventions as possible does" (p. 43).

For a woman late in pregnancy feeling "huge and uncomfortable and anxious" (Goer, 1999, p. 51) the idea of "having a baby today" can be seductive, and it is all too rare that she will ask for or be provided with an informed consent for the induction procedure that details all the known and possible risks of starting labor at a time that is not of nature's choosing. It is equally likely that a woman (or her anxious partner) whose doctor expresses concern that her baby is becoming quite large (macrosomia, variously described as a birth weight over 4,000 g [8 lbs 13 oz] or 4,500 g [9 lbs 14 oz]), that her pelvis may not be all that big, that she has insufficient amniotic fluid (oligohydramnios), or that her placenta's functioning may be starting to deteriorate may also acquiesce to the suggestion that an induced labor will help her avoid the perceived risks to herself or her baby. Such perceived risks can include fetal demise, inability to deliver the baby vaginally, or a shoulder dystocia—a stuck shoulder, which can result in fetal death or brain damage if not resolved quickly, because the umbilical cord is compressed, limiting oxygen supply to the baby's brain, or can lead to a possible brachial plexus injury or broken clavicle in the attempt to free the shoulder.

According to medical writer Henci Goer's (1999) examination of the available research, however, the facts are otherwise. Ultrasound estimates of fetal size become increasingly inaccurate as pregnancy progresses, and normal gestations are considered to last approximately 40 to 41 weeks only because of a single German obstetrician, Franz Carl Naegele, who in the late 19th century declared that a pregnancy should last 10 lunar months (i.e., 40 weeks). Later research (Mittendorf, Williams, Berkey, & Cotter, 1990) demonstrated that first pregnancies tend to last an average of 8 days longer, but with no reliable way of accurately estimating the due date, the risk of delivering a smaller than estimated or even preterm baby is, in fact, higher than the risk of birthing an infant too big to negotiate the mother's pelvis. Inductions, originally employed only for prolonged pregnancies of 44 weeks or more, began to be used in those of 43 and 42 weeks, and then even earlier. In addition, research does not support induction for suspected macrosomia.

Figure 2.2 indicates the continued increase in rates of preterm birth, apparently paralleling the increase in labor inductions and cesarean sections over the same time period. Chalmers and Richards (1977, as cited in Menticoglou & Hall, 2002), the authors of a chapter entitled "Intervention and Causal Inferences in Obstetric Practice," pointed out that in situations of increasingly earlier inductions, "As the indications expand, the benefit weakens but the hazards remain constant. As a result, the hazards outweigh the benefits" (Menticoglou & Hall, 2002, p. 490). In addition, one of the feared risks of postdate deliveries, dystocia, is less tied to fetal size than is popularly assumed, and shoulder dystocias, although dangerous, rarely result in permanent injury when properly managed.

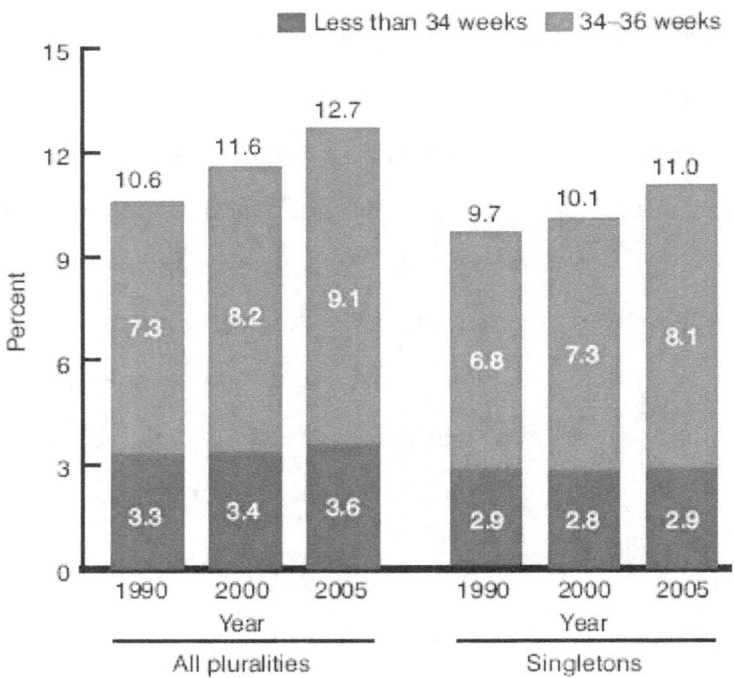

Figure 2.2. Preterm birth rates for all births and for singletons only: United States, 1990, 2000, and 2005.

From CDC/NCHS National Vital Statistics System (Martin et al., 2007). Document in the public domain.

An evidence report commissioned by the Agency for Healthcare Research and Quality (Myers et al., 2002) searched six databases (MEDLINE, HealthSTAR, CINAHL, EMBASE, the Cochrane Database of Systematic Reviews, and DARE) for studies between 1980 and 2000, in order to examine measures for assessing the risks to fetuses and mothers of prolonged pregnancy, the likelihood of successful labor induction, the benefits of labor induction as opposed to expectant management, the comparative benefits and risks of different methods of induction, and the implications of prolonged pregnancy for different populations. Among the report's conclusions is that although the risk of stillbirth is increased after 41 weeks, the absolute risk is still low, and that at least 500 women would need to be induced to prevent one stillbirth at or beyond 41 weeks, with no other benefits of induction identified. Myers et al. also reported that, aside from membrane sweeping, methods of induction involved either risk-benefit trade-offs or uncertainty about harms.

Similarly, a 2006 Cochrane review (Gülmezoglu, Crowther, & Middleton, 2006) of 19 trials involving a total of 7,984 women, reporting on induction of labor at or beyond term (41 weeks), concluded that although a policy of labor induction at 41 weeks or later is associated with fewer perinatal deaths than is a policy of expectant management, the absolute risk is extremely small. Gülmezoglu et al. advised counseling women on both relative and absolute risks, considering expectant management to be a legitimate choice for women wishing to avoid "the more 'medicalized' experience of an induced labor" (p. 754).

Menticoglou and Hall (2002) of the University of Manitoba's Department of Obstetrics, Gynecology and Reproductive Sciences took to task the assumption that meta-analysis of randomized controlled trials "has settled the question in favour of routine induction" (p. 485) by providing the best available evidence to determine the most appropriate care. The authors examined the data from the largest included trial (Hannah et al., 1992), which was conducted in Canada and contained over half the cases examined (3,407), noting that the clinical practice guidelines subsequently issued by the Society of Obstetricians and Gynaecologists of Canada in 1997 resulted in a "mutation" from guideline to standard of care (i.e., routine induction at 41 weeks), whereas further inquiry might be inhibited following such a consensus.

Menticoglou and Hall (2002) scrutinized the reports of the seven neonatal deaths in the expectant arms of the clinical trials and effectively disputed the inclusion of all but two of these, compared to one death in the induction group, thus casting doubt on the purported higher risk that induction at 41 weeks is claimed to reduce. The authors also identified three types of bias that may have resulted in the higher rate of cesareans in the expectant management group, including the higher rate of cesareans for "fetal distress," which they believed (and substantiated with examples) were a result of "availability error" in decision-making—the probability that monitoring itself "created and reinforced bias towards inference of fetal distress and made it more likely that caesarean delivery would be the response to that inference" (p. 487).

Menticoglou and Hall (2002) described the significantly greater workload resulting from 15% to 20% more inductions per year on the basis of arrival at a gestational age of 41 weeks alone, with no other indications, and even though the guidelines allow for induction to take place anywhere within the 6 days following the 41-week point. They observed that in practice obstetricians schedule inductions by or before 1 week past the estimated due date. They pointed out that, in addition, there is a difference in the duration of labor between a woman who arrives in labor and delivers 5-10 hours later and a woman who arrives for scheduled induction with an unfavorable cervix which will almost certainly result in a significantly longer labor, placing an additional strain on resources for an outcome whose improvements in risk reduction they consider dubious, at best, if not indefensible.

Citing their own experience of a maternal mortality resulting from the unavailability of beds because of scheduled inductions, and a serious morbidity that was unreported in the Canadian trial, Menticoglou and Hall (2002) speculated about the possibility of near misses and catastrophes that may occur on labor wards and that might be anticipated and prevented were the staff not so busy with scheduled inductions. They concluded that the evidence for scheduled induction at 41 weeks is "seriously flawed and an abuse of biological norms" and called for "this nonsensus consensus" to be withdrawn (p. 490).

Pitocin and the Intervention Cascade

As far back as 1922, there were objections to the overuse of Pitocin's predecessor, Pituitrin, to induce or augment labor (Brumbaugh, 1922). Pitocin inductions tend to initiate what is sometimes described as a cascade of interventions when contractions become considerably more intense and closer together, and their duration longer, sometimes with painful double peaks that are difficult for the mother to tolerate. Rather than reducing the concentration of Pitocin in the IV if the mother's pain becomes unbearable, which risks slowing the labor, medical staff may offer the mother epidural anesthesia or narcotics to counteract the pain without diluting the stimulating effects of the Pitocin.

The stronger contractions also may deprive the fetus of needed oxygen. Caldeyro-Barcia et al. (1957, as cited in Arms, 1997) concluded, after a collaborative study in 12 Latin American medical centers, that in oxytocic-induced labors, even with proper precautions—such as the lowest effective dosage given and proper monitoring of mothers—almost 75% of the mothers' uterine contractions were shown through fetal heart monitor tracings to result in a reduction of oxygen to the baby's brain.

Mothers receiving IV Pitocin require continuous fetal monitoring for possible fetal distress and are likely to have had the amniotic sac artificially ruptured, so they rarely enjoy the option of using mobility and position changes to assist the baby in its descent through the birth canal. The baby loses the fluid cushion protecting it from the mother's pelvic bones and effectively finds its head being used as a battering ram to dilate the mother's cervix. A baby presenting in a difficult position for birth, or unable to descend because of poor positioning, is then likely to receive the assistance of forceps or vacuum extraction in order to be born, thus likely adding to the trauma of rapid molding to the fetal cranium. The alternative response to a problematic presentation is cesarean section, with its own attendant risks and the consequences of anesthesia use and major abdominal surgery for the mother of a newborn.

The Hormone Oxytocin and its Artificial Correlate, Pitocin

Oxytocin is a hormone unique to mammalian species and is produced in the area of the brain known as the limbic system, sometimes referred to as the "old mammalian brain." It is also transported to areas of the brain related to maternal and social behaviors. Its half-life in the blood (i.e., the time it takes to reduce levels by half) is short, with estimates at under 15 minutes, and in pregnancy the placenta produces oxytocinase, an enzyme which breaks down oxytocin, resulting in even more rapid clearance (Buckley, 2007). The half-life of oxytocin in the brain is estimated to be around 28 minutes. Oxytocin or its receptors are found not only in the female mammalian uterus and the reproductive tract of both males and females but also in the thymus, adrenals, fat cells (Gimpl & Fahrenholz, 2001), pancreas, blood vessels, heart, breasts, and kidneys (Lippert, Mueck, Seeger, & Pfaff, 2003).

The heart and the pituitary gland in the brain both secrete oxytocin in similar concentrations (Gutkowska, Jankowski, Mukaddam-Daher, & McCann, 2000; McCraty, Atkinson, & Tomasino, 2001; Russell, Leng & Douglas, 2003). Oxytocin also plays a significant role in digestion: Its release activates the vagal nerve, which increases the activity of the gut hormones, enhancing nutrient storage and digestion (Buckley, 2007). In addition, in a positive feedback loop, vagal nerve stimulation through eating stimulates oxytocin release in the brain, which results in the calm and connected feeling that facilitates social behaviors (Uvnäs-Moberg, 2003).

Unlike intravenously administered Pitocin, oxytocin was found to be emitted in a pulselike pattern in prairie voles (Cushing & Carter, 2000). Other researchers have identified pulsatile oxytocin release during birth and breast-feeding (Russell, Douglas, & Ingram, 2001), and Fuchs et al. (1991) found that oxytocin pulses increased in frequency as labor progressed, from 4.2 pulses per 30 minutes in early labor to 6.7 pulses in the second and third stages, peaking in maternal plasma with each contraction (Nagata et al., 1983). Oxytocin also was found to increase in the cerebrospinal fluid of laboring women (Takeda, Kuwabara, & Mizuno, 1985).

During pregnancy in humans, oxytocin receptor numbers increase in the uterus, beginning at six times the number in a nonpregnant uterus and representing up to an 80-fold increase at term (Fuchs & Fuchs, 1984). Meanwhile, the pregnant uterus has over 300 times the receptor messenger RNA at parturition than does the nonpregnant uterus (Kimura et al., 1996). These changes prepare the pregnant mother for a coordinated oxytocin release during labor and for appropriate responses to the newborn. The changes also explain the increasing sensitivity of the uterus to artificial oxytocin as the woman gets closer to the spontaneous onset of labor.

Buckley (2007) noted that there is wide individual variation in oxytocin levels and that intermittent measurements may be inaccurate because of the pulsatile release pattern of oxytocin during labor. There also are variations in the numbers of oxytocin receptors in different parts of the uterus and changes in uterine configuration as labor progresses. According to Gimpl and Fahrenholz (2001), the olfactory bulb is also involved, emphasizing the importance of smell in mammalian maternal behavior, especially in the minutes and hours following delivery, when mother and baby bond and breast-feeding is initiated.

A unique phenomenon known as "burst firing" happens during the perinatal period: groups of neurons fire together in a series of very rapid, coordinated spikes, separated by a few seconds. This results in large spikes of oxytocin during childbirth and lactation, resulting in the milk ejection reflex. During birth this release of oxytocin from oxytocin neurons appears to stimulate further oxytocin release, forming a positive feedback loop in the hypothalamus to enhance oxytocin's effects (Russell et al., 2003). Neither the pulsatile pattern of oxytocin release nor the burst firing are replicated when Pitocin is used during labor.

Natural oxytocin is described as the hormone that is a major component of the "calm and connection system" (Uvnäs-Moberg, 2003, p. 7) and its mode of operating in situations of stress is viewed as the counterbalance to the more well-known aspect of the psychophysiological system that is activated in situations perceived by the individual as threatening, harmful, or demanding and in which fight/flight and stress responses play a significant role. The release of oxytocin in such situations helps restore homeostasis in the individual.

In her examination of the hormonal physiology of childbirth, Buckley (2007) drew on Insel's (1997) article on the neurobiology of attachment, in which Insel extrapolated from animal research the role of oxytocin and vasopressin and postulated that they play an important role in human attachments, concluding that human research has "confirmed that oxytocin is involved in many aspects of mammalian social attachment, including mother-infant attachment; paternal and parental behavior; social recognition; courtship and monogamous pair bonds; and wider social relationships" (Buckley, 2007, p. 22). Oxytocin apparently enhances both the need for social interactions and the rewards these interactions bring, both between infant and mother and between unrelated adults (Carter, 1998; Insel, 2003).

When artificial oxytocin is delivered intravenously, it fails to deliver the calming, healing, and loving effect described by Uvnäs-Moberg (2003) and familiar to lovers and mother-infant dyads. Moreover, its effects on uterine contractions may elicit feelings of fear and panic in laboring mothers unable to cope with the increased pain and intensity. It is further believed that Pitocin temporarily blocks the oxytocin receptors that are designed to enhance bonding and attachment at birth and thereby obstructs the amelioration of birth stresses through the attachment behaviors fostered by natural oxytocin production (Gale et al., 2003; Hollander, 1996; Wahl, 2004).

A study by Nissen, Lilja, Widstrom, and Uvnäs-Moberg (1995) demonstrated that the "sensitive period" for postpartum bonding is reflected in elevated plasma oxytocin levels at 15, 30, and 45 minutes following delivery when infants are placed skin-to-skin on their mothers' chests, returning to normal levels at 60 minutes postpartum. Research by Dawood, Wang, Gupta, and Fuchs (1978) and Kumaresan, Han, Anandarangam, and Vasicka (1975) indicated that newborns have oxytocin levels equivalent to or higher than their mothers', following a vaginal birth. Moreover, these studies have found higher oxytocin levels in the umbilical artery than in the umbilical vein, indicating that the baby is producing oxytocin during labor and that this oxytocin may flow to the maternal circulation. By contrast, newborn oxytocin levels are reduced following oxytocin administration in labor, with a reversal of the ratio of oxytocin in the umbilical artery and vein, suggesting that oxytocin may be transported through the placenta to the baby (Dawood et al., 1978).

Buckley (2007) noted that animal researchers concluded that social interactions during the neonatal period influence adult behaviors by altering the offspring's sensitivity to neuropeptides such as oxytocin, arginine vasopressin, and other chemicals in specific areas of the brain, and postulated that the same is true of humans. Based on their study of neurobiological attachment mechanisms in previously institutionalized children Fries, Ziegler, Kurian, Jacoris, and Pollak (2005) suggested that when young children fail to receive species-typical care, normal development of the oxytocin and arginine vasopressin systems is disrupted, which implies that maternal care patterns resulting in oxytocin release in the offspring may play an important role in adult health and well-being. Hormonal manipulation has not been adequately studied and may have adverse effects on neural systems in the neonate. Studies suggest that these neural changes may be long-lasting and could affect neuroanatomy, physiology, and behavior (Bales et al., 2007).

We are only now beginning to obtain a glimpse of the intricacy of the hormonal and physiological dance that takes place between mother and baby when they are left to their own devices for birthing and the postpartum period—certainly we still have little understanding of how serious a derailment of that dance may take place when labor is induced or augmented with artificial oxytocin.

Pitocin Use at Birth

A review was conducted of the literature on Pitocin as a labor induction agent, with a particular emphasis on identifying research pertaining to possible effects on the infant. Studies of the effects of Pitocin inductions on the neonate are generally confounded by the variety of other variables that may affect the results, such as the reason for the induction itself—whether elective (for doctor's, hospital's, or family's convenience) or medically indicated, legitimately or otherwise; the length and manner of administration and dosage; and whether other events or interventions (e.g., premature, spontaneous, or artificial rupture of membranes; epidural or other narcotic or sedative use; episiotomy; instrument delivery; or cesarean section) preceded, accompanied, or followed its use. Additional confounding factors may include characteristics of the mother or the child, such as temperament, and the nature of their early relationship, in addition to the contribution of the father and siblings to the mother-infant relationship.

The literature review revealed an increased risk of nuchal cord (umbilical cord wrapped around the baby's neck) (Rhoades, Latza, & Mueller, 1999); that twin pregnancies are associated with fewer side effects from oxytocin stimulation (e.g., interruptions for fetal heart rate abnormalities and hyperstimulation of the uterus) than are singleton pregnancies (Fausett, Barth, Yoder, & Satin, 1997); and an ongoing debate about whether oxytocin itself, which acts as an antidiuretic, or its administration in large volumes in IV solutions, is responsible for higher incidences of neonatal jaundice among infants exposed to Pitocin than among infants not thus exposed (D'Souza, Lieberman, Cadman, & Richards, 1986; Johnson et al., 1984; Singhi & Singh, 1979).

Several studies (Ekman, Granstrom, & Ulmsten, 1986; Goeschen, 1989; Rojansky, Reubinoff, Tanos, Shushan, & Weinstein, 1997) compared the effects of oxytocin induction unfavorably with those of prostaglandin F2 alpha induction (which ripens the cervix), whereas one (Fuchs, Goeschen, Husslein, Rasmussen, & Fuchs, 1983) pointed out that both increased oxytocin levels and increased prostaglandin levels (PGF2 alpha) are required for adequate stimulation of the human uterus during labor—apparently oxytocin initiates labor and PGF2 alpha is responsible for the progress of labor.

In a review of research concerning the management of premature rupture of membranes Goer (1995) summarized several studies whose results showed unfavorable outcomes with oxytocin induction, finding longer intervals between premature rupture of membranes and delivery with concomitant increases in neonatal infection, an increase in epidural use, and more fetal distress detected by electronic fetal monitoring, leading to more operative vaginal deliveries and cesareans. On the other hand, a study of the neurophysiologic responses (as measured by electroencephalogram and heart rate) of newborn infants delivered after spontaneous onset of labor, compared with those of infants whose mothers had labor induced with oxytocin or prostaglandin F2 alpha, found significant differences in resting brain activity, with "some attenuation of activity in the two induction groups prior to stimulation" (Crowell et al., 1980, p. 52). The differences were greatest between the group with normal onset of labor and the group induced with prostaglandin F2 alpha. The authors were unable to define the mechanisms underlying the effects revealed by electroencephalogram and called for further study "to determine whether the effect is transitory or persistent and related to any behavior patterns" (p. 52).

Two studies (Cahill, Boylan, & O'Herlihy, 1992; Pates & Satin, 2005) suggested that the use of high-dose artificial oxytocin to augment labor as part of an active management protocol does not increase adverse fetal outcomes such as perinatal mortality or morbidity, fetal distress, neonatal seizures, or abnormal neonatal neurologic behavior.

In contrast, a survey conducted in Sweden (Milsom et al., 2002) found a nearly threefold increased risk of asphyxia at birth among babies born after oxytocin augmentation. Cammu, Martens, Ruyssinck, and Amy (2002) found increased rates of cesarean deliveries, instrument deliveries, use of epidural analgesia, and transfers of babies to the neonatal ward with induced labor. Buckley (2007) postulated that the surge of catecholamine triggered by pressure on the fetal head close to the moment of birth normally protects the fetus's ability to tolerate low oxygen levels during labor but that this surge is less likely to be available during labors induced with Pitocin because the baby is often still high in the pelvis.

The package insert from the manufacturer of Pitocin warns of a number of adverse reactions that have been reported in the fetus or neonate, including low 5-minute Apgar scores, neonatal jaundice, bradycardia, arrhythmias, permanent central nervous system or brain damage, neonatal seizures, and fetal death. In a box at the beginning of the package insert's indications and usage section it is clearly stated, "Since the available data are inadequate to evaluate the benefits-to-risks considerations, Pitocin is not indicated for elective induction of labor" (Monarch Pharmaceuticals, 2004, p. 1).

Buckley (2005) noted that in addition to the risks of using medications for induction and augmentation that result in abnormal labor among healthy mothers, these medications also may disrupt the normal functioning of birth hormones in both mother and baby, with largely unknown consequences.

A search of the Cochrane Library database on the term *labor induction* resulted in 29 reviews of clinical trials, 26 of which focused on different methods of induction or on comparisons of such methods. Methods included the use of various medications—corticosteroids, estrogen, hyaluronidase, mifeprostone, misoprostol, oxytocin, prostaglandin, and relaxin—variously administered topically (for cervical ripening), intravenously, or orally. Other trials of induction methods reviewed included acupuncture, amniotomy, breast stimulation, membrane sweeping, castor oil, bathing, enema, mechanical induction methods, and sexual intercourse. One review focused on comparing expectant management with induced labor following prelabor rupture of membranes at term (37 weeks or more), whereas two more examined the use of interventions, induction, or both for the improvement of outcomes at or beyond term.

Although the words *fetal, neonatal,* and *baby* were employed in the majority of these reviews, no review focused specifically on any possible association between induction of labor of any type and later functioning in the child. Reviews that discussed any such effects did so in passing, with references to decreasing morbidity and mortality; hypoglycemia; brachial plexus injuries or fractures; concerns about size, weight, and growth rate; the risk of overstimulation causing the baby difficulties during labor;

monitoring of fetal heart-rate or movements; or frequency of neonatal intensive care unit admissions as a result of concern about possible infection following prelabor rupture of membranes at term. An additional search on the term *Pitocin* resulted in five reports of individual clinical trials conducted in the 1980s and 1990s. None of these trials involved follow-up with regard to potential associations between induction and later functioning.

Although the Cochrane Collaboration's reviews of randomized controlled trials are considered to be the gold standard for meta-analysis of the most respected form of research methodology in the obstetrical field, resulting in periodic changes in clinical practice guidelines, they are limited to the type of studies (i.e., clinical trials) that are not normally conducted to answer research questions requiring longer-term follow-up. Furthermore, the possibility of an association between obstetrical interventions such as induction with artificial oxytocin and later psychosocial functioning in the child is not generally seen to be within the purview of obstetrical research because the care of the child falls first to the hospital's pediatric team and later to a pediatrician of the parents' choice. In some cases, the authors of the reviews admitted that their review contributes little to an understanding of the importance of how mothers think and feel about the options available to them in giving birth and about the birth itself. In areas such as these, it is possible that other research methodologies may shed more light on directions for clinical practice—the Listening to Mothers surveys (Declercq, Sakala, Corry, & Applebaum, 2006; Declercq, Sakala, Corry, Applebaum, & Risher, 2002) being recent examples of such an alternative methodology.

Perinatal Risk Factors for Various Disorders and Later Effects

Studies Implicating Oxytocin in Specific Disorders

Dr. Eric Hollander (1996) of New York's Mount Sinai School of Medicine noticed in the 1990s that 60% of his autistic patients had experienced Pitocin-induced births and hypothesized that a consequent dysfunction in the newborn's natural oxytocin production might play a role in the social deficits inherent in autism. In later studies, Hollander et al. (2003) found that oxytocin administered by intravenous infusion at 2- to 3-week intervals significantly reduced repetitive behaviors in 15 adults with autism or Asperger's syndrome, compared to placebo. The effects were measured by an instrument rating six repetitive behaviors in a double-blind crossover design. In 2007 Hollander et al. used a randomized, double-blind crossover, placebo-controlled methodology, and determined that the treatment facilitated social information processing, as measured by retention of affective speech comprehension in 15 individuals with either an autism or an Asperger's disorder diagnosis. Hollander et al. (2007) noted the support of the findings of Kosfeld, Heinrichs, Zak, Fischbacher, and Fehr (2005) that trust was increased among healthy male participants when oxytocin was administered intranasally, and of Kirsch et al. (2005) that oxytocin served to dampen the amygdala's responsivity to threatening social stimuli.

A retrospective study by Fein et al. (1997) of 633 autistic preschool children tested the hypothesis that the use of artificial oxytocin at birth might result in autism in genetically susceptible infants and found that the frequencies of labor induction for this group, compared with other clinical groups, were extremely close to those expected, not supporting Hollander's (1996) earlier hypothesis.

Glasson et al. (2004) examined the association of obstetric factors found in the Maternal and Child Health Research Database of Western Australia with autism spectrum disorders and found that, among 481 siblings and a random population-based control group of 1,313 others, 465 children with a diagnosed autism spectrum disorder had significantly older parents and were more likely to be firstborn. Labor induction was found to be one of a group of prenatal and perinatal events (including threatened abortion, epidural use, labor duration of less than 1 hour, fetal distress, delivery by elective or emergency cesarean, and 1-minute Apgar scores of less than 6) that was more likely to have been experienced by these children. Glasson et al. also found that these children had more complications than did children with the diagnosis of pervasive developmental disorder not otherwise specified or Asperger's syndrome. The authors concluded that autism development could not be predicted from the observed complications, which were generally nonspecific, and attributed the development of autism spectrum disorders to the genotype, which results in a compromised prenatal experience and leads to obstetrical complications.

A study of a group of perinatal risk factors, including induction of labor, failed to find a relationship between each risk factor in isolation and temperament, as measured by the Temperament Assessment Battery for Children–Revised (Kirsch, 1997). On the other hand, induction of labor (along with breathing problems or need for oxygen, and breech birth) was one of the neurodevelopmental risk factors associated with the etiology of schizotypy (Bakan & Peterson, 1994) and was significantly associated with Sudden Infant Death Syndrome, as were a number of other prenatal and postnatal correlates (Fedrick, 1974).

Both schizophrenia and autism, as well as other common brain/behavior problems, appear to involve malfunctions of the oxytocin system (Green et al., 2001; Jacob et al., 2007; Modahl et al., 1998; Wu et al., 2005), suggesting that labor induction with artificial oxytocin may play a role in their etiology; however, research to date appears to have failed to find a definitive relationship between labor induction and either diagnosis.

Zappitelli et al. (2001) reported on a review of 51 research reports, dated between 1976 and 2001 and identified via Medline and PsychINFO searches, examining the relationship between prenatal, perinatal, or postnatal stress and attention-deficit/hyperactivity disorder. The studies reviewed were selected for their research focus on obstetrical and delivery complications and ADHD. In the section of the article reviewing studies of perinatal events and ADHD, the authors addressed two areas in which studies have been conducted: hypoxia and low birth weight. They noted that studies have indicated an association between ADHD and a dysfunction in dopamine transmission in the right prefrontal cortex and striatum, and they suggested that events during birth that result in hypoxia may affect the developing brain in a way that results in abnormalities of the dopaminergic system, which in turn can manifest as symptoms of ADHD.

Zappitelli et al. (2001) also pointed out that intraventricular hemorrhage secondary to perinatal asphyxia can lead to intellectual and neurological dysfunctions as well as the possibility of psychiatric disorders. Numerous factors can result in perinatal asphyxia—fetal distress for any reason or a long labor are two that are cited. However, the studies reviewed in this article do not specifically identify labor induction with artificial oxytocin per se as one of these factors. The research appears to be contradictory on this matter, with one study (Milsom et al., 2002) finding three times the likelihood of asphyxia with oxytocin augmentation of labor whereas others found no additional risk with oxytocin use.

Zappitelli et al. (2001) concluded that further, more detailed study is clearly needed, noting that many of the studies reviewed were seriously limited by not accounting for confounding variables in studying a clearly multifactorial disorder, given that socioeconomic status, family history, and the presence of learning disorders have been specifically identified as significant to the disorder under study, ADHD. They consider large-scale prospective studies with sound diagnostic methods to be the ideal, and they recommended the inclusion of data from both parents and teachers, with the addition of relevant data from medical records. Zappitelli et al. stated that it would be wise to examine the relationship of prenatal or perinatal factors with both the severity and the varied phenotypic expressions of ADHD.

Claycomb et al. (2004) reported on their investigation of possible relationships among ADHD, induced labor, and a number of physiological and demographic variables. Similar to the studies reviewed by Zappitelli et al. (2001), Claycomb et al. (2004) cited prior studies suggesting that environmental toxins, genetic factors, and maternal stress during pregnancy may contribute to the existence of ADHD. They also focused attention on the possibility that disrupted oxygen flow to the striatum results in compromised function in the faculty of awareness and ensuing problems with impulsivity, hyperactivity, and inattention. Claycomb et al. noted that such a compromise is relatively commonplace with prematurity, which is known to be associated with an increased risk of ADHD. They argued that labor induction may increase maternal stress and therefore increase fetal exposure to glucocorticoids, a known risk factor for ADHD, and commented that "the literature is silent concerning" this possibility (p. 690). They cited literature reporting that excessive use of artificial oxytocin during labor may result in variations in fetal heart rate and central nervous system damage and noted the absence of research specifically intended to examine the relationship of labor induction with a later diagnosis of ADHD.

Claycomb et al. (2004) did not cite the Zappitelli et al. (2001) review, nor did they reference any of the studies examining possible relationships between oxytocin use for induction and later functioning, or studies that found hypoxia to be one of the effects of Pitocin inductions. Their study found no statistically significant relationship between induction and later ADHD, but the study had significant methodological flaws that compromise the validity of its findings. For example, the brief, 17-item questionnaire employed asked mothers to respond only to a yes/no question concerning induction, lacking specificity and detail (e.g., time and duration of administration), and did not state how many of the 130 mothers surveyed were induced at the birth of their ADHD children.

Studies Associating Obstetric Conditions With Adult Substance Abuse and Suicide

In the 1980s and 1990s, a series of studies explored the possibility of relationships between maternal and perinatal conditions and later drug abuse or suicide in the offspring. Citing Canadian and U.S. studies of birth cohorts in 1980 that demonstrated consistently rising rates of adolescent suicide over the previous 25 years, a study by Salk et al. (1985) investigated a possible relationship between these rates and the falling rates of perinatal mortality over the same time period. They noted that the

1985 rate of suicide among teens and young adults was approximately 300% higher than in 1955, although in the same time period there had been little variance in suicide rates among the overall population.

Salk et al. (1985) conducted a blinded review of the birth records of 52 individuals who had subsequently committed suicide. These individuals were matched with two control groups comprising the closest birth preceding that of each case and the closest birth following each case, matched for sex, race (all Caucasian), and hospital of birth. The researchers reported controlling for socioeconomic factors and "other family conditions." The individuals were all adolescents (43 males, 9 females) who died of recorded suicide before age 20, between February 1975 and March 1983, in Rhode Island. Prenatal, birth, and neonatal records of nine hospitals were accessed for all subjects and controls.

Salk et al. (1985) used a system of tabulation to itemize 36 risk factors for the prenatal and birth period and 10 factors for the infant's condition at birth. All factors were summed for each subject and each control. Specific risk factors for each case and the controls were tallied and Student's *t* test was used for matched pairs. All risk factors were extracted whose incidence in any one group was twice as high as for either of the other groups, with at least four cases in the group with high scores. Salk et al. found 10 variables meeting these criteria, 9 of which showed a higher incidence in the group of suicide victims than in the controls, with no statistical differences found between the controls.

The risk factors most commonly found in the suicide victims were compared across the three groups (Salk et al., 1985). These were (a) lack of prenatal care before 20 weeks (30.8%, compared with 3.8% in Control Group 1 and 11.5% in Control Group 2); (b) chronic disease of the mother during pregnancy (21.2%, compared with 0% in Control Group 1 and 5.8% in Control Group 2); and (c) respiratory distress for more than 1 hour at birth (19.2%, compared with 7.7% in Control Group 1 and 3.8% in Control Group 2). Combined, these three risk factors differentiated suicide victims from matched controls better than any factor individually. Each risk factor was found to occur alone in 81% of suicide cases and combined with one other risk factor in 19% of suicide cases. There were no cases of all three risk factors found together.

Salk et al. (1985) suggested that the reduction in perinatal mortality signifies that more babies are being successfully resuscitated who would formerly have died. Indeed, prior to the 1953 introduction of Virginia Apgar's system of scoring the condition of newborns at 1 and 5 minutes after birth, according to

Gawande (2006), babies who were malformed, small, or simply blue and not breathing well were typically listed as stillborn, and no resuscitation efforts were made. Salk et al. (1985) noted that many babies survive various forms of perinatal adversity, so one cannot assume a direct connection between such events and later suicide, but they proposed that if there are indeed triggering factors to such suicides, perinatal conditions may render these individuals more vulnerable.

The study by Salk et al. (1985) has the disadvantage of being retrospective, with the possibility that the researchers may have missed some common circumstance or event affecting the individuals who eventually committed suicide. In addition, their discussion of the findings focused, curiously, almost entirely on the perinatal risk factor of respiratory distress for more than 1 hour at birth, although the percentage difference between the suicide group and the control groups for this factor was smaller than the percentage difference between the suicide group and the controls for the two prenatal risk factors: lack of prenatal care before 20 weeks and chronic disease in the mother during her pregnancy. One might consider these two risk factors during the prenatal period to be symptomatic of ongoing health or family problems or challenges that might be significant contributors to the ultimate suicides, which thereby confounds the findings of the study.

A similar study, published 2 years later and described by its authors as a pilot study (Jacobson et al., 1987), sought to examine more closely the specific relationship between obstetric procedures and eventual adult behaviors. Like the study by Salk et al. (1985), the Jacobson et al. (1987) study was retrospective, employing birth record data for 2,901 controls and 412 forensic victims who were born in identified Stockholm hospitals after 1940 and who died there between 1978 and 1984, having committed suicide or having been alcoholics or drug addicts. Criteria for suicide victims comprised a suicide note or clearly stated intention to end one's life; for alcoholics, characteristic tissue changes in liver and pancreas indicative of known alcohol abuse were confirmed by social authorities; for drug addicts, multiple injection scars and confirmation by police records or social authorities. All cases were confirmed by autopsy and analyses were conducted for alcohol and drugs, including narcotics.

This study (Jacobson et al.,1987) analyzed 8,720 hospital birth records to determine annual percentages of administration of opiates and barbiturates, although the authors admitted that records of nitrous oxide analgesia and chloroform anesthesia were not accurately recorded and so their role as risk factors could not be accurately evaluated. The researchers found significant associations between the perinatal administration of either opiates, barbiturates, or both during labor and later drug addiction; asphyxia at birth was closely associated to suicides by violent means (e.g., hanging, strangulation, drowning, or poisoning by gas); mechanical birth traumas (e.g., breech presentation, forceps delivery, or nuchal entanglement with multiple loops) were associated with suicides by violent mechanical means (e.g., hanging, strangulation, jumping from heights, or firearms); and opiate or barbiturate administration to laboring mothers was associated with drug addiction in the offspring. Drawing on ethological research in this area, the authors suggested that the means by which these experiences at birth were played out in adulthood might be analogous to imprinting. They noted that it seems less likely that humans do not have an imprinting mechanism than that, as in many other species, this mechanism exists in our species to enhance survival. This study did not control for parental socioeconomic circumstances or specific type of addiction.

Jacobson et al. (1988) published a study that focused on testing the hypotheses that the administration of obstetric medications at delivery constitutes a risk factor for later drug addiction in the child and that adult behavior patterns can result from perinatal imprinting of specific risk factors. They theorized that the administration of nitrous oxide would be more likely to result in amphetamine addiction than would other obstetric medications and that amphetamine addiction would be correlated with the duration of the nitrous oxide administration. Their study of 200 amphetamine addicts and 195 sibling controls born at one of seven major hospitals in Stockholm between 1945 and 1966 and raised by their biological mothers began by recruiting subjects through interviews with all people arrested on certain days between November 1986 and September 1987 who had chronic injection scars. These individuals were asked for their mother's name, the hospital at which they were born, their drug preferences, their number of siblings and if they were raised in the family, and if any siblings were drug addicts. The authors acknowledged that females were underrepresented in their data because they are less likely to be arrested than males.

The Jacobson et al. (1988) study attempted to remedy the deficits of the prior study (1987), controlling for socioeconomic circumstances by using siblings as controls. The researchers also created a control database of hospital data, whereas a blind evaluation of the records of study participants (addicts and control siblings) and a quality check on control data revealed incomplete records, particularly with reference to missing data concerning the administration of nitrous oxide, in order to take these factors into account.

Findings included that one of the seven hospitals accounted for 27% of the addicts but only 14% of all births, with this distribution not accounted for by socioeconomic factors (Jacobson et al., 1988). The authors were unable to explain this finding with any certainty. Overall, nitrous oxide was administered for longer periods, more often, among mothers of future addicts than among controls, and chloroform was administered in larger doses to mothers giving birth to future addicts in 26 instances, compared to 20 instances for nonaddicted siblings. Using logistic regression, the duration of nitrous oxide administration was tested against 12 potential confounding variables: hospital; birth year; birth weight; birth order; labor duration; nonvertex presentation; asphyxia; meconium-stained amniotic fluid; instrument delivery (forceps or vacuum extraction—no cesareans took place in this sample); and administration of opiates, barbiturates, or chloroform. The researchers found that the administration of nitrous oxide to the mother for at least 4.5 hours yielded a relative risk that the infant was 5.6 times more likely to become a drug addict than was the infant of a mother who received nitrous oxide for 15 minutes or less. They admitted being unable to control for criminal behavior as a confounder but noted that even if criminal behavior were a factor in explaining the data, nitrous oxide administration would have had to lead first to criminal behavior, and thence to drug addiction, rather than the reverse.

Jacobson et al. (1988) cited an article by Salk (1966) on the role of imprinting in early development and an article by Kimball (1967) on the role of ethology in clinical obstetrics to suggest that imprinting mediated by catecholamines is well documented as a survival mechanism in many species. Jacobson et al. (1988) noted that such hormones are at their peak during the birth process, enhancing the neonate's chances for survival, although the concept appeared to have become a controversial issue when applied to patterns of behavior in adult humans.

Jacobson et al. (1988) believe that the risks determined in the study are probably underestimated, because nitrous oxide was measured only by duration of administration rather than by dosage. They noted that at the time of the births of the study subjects, 3 to 5 liters of pure nitrous oxide were administered intermittently during contractions, whereas currently it is mixed with oxygen. They also stated that omitting the factor of being born in the particular hospital that increased the risk of becoming an addict made the estimated risk more conservative. They concluded by asserting that the administration of obstetric pain relief medications that pass through the placenta is closely associated with eventual drug addiction in offspring.

Although this study (Jacobson et al., 1988) still follows the model of retrospective examination of birth records, taking care to seek out and control for confounders, and although interviewing living addicts lends the study some strength in relation to the earlier studies, the interviews do not appear to have been intended to explore the addicts' own perceptions of their history and path toward drug addiction, which might have served to contribute valuable qualitative data to the study. Genetic and socioeconomic factors were controlled for by matching subjects with their siblings.

Some of these researchers sought to weigh against each other the possible risk factors for drug addiction: perinatal obstetric medication against familial socioeconomic conditions at time of birth (Nyberg, Allebeck, Eklund, & Jacobson, 1992) and obstetric care at specific hospitals of birth against residential area during adolescence (Nyberg, Allebeck, Eklund, & Jacobson, 1993). In the former study (Nyberg et al., 1992), a low socioeconomic level appeared to be a possible risk factor for amphetamine addiction but not for opiate addiction. Meanwhile, the uneven distribution of births among the hospitals, which was most pronounced for amphetamine addicts, appeared to support the authors' hypothesis that obstetric practices could be risk factors for adult drug addiction.

The second study (Nyberg et al., 1993) focused on 200 amphetamine and 200 opiate addicts born between 1945 and 1966. The relative risk of future addiction through "contagious transmission" was determined for eight residential areas, for the seven Stockholm hospitals, and for four periods of birth. In the case of opiate addicts, the researchers found only one weak association for residential area, which did not fully account for a clustering of births at any particular hospital, whereas among amphetamine addicts the hospital of birth remained an important risk factor after controlling for residential area, thus confirming the findings of the Jacobson et al. (1988) study. Studies in areas such as Stockholm have the advantages of detailed record keeping over a period of many years and a relatively nonmobile population.

Jacobson et al. (1990) published an additional retrospective study in Stockholm investigating the relationship between the obstetric administration of opiates, barbiturates, and nitrous oxide (for a period greater than 1 hour) and opiate addiction. In this case, the participant sample comprised 41 of the interviewees from the earlier (Jacobson et al., 1988) study, 75 individuals confirmed dead from opiate addiction between 1978 and 1988, and 84 individuals accepted for a methadone program. After exclusions, the sample contained 139 cases matched with 230 siblings to control for genetic and socioeconomic confounders.

As in the Jacobson et al. (1988) study, data in Jacobson et al. (1990) were extracted by an experienced midwife blinded to the test hypotheses, and data analysis was conducted via logistic regression, with stepwise regression used to exclude confounders. Findings included that siblings were exposed to a significantly lower administration of obstetric drugs than were the addicted individuals. The hypothesis that opiates and barbiturates constitute risk factors for eventual opiate addiction in the offspring when these drugs were administered between 1.5 and 4.5 hours prior to delivery was not disproved, with the relative risk increasing with the number of administrations.

Jacobson et al. (1990) found that asphyxia at birth was not statistically significant, but they nevertheless speculated that minimal brain damage might result from hypoxia caused by the administration of 100% nitrous oxide prior to birth, and that such injury might contribute to emotional instability, making the individual more susceptible to drug addiction. They found, unexpectedly, that nitrous oxide administration, already shown to be associated with amphetamine addiction, also contributes to the risk of opiate addiction. They cited animal studies indicating that effects of nitrous oxide are mediated through two mechanisms, one involving catecholamines, including dopamine, thereby possibly imprinting a sensation of elation and thus explaining a preference for amphetamines, and the other involving opioids, similar to the mechanism for opiates.

In this article, Jacobson et al. (1990) explored more thoroughly their reasons for believing that imprinting is the mechanism involved in drug addiction in adult offspring of mothers administered opiates, barbiturates, or nitrous oxide during delivery. They suggested that what is imprinted is a propensity for using/abusing opiates to alleviate anxiety, because catecholamines are at a peak late in labor and prior to birth, and cited prior studies describing such a process with both animals and human infants. They asserted that no other explanation makes as much sense of their findings, noting that chloroform, which provides few subjective sensations other than a reduction of consciousness, was not found to be a risk factor for drug addiction. They also noted that the three drugs tested in the study have different chemical structures yet contribute equally to the risk, making it unlikely that the effect is mediated through toxicity to the brain tissue, as opposed to a more psychobiological process.

Jacobson et al. (1990) also noted that drug addiction is more commonplace among males, who have higher levels of circulating testosterone at birth, which is among the substances that facilitates imprinting; that imprinting, considered to be an irreversible memory process that causes specific neuroanatomical changes in animal brains, may explain the difficulties of treating addiction and avoiding relapse; and that the significant increase in drug misuse and abuse occurred in the 1960s, whereas the first generations exposed to heavy analgesia and sedation at birth were born in the postwar years (mid-1940s) and thereafter, suggesting a causal connection. The possibility of genetic or socioeconomic confounders during the postwar years was ruled out by the use of sibling controls, and other perinatal factors were controlled for by multivariate analysis.

In 2000, one of the researchers in several of the earlier studies, Karin Nyberg, published a study with American colleagues (Nyberg, Buka, & Lipsitt, 2000), using a North American sample, with the goal of examining the relationship between perinatal exposure to obstetric medications and adult drug abuse, using the sibling-control design employed in some of the earlier studies. The study utilized the National Collaborative Perinatal Project, in which 4,140 pregnancies were enrolled between 1959 and 1966, with extensive prospective collection of obstetric, neurological, psychological, and sociodemographic data from the prenatal period through age 7, and follow-up procedures at the ages of 18 to 27.

Of the offspring followed, 693 were interviewed and psychiatric diagnoses were assessed using the Diagnostic Interview Schedule Version III in order to identify psychiatric and substance abuse disorders (Nyberg et al., 2000). The researchers identified 69 subjects meeting the *Diagnostic and Statistical Manual of Mental Disorders* (3rd ed.) criteria for diagnoses of drug abuse or dependence on cocaine, hallucinogens, narcotics, and other "hard drugs." A case-control design was used, comparing participants with 33 nonabusing siblings (also National Collaborative Perinatal Project participants) with regard to opiate and barbiturate medication given to their mothers between 10 hours prior to delivery and birth, and with regard to obstetrical complications (perinatal asphyxia; i.e., Apgar less than 7 at 5 minutes), meconium-stained amniotic fluid, labor longer than 12 hours, birth order, and low birth weight (under 2,500 g). Medications administered to the mothers were phenobarbital (100 mg to 150 mg/dose), secobarbital (1.5 g to 3 g/dose), and meperidine (50 mg to 100 mg/dose).

Data were abstracted blindly from research protocols completed at delivery (Nyberg et al., 2000). Sibling controls were selected to control for possible confounding by environmental, genetic, and socioeconomic factors, resulting in 33 eligible controls for the 69 subjects. The results were provided with 95% confidence limits.

In contrast to the studies conducted in Sweden (Jacobson et al., 1988; Jacobson et al., 1990), Nyberg et al. (2000) had the advantage of Apgar scores for evaluating perinatal asphyxia, and the sample was followed prospectively, with extensive data-gathering concerning perinatal and obstetric conditions. None of this sample was exposed to nitrous oxide, thus ruling out the possibility of asphyxia resulting from the administration of 100% nitrous oxide and leading to later addictive behaviors, which was an alternative hypothesis to explain the findings of the Swedish studies (Jacobson et al., 1988; Jacobson et al., 1990) referenced by Nyberg. Perinatal risk variables (asphyxia, low birth weight, birth order, and prolonged labor) were distributed similarly between subjects and controls (Nyberg et al., 2000), as it was in these previous studies.

Nyberg et al.'s (2000) findings replicated those of the prior studies, with individuals exposed to high doses of obstetric medications at birth showing a four- to fivefold increase in the likelihood of adult drug abuse or dependence. Because the sample was drawn from an American population in contrast to the prior studies conducted in Sweden (Jacobson et al., 1988; Jacobson et al., 1990), this study, though small, supported the conclusion that ethnic, local, or environmental factors cannot account for the findings.

A study by Neugebauer and Reuss (1998) attempted to replicate Salk et al.'s (1985) study, using a similar methodology with a sample of 189 individuals aged 15 to 22 who were born and, between 1985 and 1991, committed suicide in New York City. Data were extracted from birth and death certificates. Controls were selected in the same manner as those in Salk et al.'s study, and in the case of the controls it was ascertained that each had survived to the age of 1 year, because pregnancy complications are associated with increased infant mortality.

Neugebauer and Reuss (1998) emphasized the importance of evaluating risk factors for suicide in people between 15 and 24 years of age, especially factors that might be amenable to intervention, such as prenatal and perinatal factors. These researchers found that the overall mean complication score was not significantly different between cases and either control group, even when adjusted for hospital service, and this finding did not vary according to ethnicity, sex, or age at death (15 to 20 years or 21 to 22 years). Neugebauer and Reuss acknowledged that the information available to them via birth certificates excluded some of the data available to Salk et al. (1985), predominantly factors pertaining to neonatal status, including respiratory distress for more than 1 hour. They attempted to control for this lack of information by computing a complication score for Salk et al.'s cases that was limited to the information available from birth certificates, but found that the new mean for the Salk et al. cases was still substantially higher than the controls'.

The Neugebauer and Reuss (1998) study also controlled for socioeconomic differences between cases and controls, which increased observed excess of complications among controls compared to cases, an anticipated finding based on the origin of the sample. The authors concluded that their inability to replicate Salk et al.'s (1985) study was indicative of a lack of consistent epidemiological support for the hypothesis of an association between maternal, prenatal, or perinatal risk complications and later risk of suicide in offspring, but called for further research in the area.

Later in the same year, Jacobson and Bygdeman (1998) published a new, prospective case-control study, following up on Salk et al.'s (1985) and Jacobson et al.'s (1987) studies, with the goal of testing whether traumatic birth might be associated with suicide by violent means. Jacobson and Bygdeman (1998) claimed to employ a stringent study design that controlled for confounding variables and used the hypothesis that individuals committing suicide might be unconsciously replicating the sensations of traumatic birth through the mechanism of imprinting. They further hypothesized that men would be affected more than women, because they believe imprinting to be facilitated by testosterone. They identified variables to contribute to a trauma score, prior to accessing birth records, and selected only cases who had died by unambiguous suicide by violent means (e.g., use of a firearm, jumping in front of a train, jumping from a height, laceration, strangulation, or hanging).

All cases were born at one of seven hospitals in Stockholm between 1945 and 1980, were Swedish citizens, and had been examined postmortem (Jacobson & Bygdeman, 1998). A total of 242 cases of suicide were matched with 403 siblings. Birth records were coded and data were extracted by two midwives blinded as to cases versus controls. Each case was assigned a trauma score based on the number of instances of certain birth events likely to cause pain to the infant: meconium-stained amniotic fluid and membranes, presentation other than vertex, internal version or instrumental delivery, and resuscitation and other complications normally requiring care.

Jacobson and Bygdeman (1998) recorded the frequency of administration of opiates (50 mg to 100 mg pethidine hydrochloride or 15 mg to 20 mg morphine) in the 24 hours before birth. They also identified and took into account several potential confounders, including both categorical (e.g., hospital; year and season of birth; socioeconomic level; birth order; duration of labor; birth weight; and administration of chloroform, barbiturates, or nitrous oxide) and indicator variables (e.g., sex, treatment with oxytocin, or neonatal asphyxia).

Three methods were used to determine the duration of labor (Jacobson and Bygdeman, 1998). Logistic regression of subjects with a variable number of siblings was employed, together with multivariate analysis after stepwise regression to estimate the relative risks for suicide, using a significance level of $p < .05$ as the criterion for inclusion. Determining the regression coefficients allowed estimation of odds ratios for the various factors, taking into account confounding variables.

Jacobson and Bygdeman (1998) found that the duration of labor decreased over the period of the study as obstetric practices changed. They found that offspring who committed suicide had been more frequently exposed to birth complications than had their siblings and that instrumental delivery or internal version, resuscitation, and other birth complications contributed more to mean trauma scores during the periods 1966 to 1970 and 1971 to 1980 than during the period from 1945 to 1960. They found that the mothers of subjects who later committed suicide were administered fewer doses of opiates during five of the six periods of the study, and that maternal age, sex of child, treatment with opiates, and the interaction of men with the trauma score were significant variables. The youngest maternal age group showed the lowest relative risk of infants eventually committing suicide and also was the group that was administered the most opiates.

Jacobson and Bygdeman (1998) reported that the findings indicated that 13 of 15 potential confounders were nonsignificant. It was noted that the increase in contribution to the trauma score of obstetric and neonatal measures after 1965 was unlikely to be attributable to improved record keeping, because the recorded number of meconium-stained amniotic fluid and membranes and presentations other than vertex did not increase, suggesting "more active obstetrical care for reducing perinatal complications" (p. 1348).

Jacobson and Bygdeman (1998) suggested that it may be the reason for the traumatic intervention, or some other subtle and unidentified high-risk factor, that gives rise to the increased risk of suicide. They noted that the risk of eventual suicide was approximately halved among children of mothers who were administered one treatment with opiates, and they posited that painful deliveries may result in ambivalence toward their infants on the part of the mothers, whose parenting might then be compromised by lack of motivation, with pain medication serving to counteract this outcome. They pointed out that the use of opiates bears its own consequences in the increased risk of subsequent drug addiction in the offspring, but emphasized the importance of reducing pain and discomfort to the infant during birth.

The conclusions of the Jacobson and Bygdeman (1998) study were disputed by Appleby (1998), a professor of psychiatry at the University of Manchester, who maintained that violent suicides, asphyxiation by exhaust fumes, and hanging are typically more common in men and that these methods are associated with severe mental illness such as schizophrenia and major affective disorder. Appleby noted that methods are typically influenced by availability of means, such as deaths from firearms in the United States and jumping from tall buildings in Hong Kong. He questioned the validity of obstetric complications, or scores derived from them, as indicators of infant pain, and the correspondences drawn by Jacobson and Bygdeman (1998) between type of perinatal experience and means of suicide.

Appleby (1998) noted that studies have indicated the likelihood of neurodevelopmental impairment, possibly resulting from fetal hypoxia, as a contributing factor to schizophrenia and possibly also to major affective disorder. He confronted what he perceived to be Jacobson and Bygdeman's (1999) assertion that the causal mechanism is imprinting, using the high testosterone level at birth as a mediating factor.

In their rebuttal, Jacobson and Bygdeman (1999) denied claiming to ascribe their findings to this hypothesis, stating that it was employed only as part of the study's design and to predict the findings. They noted that they had stated that they could not exclude the possibility that it may be the circumstances giving rise to the need for intervention that result in eventual suicides. They added that the findings of their study failed to support the hypothesis that fetal hypoxia may be a causal factor.

In spite of Jacobson and Bygdeman's (1999) assertion that the imprinting hypothesis was employed merely to predict results prior to beginning their most recent study, this hypothesis is a theme throughout this series of studies, an attempt to explain associations between obstetric complications and interventions and serious problems of drug addiction and suicide in adult life. Only two of this group of studies (Neugebauer & Reuss, 1998; Salk et al., 1987) were conducted by researchers not known to be connected to the other studies in the series. The majority of the studies were conducted by researchers associated with the Swedish Karolinska Institute, from which a considerable body of birth-related research has been generated, in part because Sweden's thorough record keeping facilitates both retrospective and prospective case-control research.

These researchers (Neugebauer & Reuss, 1998; Salk et al., 1987) have discussed the shortcomings of their studies as they saw them and have attempted to remedy these shortcomings in more recent efforts, and although the series cannot prove that imprinting is the mechanism by which events in adult life are significantly influenced, the question of why imprinting should not be a survival-enhancing mechanism that humans share with many other species is a salient one. Neither these studies nor Appleby (1998) reference imprinting studies in animals that identify the time around birth as a critical period for such a process to take place, not only in animals but also quite possibly in humans.

This is a significant deficit in all the studies focused on the relationship between obstetric complications and later suicide, although none of the studies specifically sought to examine the possibility of mental illness being a causal or mediating factor in the suicides under examination. It is nonetheless possible that there is some truth to both positions: obstetric complications and interventions may indeed result in some form of imprinting effect, and mental illness may be a contributing factor in the eventual suicide but may have origins that lie in prenatal or perinatal events.

Of the series, only Nyberg et al.'s (2000) U.S. study employed standardized diagnoses, and then only to establish substance abuse—the study did not address suicide. Research with mothers (Kitzinger, 2006) confirmed that birth experiences can result in maternal trauma and mental illness, and mothers profoundly influence their infants' moods and experiences not only by virtue of their parenting and mood but also biochemically, prior to birth. In addition, if what happens to a mother at birth is traumatic, can we assume that it would not also be traumatic for her baby?

Nyberg (2000) addressed the question of why this series of studies has not been replicated by others, citing the fact that the record keeping of other countries, including the United States, may preclude conducting studies requiring such detail about the circumstances of birth. Moreover, prospective studies would require enormous cohorts and a willingness to wait 20 or 30 years to examine outcomes. The gold standard for obstetrical studies is the randomized controlled trial, and epidemiological studies are typically given less credence by the medical field.

In addition, it is difficult to challenge common practice, especially when this research carries the implication that what is done to newborns at birth may have long-term effects. Nyberg (2000) noted that more recent studies examining the effects of perinatal events on the future health of individuals have explored ties with autism and schizophrenia and expressed hope that these studies will stimulate further interest in the possibility that short-term exposures in the period surrounding birth might have significant effects.

Studies of the Effects of Obstetric Conditions on Newborns and Young Children

Dean, Gray, and Anderson (1996) reviewed a number of studies conducted in the 1970s and 1980s that reported a relationship between perinatal factors and cognitive outcomes, and other studies demonstrating links between perinatal events (e.g., pregnancy factors, gestational age, birth weight, or obstetrical complications) and children's behavioral and educational performance, although they noted that other studies conducted during the same time period failed to find such a relationship. The authors attributed these discrepancies to the univariate design used in the majority of the cited studies, observing that perinatal events have a multivariate nature.

Consequently, Dean et al. (1996) examined the underlying factor structure of perinatal events for 847 children (272 with normal development, 117 developmentally disabled, 37 speech disordered, 221 learning disordered, 91 emotionally disturbed, and 109 Head Start children), subjecting to principal component analysis the pertinent information from the mothers' responses to the Maternal Perinatal Scale. The resulting 10 factors accounted for approximately 57.9% of the total variability. Labor induction loaded with "time from rupture of membranes to start of labor" in a factor interpreted as "labor" that accounted for 5.3% of the total variability.

However, as is frequently the case in studies of multiple perinatal events, the forms of labor induction reported were not differentiated. Dean et al.'s (1996) emphasis in the article was predominantly on the efficacy of the chosen paradigm for data reduction and the advantages of examining multiple factors, rather than on individual events, in predicting perinatal outcomes. Although the study did not provide definitive data concerning the use of oxytocin during labor induction and its relation to the childhood disorders in the study population, it makes a salient point concerning methodologies for studying the effects of perinatal events.

The Medline database contains records of studies of labor induction dating back to 1949. Although these articles address a variety of approaches and medications used to induce labor, a considerable number of them focus on the use of Pitocin. Niswander, Turoff, and Romans (1966) cited two earlier publications (Keettel, Randall, & Donnelly, 1958; Niswander & Patterson, 1963) on the "hazards of elective induction of labor," demonstrating what is now clearly a long-standing concern about the use of labor induction in the absence of medical indications. The subtitle of the Niswander et al. (1966) article indicates that it is a report on a 4-year follow-up study and that the authors had described in two prior articles (Niswander & Patterson, 1963; Niswander, Patterson, & Randall, 1960) the preliminary and final results of a retrospective study of elective induction of labor involving 2,862 mothers.

Based on the perception that the literature on elective induction at that time was "both voluminous and contradictory" (Niswander et al., 1966, p. 15), the article detailed the findings of the follow-up study on the developmental status of children delivered by elective induction of labor. The authors suggested that expected outcomes might include higher perinatal mortality, which implies an increased risk of neurological damage in surviving infants, increased frequency of perinatal anoxia, increased numbers of babies with depressed Apgar scores, and the authors' own prior findings of a "significantly increased number with neonatal respiratory problems" (p. 15). They cited the concept of a "continuum of reproductive causality" postulated by Lilienfeld, Pasamanick, and Rogers (1955) in reporting on a series of epidemiological studies, with a "lethal component" resulting in fetal or neonatal death and a "sublethal component" resulting in various degrees of disability, including "certain behavior disorders of childhood" (Lilienfeld, Pasamanick, & Rogers, 1955, p. 641).

Niswander et al. (1966) posited that "induction, constituting a minor trauma for some surviving infants, might be associated with a concomitant increase in the number of such surviving babies having behavioral and/or intellectual deficits probably based on underlying neurologic impairment" (p. 15). In this follow-up study, Niswander et al. randomly selected equal numbers of 4-year-olds whose mothers had had electively induced labor ($n = 131$) or spontaneous labor ($n = 147$), born between 38 and 42 weeks of gestation. All parents were Caucasian. Past obstetric histories of the mothers in the two groups were found to be almost identical, and cases of presentations other than vertex, spontaneous rupture of membranes prior to onset of labor, and all other medical complications were excluded. Other small differences between the induced and control groups (maternal age, parity, and socioeconomic status) were identified and found to be not statistically significant.

The authors stated in the second article of the series (Niswander & Patterson, 1963) that they had elected to extend the original study for 2 more years (i.e., from 1955 to 1961, overall) in order to include a larger number of labors in which induction was purely by oxytocin (usually administered intravenously) rather than with a preliminary artificial rupture of membranes (amniotomy), believing that the latter was more likely to result in the birth of premature infants. A significant finding of this study ($p < .01$) was that electively induced babies were more likely to experience some degree of respiratory distress. This second article (Niswander & Patterson, 1963) anticipates the follow-up study (Niswander et al., 1966) and the methodology employed in that study, stating that the authors were unconvinced that induced labors are safe and have no effect on fetal morbidity and that they saw the need to employ "careful functional and psychologic testing of the preschool child" (Niswander & Patterson, 1963, p. 232) in order to explore these concerns further.

Niswander et al.'s (1966) study of 278 children found that 70% of the induced group, as opposed to 40% of the control group, had gestational ages of 38 or 49 weeks, which was an expected finding. Females were found to have significantly higher IQs ($p < .05$), and so the findings were reported in four categories: control females, induced females, control males, and induced males. Thirty-two percent of the selected individuals could not be located. These were divided equally between the study group and control group, resulting in the final sample comprising 131 children in the induced group and 147 controls. Follow-up procedures (analyzing patient refusal pattern, and follow-up phone calls to ascertain reasons for refusals to participate) were documented, and it was noted that information regarding reasons for nonparticipation was incomplete. The researchers speculate that families of impaired children might "be reluctant to present the child for a testing procedure" (p. 17). Among those located (numbers were not provided), the induced group contained 2 children who were mentally retarded and 4 with nonfebrile convulsions, compared to 1 with mental retardation and 2 with nonfebrile convulsions in the control group, but the researchers were unable to identify any etiology of these findings or a relationship with the type of labor.

Noting that "there is a dearth of sensitive psychologic instruments designed to measure minimal brain damage at 4 years" (Niswander et al., 1966, p. 17), the authors selected the Stanford-Binet IQ test to measure intelligence, together with other standardized methods (Porteus mazes, a peg board, and the Graham-Ernhart Block Sort Test) to test fine motor skills, gross motor functioning, and conceptual ability. Based on the understanding that the brain-damaged child can be identified via behavioral characteristics, the researchers stated only that these were "looked for and noted, and an overall estimate of social-emotional adjustment was based on observation during the examination" (p. 17).

Niswander et al. (1966) reported that a significantly greater percentage of females than males was found to have normal functioning on fine and gross motor and overall evaluations, but there were no statistically significant differences between induced and control groups on these measures. A higher median IQ was found among the females than among the males, with overall difference in distribution of scores at the 5% level. The authors were surprised to find a higher median IQ among the total induced group than among the controls, although this finding was not statistically significant. Another unexpected and apparently inexplicable finding was that children born following an electively induced labor of under 3 hours had a statistically significant higher mean IQ than those born following spontaneously initiated labor of the same duration. At 3 hours or more of labor, the difference in mean IQ was not significant.

The findings of the behavioral observations were reported only in a table and do not appear to differentiate between study children and controls to a statistically significant degree. Niswander et al. (1966) noted that they excluded from the follow-up study all premature induced infants and suggested that, given that it has been shown that prematurity has adverse effects on neurological development and that it is a known risk of elective induction, inclusion of these infants in the study might have altered the findings.

There are several problems with these studies: the initial study, documented in a preliminary report (Niswander, et al., 1960) and a second article (Niswander & Patterson, 1963), and the follow-up study reported by Niswander et al. in 1966, especially with how they were documented. First, the article describing the follow-up study (Niswander et al., 1966) contained neither details concerning the induction of labor in the deliveries of the children studied nor a direct reference to the prior study (Niswander et al,, 1960; Niswander & Patterson, 1963) as the source of the sample of children in the follow-up study (Niswander et al., 1966), leaving the reader to seek out the prior publications and assume the relationship between the initial study and the follow-up with the offspring.

Second, remarkably (for a study investigating the possibility of minimal brain damage resulting from induction of labor), in reporting that the type of delivery did not vary between the two groups, Niswander et al. (1966) stated that 93.9% of the control group and 93.1% of the induced babies were delivered by outlet forceps but did not address the possibility that injury, possibly undetected, as a result of this intervention could be a significant confounding factor in any findings—that any impairments found might be the result of injuries resulting from forceps use rather than from labor induction. The value of studying children born by elective induction is that there are no preexisting or emergent conditions necessitating the induction that might confound any significant findings about induction itself. Given that the benefits of forceps delivery and the risks of cranial and other injuries resulting from the procedure have been debated in the literature since it was first employed to extract live infants (e.g., Gawande, 2006), ignoring the possible influence of so significant a variable seems to undermine the attempt to examine the relationship between elective induction of labor and subsequent evidence of brain damage.

Third, although the details of oxytocin dosage and administration (but not duration) were documented, there was no mention of whether any type of anesthesia was used during labor, which might have served to explain the almost universal use of forceps in delivery, unless their use was dictated by hospital policy or standard procedures of the time—information which also was not provided.

In addition, although the use of standardized and well-known measures of IQ and perceptual, visual, and motor functions was documented, Niswander et al.'s (1966) efforts to study behavioral characteristics and socioemotional adjustment were described in a single sentence, leaving it unclear exactly what characteristics were looked for, how systematically these were noted and the socioemotional adjustment estimated, and how these were expected to manifest in the context of the testing situation. No information was provided about the training of testers, if any, nor whether they were blinded to the group to which each child tested belonged. No observation protocol was reported and nothing was stated about whether the testers' observations were validated by others. The findings of this part of the study were reduced to two lines in a table indicating the numbers and percentages of males and females in the induced and control groups who were perceived to be "normal" or "not normal" in their observed behavior.

Finally, Niswander et al.'s (1966) failure to include the duration of oxytocin use when the researchers apparently had access to this data from the original study (Niswander et al, 1960; Niswander & Patterson, 1963) limited their ability to link the total amount of medication administered during induction to any findings of the measures used with the studied offspring at age 4. Furthermore, because this study was a follow-up to a very large study, a prospective design might have permitted recruiting and following a larger number of children and documenting their functioning at several intervals (e.g., during infancy, at age 2, and at age 4) in order to explore continuity and change in any findings between birth and age 4.

An Australian retrospective study (McBride, Lyle, Black, Brown, & Thomas, 1977) cited prior studies that resulted in conflicting findings concerning possible ill effects of labor induction with amniotomy, and sought to reassess the findings of the studies of Niswander et al. (1966) "with more precise control of potentially confounding variables" (p. 457).

McBride et al. (1977) compared two methods of elective induction—amniotomy alone and amniotomy together with oxytocin—among a group of 101 children at age 5, with a follow-up at age 8 (Black & McBride, 1979). Socioeconomic data were obtained via standard interview with the mother, ranking the father's occupational status on a 7-point Congalton scale and the mother's educational status on a 12-point scale. Mothers also participated in a written intelligence test (ACER Form M, Section L). Mothers were screened to eliminate from the sample those whose first language was not English (in order to ensure facility in English for the intelligence testing of the children) and unmarried mothers, "most of whom had surrendered children for adoption" (McBride et al., 1977, p. 457). Cases of breech presentation, multiple births, and instrument deliveries also were excluded from the sample. This resulted in a relatively small sample size of 32 mothers in the spontaneous labor group, 31 in the amniotomy group, and 38 in the amniotomy plus oxytocin group.

McBride et al. (1977) used four verbal and four nonverbal subtests from a standardized intelligence scale (the Wechsler Preschool and Primary Scale of Intelligence), tests of fine motor movement and balance, an audiometric screening test for auditory acuity, visual tests (the Titmus Vision Test for Preschoolers and the Titmus Fly Test of stereopsis), height and weight measurements, a pediatric examination scoring from *no abnormality* to *very significant defect* on a 4-point scale for each of 18 items, and a developmental history obtained from the mother. All tests except the pediatric examination were conducted by the same two psychologists, who were blinded as to which group each child represented.

McBride et al. (1977) found no differences between children born after elective induction of labor (via amniotomy or amniotomy with oxytocin) and those whose labors began spontaneously. The components of the children's test batteries were found not to approach significance ($F < 1$), and the researchers stated that they did not conduct statistical analyses of the sensory tests or pediatric examination because of very small variances of the distribution of scores. The only finding of significance was that induction shortened the first stage of labor ($p < .01$).

In the follow-up study 3 years later, Black and McBride (1979) referenced a text on learning difficulties, suggesting that "some forms of minimal brain dysfunction occur in children of normal intelligence, and are manifest as specific learning difficulties detectable only after the beginning of formal schooling," and speculating that global IQ scores might be too insensitive to detect "subtle differences due to perinatal factors" (p. 362). Nine children were not retested for follow-up, 3 in each group, and of these, only 1 was contacted and declined to participate, whereas the others were either known to have moved out of the area or were suspected to have moved, with current addresses unavailable.

Black and McBride (1979) used standardized tests of school achievement in reading (the ACER individual reading test, word reading, and the ACER primary reading survey) and arithmetic (the arithmetic subscale of the WISC-R); the Bender-Gestalt test for young children, for signs of brain damage and emotional disturbance; the Wepman test of auditory discrimination; and the Belmont and Birch test of auditory-visual integration. They also employed a behavioral checklist (Rutter, Tizard, & Whitmore, 1970) completed by a parent and scored for severity of problems, neuroticism, and antisocial behavior. Parents also rated their child's school performance on a 7-point scale.

Employing one-way analyses of variance for each variable, Black and McBride (1979) found no adverse effects either in terms of learning disabilities or behavior. In fact, this follow-up study found that the children who were induced (in both induction and amniotomy plus induction groups) performed better on scores for reading comprehension and neuroticism than did the spontaneous-labor group. The pattern for total behavioral problems and antisocial behavior was similar, although not statistically significant. The authors noted, "It appears that there are no detectable adverse effects of induction of labour in terms of specific learning disability at the age of eight years" (p. 363). This study may have been the first to suggest that induced labor could result in subtle effects difficult to detect with more global measures.

Although McBride et al.'s (1977) intention to separate out and compare the types of induction represents a refinement in comparison to the Niswander et al. (1966) study, this sample included three different types of oxytocin administration: intravenous infusion, intramuscular injection, and buccal tablets, the proportions of which were not reported, nor was the dosage or duration of administration. It is unfortunate that it was not possible to compare outcomes of these different forms of administration.

Another small, matched control study (Friedman, Sachtleben, & Wallace, 1979) examined 156 children between 23 and 62 months after births associated with three types of labor: spontaneous, induced with oxytocin, and induced with prostaglandin E2. Although the frequency of neurological or developmental abnormalities not attributable to postdelivery events was found to be the same overall in both the induced and the spontaneous labors (19.2 per 1,000 labors), the authors reported that those occurring after labor induction all were associated with oxytocin rather than with prostaglandin E2.

Introducing a large-cohort retrospective study, Sorensen et al. (1999) described some of the possible effects on the fetus of inappropriately high doses of oxytocin when used as an uterotonic: abnormal heart rhythms, circulatory collapse, and preterm delivery with its accompanying increased risk of respiratory distress and central nervous system damage. They noted a paucity of knowledge concerning the long-term consequences of exposure to uterotonic drugs. Their study of 4,300 Danish men who took a standardized 45-minute Boerge Prien intelligence test when registering with the draft board attempted to discover whether artificial oxytocin use in labor, which could result in neonatal hyperbilirubinemia (jaundice), might affect later cognitive functioning. The authors reported that the test used, developed in 1957 for the Danish draft board, correlates highly with the Weschler adult-intelligence scale's verbal intelligence quotient (.78), the performance-intelligence quotient (.71), and the full-scale intelligence quotient (.82).

Data from this examination were linked with the Danish Medical Birth Registry, and the mean Boerge Prien test score was examined according to perinatal exposure to uterotonic drugs, with oxytocin being the most commonly used of these at the time of the births of the men studied. Sorensen et al. (1999) stated that their analysis accounted for possible confounding variables.

The findings of their multiple linear regression analysis, including all confounders, found the difference in Boerge Prien score to be -0.58 (95% Confidence Interval; 1.25 to 0.08) between individuals exposed and those not exposed to uterotonic drugs. Sorensen et al. (1999) noted that Friedman et al. (1979) studied children at 23 to 62 months after birth and found that, although the number of neurological or developmental abnormalities not attributable to events following birth were not statistically different in induced and spontaneous labors, abnormalities that occurred following labor induction were all associated with the use of oxytocin. Sorensen et al.'s (1999) own findings, looking at males between 18 and 20 years of age, appear to concur with Friedman et al.'s (1979), failing to find an association between oxytocin use at birth and later inferior cognitive function. The strength of the Sorensen et al. (1999) study lies in its large-scale and population-based design; however, as in the other studies reviewed so far, the focus appears to be on identifying possible outcomes of affected cognitive functioning, in this case via the common consequence of oxytocin use: neonatal hyperbilirubinemia (jaundice).

A Dutch prospective study, coauthored by obstetrician/gynecologist Mark Vierhout and psychologist Jan Out and reported in a series of two articles, examined obstetric and neonatal effects (Vierhout, Out, & Wallenberg, 1985) and psychological effects of elective induction (Out, Vierhout, Verhage, Duivenvoorden, & Wallenburg, 1985). The latter article asserted that "only in a prospective study, preexisting psychological differences between women opting for elective induction and women choosing a spontaneous onset of labor can be assessed" (p.163). Study participants were drawn from a group of healthy women receiving prenatal care in the clinic of University Hospital, Dijkzigt, Rotterdam, starting during the first trimester. Gestational age was verified by ultrasound between 18 and 20 weeks and only singleton pregnancies were included. At 36 weeks gestational age, women whose fetus was assessed to be in a vertex position without cephalopelvic disproportion were given written and verbal information about elective induction of labor and were "at all times allowed a free choice of elective induction or spontaneous labor" (Vierhout et al., 1985, p. 156).

Each participant was matched with a healthy woman with an uncomplicated pregnancy whose labor began spontaneously, based on three criteria: age group, parity, and cultural nationality (Dutch or non-Dutch) (Vierhout et al., 1985). The reference group also was selected at 36 weeks. Of this group, 28 women had complications arise between the 36th week and delivery, resulting in a group of 156 women in the reference group, with 184 women in the induction group, leaving 28 women in the induction group without a reference group match. The researchers reported that cervical ripeness was assessed during the 38th week of pregnancy, using the Burnhill score: when the score was greater than 4, a date was set for induction of labor. No information was provided concerning the interval between the evaluation of cervical ripeness and the induction date.

When the induction took place it involved a total of four procedures. Induction was initiated by artificial rupture of membranes, a catheter was inserted through the cervix to record uterine activity, and an electrode was attached to the fetal scalp to monitor the fetal heart rate. The fourth procedure involved the use of intravenous oxytocin to induce uterine contractions, and details of incremental dosage and desired range of uterine activity were documented in the article (Vierhout et al., 1985).

In the reference group the beginning labor was defined as the point at which contractions became regular with a 4- to 5-minute interval, or as the moment when membranes ruptured spontaneously. In this group, internal fetal monitoring was used only when fetal distress was suspected (n = 29) or "when it appeared to be necessary to augment uterine activity" (n = 15) (Vierhout et al., 1985, p. 156). Whether a transcervical catheter was used to record uterine activity is not reported. Both induction and reference group participants received a "standard dose of 75 mg of pethidine-HCL 1. M. for pain relief," if necessary (p. 156). It appears from the report that no one in either group received any form of anesthesia.

Following delivery the infant was placed on the mother's abdomen and the umbilical cord was clamped (Vierhout et al., 1985). Apgar scores were recorded at 1 minute and 5 minutes. Cord blood yielded the acid-base status, and bilirubin concentration in serum was determined on the third day postpartum in all newborns still in the hospital. Prechtl's (1977, as cited in Vierhout et al., 1985) neurological screening was performed in a random sample of 125 infants, presumably (though this is not explicitly stated) also on the third postpartum day, because it would appear that some families would already have been discharged, and that the third day might therefore be expected to be the last in the hospital, if no complications arose.

The researchers also followed the infants' development over a 1-year period, using a "Psychomotor Development Scheme 0–15 months" (Vierhout et al., 1985, p. 157). Data were analyzed using the Statistical Package for the Social Sciences system. Student's t test and chi-square test scores were used, where appropriate, for statistical analysis between induction and reference groups, and Spearman's rank correlation test was used to assess correlations between variables.

The obstetric and neonatal findings included a lower incidence of meconium-stained amniotic fluid (2.7% compared to 8.3%), confirming but not explaining the findings of prior studies (Cole, Howie, & MacNaughton, 1975; Tilch, Unger, & Stark, 1979, as cited in Vierhout et al., 1985); the administration of twice as much pain medication (39.5% compared to 24.4%); and a higher percentage of vacuum and forceps deliveries in the induction group than in the reference group (13 women, or 11.9%, compared to 5 women, or 4.5%), which could be explained neither by a higher frequency of fetal distress nor by a longer second stage. Vierhout et al. (1985) suggested that continuous fetal monitoring may have been a contributing factor, together with the possibility that having intervened by inducing the first stage of labor the obstetrician will then attempt to ensure a successful delivery by further intervention. They noted that nearly 85% of the induction group's deliveries took place during the daytime, compared with 45% of the reference group's deliveries. Mothers in the induction group also delivered an average of 3 days earlier than those in the reference group. No differences were found in the duration of labor.

Neither the neurological screening nor the 1-year follow-up study yielded significant differences between the 67 infants in the induction group and the 58 in the reference group; hence, the authors concluded that, in the absence of "somatic obstetric or neonatologic arguments" (Vierhout et al., 1985, p. 159) for or against elective induction of labor, decisions to induce labor electively must be based on other considerations.

In the companion article focusing on psychological effects (Out et al., 1985), the authors referenced literature warning about possible negative effects of some complications of labor induction on the mother-infant relationship but lacking citations of studies demonstrating such effects. The authors' review of the contemporary literature cited two studies, each of which looked at over 2,000 women (Bolte, Breuker, Haase, & Stille, 1976; Cartwright, 1977) and both of which failed to demonstrate early mother-infant separation as a negative psychological consequence of labor induction. They noted that Kitzinger (1975), on the other hand, found more cases of mother-infant separation with induction, and Ounsted, Hendrick, Mutch, Calder, and Good (1978) found that women who were induced for medical reasons were less likely to follow through on the intention to breast-feed than were women whose labors began spontaneously. Out et al. (1985) referred the reader to the previous article (Vierhout et al.,

1985) for details about selection criteria and methodology, and the articles were published sequentially in the same edition of the same journal. Out et al. noted that cases in which induction was advised by the obstetrician were excluded from the study.

For the purposes of this study (Out et al., 1985) of psychological effects, during the 36th week all participants completed a 91-item questionnaire about their pregnancy and expectations for labor, delivery, and motherhood. During Week 37 mothers received written information about induction, and during Week 38 they were asked to choose between elective induction and spontaneous onset of labor. A subgroup of 14 electively induced and 19 spontaneous-labor mothers was videotaped for the first 10 minutes of their interactions with their newborn, and trained observers subsequently evaluated the videotapes for attachment behaviors and the emotional involvement of the mothers with their infants. Observers were not informed of the purpose of the study.

Two hundred nine women were interviewed on the fourth or fifth day postpartum about their experience of labor, delivery, and motherhood. Fifteen electively induced mothers and 47 women with spontaneous labor had already been discharged on the first day after delivery and so were not interviewed. Six months later a questionnaire was mailed to all 271 participants in order to obtain their opinions about their labor and to get an update concerning the state of their health and that of their babies, together with information about nursing. There was a 92% return rate. Wilcoxon's tests and chi-square tests were used for the statistical evaluations of outcome differences between the induction and reference groups (Out et al., 1985).

Out et al. (1985) found that on 11 of 13 criteria for evaluating maternal attachment, mothers with spontaneous labor were considered to be more attached, although the differences did not attain statistical significance. Mothers choosing elective induction were reported to be more confident that they could care for their infant than were women in the spontaneous labor group. However, the conditions under which the latter group of women labored, and the kind of support they received, are not described, leaving open the possibility that the closely monitored mothers in the induction group received more attention than mothers in the spontaneous-labor group, which in itself may have influenced confidence. An alternative explanation may lie in the reasons these women chose induction, although the authors suggest that initially less confident women, in choosing induction, might gain confidence by having taken charge of their labor.

Out et al. (1985) reported that their interviews with the mothers failed to reveal marked differences in how the women experienced labor. Half the women in both groups found it to be better than they had expected, and although the mean duration of labor was 7 hours and 4 minutes for women in the spontaneous-labor group and 5 hours 12 minutes for those who had elective induction ($p < .001$), the women's subjective perception of duration was equal in both groups. A larger percentage of women received pain medication in the elective-induction group (53%) than in the spontaneous labor group (27%), and this difference was significant ($p < .001$). An interesting finding was that babies of mothers whose labor began spontaneously were perceived to cry more than those of mothers whose labor was induced ($p < .05$). The authors analyzed these perceived differences but found no other variables contributing to them.

Although the number of mothers who breast-fed their infants was significantly larger in the spontaneous-labor group than in the induced group, the duration of breast-feeding was not different at the 6-month follow-up. Five variables were found to relate to the frequency of breast-feeding: (a) intention to breast-feed, (b) participation in childbirth education, (c) absence of pregnancy complaints, (d) a positive experience of pregnancy, and (e) education level. Out et al. (1985) proposed that the intention to breast-feed being abandoned by more women in the elective-induction group suggests that the procedure has an influence on attachment (or, more accurately, bonding) behavior. However, the number of mothers in each group who did so was small: 8 in the elective induction group (28%) and 12 in the spontaneous labor group (11%), and the difference was not statistically significant. Out et al. asserted that it was "not necessary to postulate a physiologic explanation for this phenomenon. Women who do not choose the natural mode of labor may also more easily abandon their plans for the most natural way of feeding" (p. 167).

In her writing on the hormonal physiology of childbirth, Buckley (2007) cited studies indicating reductions in numbers of oxytocin receptors and amount of oxytocin receptor activity in the uterus following exposure to artificial oxytocin during labor (Phaneuf et al., 1998; Phaneuf, Rodríguez Liñares, TambyRaja, MacKenzie, & López Bernal, 2000) and speculated about whether a similar down-regulation of oxytocin receptors could take place simultaneously in brain areas associated with maternal behavior. Certainly, the fact that exogenous oxytocin—Pitocin—binds to oxytocin receptors during the passage of the baby through the birth canal and endures for some minutes after birth, thus possibly impairing early attachment and bonding efforts mediated by the production of endogenous oxytocin, lends support to

Buckley's speculation. In turn, this may offer an alternate, physiological, explanation for the finding of Out et al. (1985) concerning the "abandonment" of the intention to breast-feed among the elective-induction group, as well as the significantly larger number of mothers in the spontaneous-labor group than in the elective-induction group who breast-fed their infants ($p < .01$).

In a later article, Out, Vierhout, Verhage, Duivenvoorden, and Wallenburg (1986), the same authors who initially reported on the psychological effects of elective induction on mothers, elaborated on their earlier findings. They described the almost 50% of women in their study who opted for elective induction as having had "more complaints during pregnancy and menstrual periods, more complications in their obstetrical history and to be more anxious about their labor" (p. 375) than the women who chose to wait for spontaneous onset of labor. Predominant motives for elective induction were described as a feeling of safety and a desire to shorten the length of the pregnancy.

Out et al. (1986) suggested that these motives and characteristics among the elective-induction group reflected "a lack of trust in physical reproductive functions" (p. 375) and concluded that, when evaluating the effects of elective induction of labor, it is important to incorporate consideration of preexisting differences between mothers choosing induction and those choosing spontaneous onset of labor. Regrettably, the researchers did not apparently include in their questionnaires or interview structures requests for information concerning the participants' own birth histories or the nature of their early attachment and bonding relationships with their mothers, which might have served to elucidate preexisting differences between mothers in the two groups.

The relevance of the study (Out et al., 1985; Vierhout et al., 1985) has to do with the researchers' focus on the induced mother's participation in the attachment/bonding process, which could profoundly affect the quality and nature of the infant's attachment to the mother. The study was conducted in the Netherlands in the 1980s; therefore, one cannot assume that the climate for elective induction of labor, the type of prenatal and perinatal care, and the informed consents received by women giving birth in the hospital where the study took place are comparable to those experienced by women giving birth in hospitals in the United States.

There are a number of concerns about and problems with the study (Out et al., 1985; Vierhout et al., 1985). The first concerns the informed consent provided to the participants when offering them the choice of elective induction or spontaneous labor. It is difficult to evaluate whether merely being recipients of this information might have constituted a mild form of coercion to the women at an emotionally vulnerable time, much as the provision of gift bags containing samples of infant formula to all mothers being discharged from hospital following childbirth may be taken to mean that the hospital recommends formula-feeding. The second is that a random sample, rather than the entire cohort of infants, was administered the Prechtl (1977) neurological screening, for no stated reason, and that the postpartum day on which this screening was performed was not explicitly identified, making it difficult to compare the findings with other studies in which the same measure was used. Third, continuous fetal monitoring was standard for all members of the induction group but was used only for medical indications in the control group, raising questions about the validity of comparisons between the two groups.

In the article focusing on psychological effects (Out et al., 1985), the numbers provided for electively induced mothers (72) and mothers with spontaneous labor initiation (199) differ from those reported in the previous article focusing on obstetric and neonatal effects (Vierhout et al., 1985), so it is unclear whether this aspect of the study focused on an entirely different group of women than in the study described in the Vierhout et al. (1985) article or there were overlaps between the populations, and if so, of what type. Several subgroups were studied in various ways. One small subgroup of mothers (33: 14 from the induction group and 19 from the spontaneous labor group) was videotaped for the first 10 minutes of interaction with their newborns; the videotape was later evaluated by trained observers to assess for attachment behaviors and mothers' emotional involvement with their infants. Another group (209 women) was interviewed on Day 4 or Day 5 postpartum, and all participants received a follow-up questionnaire 6 months after the births (Out et al., 1985).

The results of Prechtl's (1977, as cited in Vierhout et al., 1985) neurological screening were reported in one sentence, and no details were provided other than that no difference was found between the two groups and that 9 infants (13.4%) in the induction group and 7 infants (12.1%) in the reference group were considered "suspect," but this term was not defined. The 1-year follow-up instrument apparently originated in Germany, and again no details of its contents are provided, affording the reader little understanding of what measures were employed. The instrument also failed to distinguish between the 67 infants in the induction group and the 58 in the reference group at the 1-year follow-up. The focus of this study (Out et al., 1985; Vierhout et al., 1985) appears to be on the mother rather than on the infant, though this was not made explicit by the authors, and this focus may have contributed in some way to the lack of statistically significant findings with regard to the effects of labor induction on the infants. As a result of the variety of groups and measures involved, together with the varying degrees of clarity provided in descriptions of how they were administered, the findings are less than optimally clear and their value is questionable.

The reviewed studies examining the possibility of longer-term effects of artificial oxytocin did not appear to consider the likelihood of a logical connection between the use of artificial oxytocin at birth and the type of effects such an intervention might have on the functioning of children born with its use. The studies typically relied upon a wide variety of (mostly) standardized measures of functioning that seemed to fail to capture the subtleties of artificial oxytocin's possible impacts on hormonal systems, belief systems, sequencing activities, endogenous rhythms, and interpersonal dynamics that clinicians experienced in working with the effects of prenatal and perinatal influences have reported to carry deep and enduring significance. Although clinical data are typically too subjective and reference too small a sample to have any generalizability to the larger population, it can provide valid directions for research. In the field of psychology, in particular, we are not well served by dismissing without further study the observations of experienced clinicians over many years, especially when assembled in the form of qualitative research data.

In contrast with the previous study reviewed (Out et al., 1985; Vierhout et al., 1985), a Japanese study (Eishima, 1992) focused on infants examined 159 newborns (80 boys and 79 girls) who were neurologically and obstetrically low-risk to discover the effects of obstetric conditions on neonatal neurological status and neonatal behavior. The researchers used Prechtl's (1977) neonatal neurological examination and the Brazelton Neonatal Behavioral Assessment Scale (Brazelton, 1984) 2 to 3 hours after feeding on the fifth day after birth. Mothers and babies shared a room during their hospital stay (at Fukuoka Central Hospital), but mothers were not present during the observations, which took place in a quiet, air-conditioned room. The assessment of obstetric conditions was gathered from transcribed medical charts and from midwives' and obstetricians' reports.

Eishima's (1992) stated intention for the study was to analyze the effects of fetal and neonatal environments on neonatal status in low-risk infants, in preparation for an additional study comparing Japanese infants with British infants, taking into consideration those factors affecting neonatal status, with an additional goal of confirming Prechtl's (1977) suggestion "that a broad view of factors is preferable to a one-to-one comparison" (p. 254) in application to low-risk infants. Eishima (1992) provides tables showing means and standard deviations for infant and maternal characteristics, results of the neurological examination, and results of the behavioral assessment, and a list showing the raw data and percentages for prenatal history, for demographic data, and for the use of anesthesia and labor induction during the birth. The relationship between obstetric conditions and neonatal neurological or behavioral status were calculated using the chi-square test and correlation coefficient.

Eishima (1992) found a significant relationship ($p < .005$) between overall obstetric conditions (as measured by Prechtl's Obstetric Optimality Score) and overall neurological status (as measured by Prechtl's Neurological Optimality Score). Eishima reports that her findings corroborate Prechtl's (1977), although with a lower degree of correlation, which Eishima suggests may be attributed to Prechtl's inclusion of high-risk groups. Eishima's (1992) study focused only on low-risk groups. Together with anesthesia, previous spontaneous abortion, previous induced abortion, and maternal alcohol consumption, induction of labor appeared to affect lability of states, alertness, orientation, habituation, activity, hand-to-mouth activity, defensive movements, head control, and resistance to cuddle, all to a statistically significant degree. Labor induction with oxytocin, specifically, was significantly correlated with inferior hand-to-mouth activity ($p < .05$), suppressed alertness ($p < .005$), and increased resistance to cuddle ($p < .005$). Eishima also found a weaker animate visual orientation (a long visual fixation) in the induced group ($p < .01$), which she believed may suggest difficulty in visual pursuit when the visual point is moved, something possibly indicative of a less mature attentive process.

Unfortunately, Eishima (1992) did not identify how many infants were exposed both to labor induction with oxytocin and to anesthesia, so that separate and cumulative effects of the drugs, or the procedures involved, cannot be differentiated. Eishima noted that a low dose of the same drug may affect different individuals to varying degrees and that effects may be potentiated by other factors, such as maternal stress. She stated, "It is uncertain which factor affects the babies, the drug, the induction itself, or the reason for the induction" and observed that "even a small difference in low-risk obstetric conditions is related to differences in neonatal neurological status and neonatal behavior" (p. 261).

Eishima's (1992) study is simpler and less ambitious than some of the previous studies reviewed, and it is perhaps because of this, to some degree, and presumably because Eishima had access to medical records permitting a high degree of accuracy, that it resulted in findings of statistical significance. However, a significant flaw of the article reporting the study is that it does not disclose whether the assessor conducting the neonatal evaluations was blinded to the obstetric conditions of the infants assessed, leaving the reported findings open to the interpretation that they may be partly attributable to researcher bias.

Eishima (1992) used two reputable measures of neurological status and behavior, allowing her to compare her findings with Prechtl's (1977) own and permitting comparisons to be made between her study and the other study that employed this screening tool (Vierhout et al., 1985). These choices also bring Eishima's (1992) study closer to the present study in terms of focus. Her analysis permitted isolation of each included obstetric condition, allowing other researchers to examine those data that pertain to their own areas of interest and the findings concerning the relationship of those conditions in relation to overall neonatal status. Studying newborns prospectively allows for better identification and control of confounding variables; however, the study is unable to predict the status of these infants at a later time, and it appears that no longitudinal follow-up was planned. This omission is disappointing in that there would be substantial value in the opportunity to reexamine the infants as they grew older in order to ascertain if and how the neonatal findings affected later functioning.

It is interesting that the Vierhout et al. (1985) study failed to find any significant neonatal differences using the same neurological screening (Prechtl, 1977) as Eishima's (1992) study. Because it is unclear in the Vierhout et al. (1985) article on what day the Prechtl screening was conducted in a random sample of 125 infants (the sentence addressing implementation of the Prechtl screening states that serum bilirubin concentration was determined on the third day postpartum, but the exact day of neurological screening is not stated), it is possible that conducting the screening on Day 5 postpartum, as Eishima (1992) reported having done, may have resulted in clearer findings. It is also possible that, rather than there being no differences found between infants receiving Pitocin inductions (together with a higher incidence of pain medication use and instrument deliveries) and infants in the spontaneous labor group, the other measures used in the Vierhout et al. (1985) study were unsuitable for identifying any such differences.

It should be noted that, despite the use of a neonatal assessment tool, the emphasis of the researchers in the 1985 study (Out et al.; Vierhout et al.) seems to have been predominantly on the psychological effects of labor induction on the mothers, and their later analysis of the characteristics and motives of mothers choosing induction of labor (Out et al., 1986) is explicit concerning their interest in discovering whether there are personality differences between women who elect induction and those who do not. By contrast, Eishima (1992) was apparently curious about, and perhaps therefore paid greater attention to, the effects on neonates of induction (among a group of obstetrical conditions), possibly resulting in more careful administration of the measures employed. Although these studies contribute to the small body of knowledge concerning the outcomes of labor induction, they also raise questions regarding both the training and the possible biases of those performing observations and administering the same measure in both studies (Out et al., 1985; Vierhout et al., 1985; Eishima, 1992).

Table 2.1 summarizes the group of studies reviewed that are most closely allied to the present study in seeking to identify what, if any, association can be found between obstetric conditions in general, or labor induction with oxytocin in particular, and later functioning, identifying the decades in which the studies were conducted, the lead author of each study, the measures employed, and the study findings.

Most of the studies investigating the possibility of enduring effects of Pitocin use at birth appear to have used a variety of mostly standardized measures, and few have found significant relationships between Pitocin and infant or child functioning. The remarkably small and geographically scattered cluster of studies conducted over the past 50 years to explore the possible effects of labor induction with artificial oxytocin on the offspring seem to have sought primarily to identify relationships between birth events and serious psychiatric or developmental disorders (e.g., schizophrenia, autism, ADHD, drug addiction, or suicide) or have employed measures of physiological, neurobehavioral, and cognitive factors to correlate with labor induction.

Table 2.1

Studies of Labor Induction and Infant and/or Child Functioning

Decade	Authors	Measures	Findings
1960s	Niswander et al.	Stanford-Binet to test intelligence	No significant difference.
		Other standardized methods (Porteus mazes, peg board, Graham Block Sort Test) to test fine motor skills, gross motor functioning and conceptual ability	Higher median IQ among females in induced group
		Behavioral observation.	
1970s	McBride et al.	Wechsler Preschool and Primary Scale of Intelligence	No significant differences.

Decade	Authors	Measures	Findings
	(age 5)	Tests of gross and fine motor movement and balance	
		Height and weight measurements	
		Pediatric examination	
		Audiometric screening test for auditory acuity	
		Titmus Vision Test for Preschoolers Titmus Fly Test of stereopsis	
		Developmental history from the mother.	
1970s	McBride et al. (age 8)	Reading tests (ACER)	Significant difference favoring induced groups (amniotomy alone; amniotomy + oxytocin) on reading comprehension and neuroticism.
		Arithmetic subscale of the WISC-(R),	
		Bender-Gestalt test for young children for signs of retardation and emotional disturbance,	
		Wepman test of auditory discrimination,	
		Belmont and Birch test of auditory-visual integration,	
		Behavioral checklist (Rutter, Tizard, & Whitmore, 1970)	
1980s	Vierhout et al.	Prechtl Neurological Screening;	No significant differences.
		Psychomotor Development Scheme (German)	
1990s	Sorensen et al.	Danish measure of adult cognitive function (Boerge Prien, 1957) correlates highly with Wechsler adult intelligence scale	No significant differences.
1990s	Eishima	Prechtl Neurological Screening;	Significant differences on both measures.
		Brazelton Neonatal Behavioral Assessment Scale	

Birth Events as Enduring Imprints

Prior to the group of studies (Jacobson et al., 1987; Jacobson et al., 1988; Jacobson et al., 1990) whose initial hypothesis was that some form of imprinting mediates a relationship between significant obstetrical conditions and events or disorders in adolescence or adulthood, Csaba (1980) coined the term "hormonal imprinting" in the 1970s to describe the long-term effects of exposure to certain hormones in the critical perinatal period, which includes the 24 hours following birth. According to Csaba, "The phenomenon is an important factor in the survival of the species, as the effect of imprinting is transmitted to the progeny cell generations" (p. 1). Casaba et al. (2004) also stated, "Perinatally, the first encounter between the maturing receptor and its target hormone results in hormonal imprinting, which adjusts the binding capacity of the receptor for life" (p. 39), and Csaba (2008) noted that "excess of the target hormones or presence of foreign molecules which are able to bind to the receptors, provoke faulty imprinting in the critical periods with life-long morphological, biochemical, functional or behavioural consequences" (p. 1).

Withuhn, Kramer, and Cushing (2003) injected into the sac surrounding the intestines of three groups of newborn rats, for 6 days, either oxytocin, an oxytocin agonist, or isotonic saline (as a vehicle control), while a fourth group was handled but not injected, and found that injection with oxytocin significantly delayed the timing and development of female sexual maturation. They concluded, "Neonatal exposure to exogenous oxytocin (OT) can have long-term effects on the subsequent expression of adult behavior and physiology" (p. 135).

Resaerchers Karen Bales and Sue Carter and colleagues have conducted extensive studies of the oxytocin system, working with prairie voles because they are monogamous, both parents care for their young, and they have a brain oxytocin system similar to that of humans. They found abnormal adult sexual behavior in males (Bales, Abdelnabi, Cushing, Ottinger, & Carter, 2004; Bales & Carter, 2003a), abnormal alloparenting behavior in males (Bales, Kim, Lewis-Reese, & Carter, 2004; Bales, Pfeifer, & Carter, 2004), and changes in patterns of intrasexual aggression in females (Bales & Carter, 2003b) when prairie voles were treated with oxytocin or an oxytocin agonist.

Speaking to a broader interpretation of the notion of imprinting, a number of prenatal and perinatal clinicians (Castellino, Takikawa, & Wood, 1997; Emerson, 1998; McCarty, 2002a) described our capacity to recapitulate, unconsciously yet with unerring precision, the movement sequences of our birth—as infants, children, or adults of any age. This suggests that birth is a sufficiently significant event in our lives that our journey into the world is accurately recorded somatically and then reproduced, in whole or in part, in response to triggering events in our lives, including therapeutic environments. These authors also described case studies offering examples of life themes and patterns of beliefs and behaviors that seemed to echo with considerable accuracy specific events and experiences that took place during an individual's birth.

A study by Cheek (1986) described hypnosis clients who spontaneously and accurately replicated their head and shoulder movements during delivery, whereas Blasco (2007) had five observers trained in prenatal and perinatal therapy view five brief videotaped clips of preverbal children (i.e., infants and toddlers) in therapy sessions for prenatal and birth issues. The observers then described which specific aspect of prenatal or birth experiences they believed each child was displaying in those segments of his or her session. Following interviews with the observers, in which they described what they believed they had observed in each segment, observers were given a brief multiple-choice questionnaire that provided a series of possible prenatal or birth events, from which they selected the events that they believed they had observed in each video clip. The high degree of agreement among observers (72%)—who were given no history, no context, and in some of the clips, no sound track to aid them—in connecting each child's behavior to a specific prenatal or birth experience is statistically unlikely to be attributable to chance. This suggests that these experiences formed enduring imprints in the children studied, who then played out the experiences in a manner identifiable by the observers with significant accuracy.

It is proposed that the use of artificial oxytocin (Pitocin) during birth results in effects that are found in the belief systems, behaviors, and interpersonal dynamics, and hence, in the evolving personality of the child, and that are played out in subtle ways throughout their lives and manifest in observable patterns. The present study seeks to clarify the hypothesized patterns and to investigate whether such patterns can be identified in 3-year-old children born following Pitocin induction or augmentation. These children were compared to those born without the use of Pitocin, through an online self-report survey completed by their mothers. If there is a relationship between Pitocin use at birth and a child's later functioning, this relationship may be sufficiently subtle to evade detection by most standardized measures and may not necessarily be associated with serious psychiatric or developmental disorders. Therefore, this study attempted to focus on the psychosocial domain described by Schore (2005) as having great significance for healthy functioning.

To date, no researcher appears to have examined the observations of clinicians who work with babies, children, and their families to resolve the effects of difficulties and stresses during pregnancy and birth, in order to learn what they have discovered about Pitocin use in labor and later functioning.

Employing a survey developed from interviews with experienced prenatal/perinatal clinicians concerning their observations of what they consider to be the effects of Pitocin, this study is intended to provide greater discriminatory power than the measures used in prior studies and to shed light thereby on the proposed relationship between Pitocin use at birth and children's psychosocial functioning.

Chapter 3. Theoretical and Empirical Framework

Because this study appears to be one of very few studies examining the relationship between the particular obstetrical intervention of the use of artificial oxytocin to induce or augment labor and children's later psychosocial functioning, I elected to use a quantitative approach to quantify relationships between the independent variables and subgroups of dependent variables. The study employed a survey developed from the findings of a preliminary study begun in 2004. The study began with interviews with 6 clinicians experienced in using a prenatal and perinatal approach to psychotherapy and healing in working with infants, children, and their families toward resolution of issues perceived to be related to prenatal or birth events. The purpose of the preliminary study was to answer the question, "If I were to survey mothers of children exposed to Pitocin at birth to discover whether the mothers' descriptions of how their children functioned were different from those of mothers of children not exposed to Pitocin, what kinds of functioning should I be asking about?"

Once asked, it became obvious that my question could best be answered by those experienced in working with children from a prenatal and perinatal perspective, and the concept of conducting the preliminary interview study was formally drafted and received institutional review board approval, and the interviews were completed. Both the preliminary study and the current survey research were based on the same premise: that one must first observe the phenomenon of interest. Thus, the clinicians' observations represent those of clinical experts in the field of prenatal and perinatal psychology, and the survey of mothers represents the observations of the "expert" on each mother's child.

The Preliminary Study

The clinicians involved were those who agreed to be interviewed, from among a group of 11 identified as possible participants. The field of prenatal and perinatal psychology is still relatively new and it encompasses professionals across a range of disciplines. All but 1 of the clinicians invited to participate were known to me to some degree. They represent a variety of disciplines and can thus reasonably be considered a representative sample. All participants practice in the United States, so their client population can be considered fairly representative of the culture of the population to be sampled with the resulting survey.

The clinicians were asked to describe their observations about what they considere to be the effects, if any, of Pitocin use at birth on children at age 3. This age group was selected because preliminary discussions of the anecdotal evidence of effects of Pitocin suggested that such effects become more evident at around this age, when more demands are made upon children for compliance with social norms in their families and as they enter more structured environments outside the home. In addition, the preschool age group is of great interest to educators because what emerges at this age has significance for how children will function upon entering school.

A further reason for studying the effects on 3-year-olds is that by age 3 the brain is essentially fully developed—with all major fiber tracts identifiable (Matsuzawa et al., 2001). According to Schore (2005), "The cellular architecture of the cerebral cortex is sculpted by input from the social environment embedded in the early attachment relationships" (p. 205). With the early maturing of the right hemisphere of the brain—which is "dominant for the emotional and corporeal self" over the later developing verbal left brain for the 3 years after birth—"the social experience–dependent maturation of the right brain in human infancy is equated with the early development of the self" (p. 205).

How the self develops, Schore (2005) reported, is through repeated episodes of "affect synchrony" between mother and infant. "Psychobiological attunement and the interactive mutual entrainment of physiologic rhythms are fundamental processes that mediate attachment," and "the spontaneous emotional communication that occurs within the attachment relationship has been described as 'a conversation between limbic systems'" (pp. 207–208). The clinicians I interviewed seemed to agree that attunement and entrainment of rhythms is a significant aspect of the mother-child relationship and one that, in their opinions, can be profoundly affected by the use of artificial oxytocin. Schore's recent publication adds credibility to their observations.

The questions I asked the clinicians focused on their observations of what they perceived to be the effects of artificial oxytocin use on the psychosocial functioning of 3-year-olds exposed to it at birth. The questions asked were as follows:

1. Have you noticed any effects of Pitocin (or Syntocinon)–induced or -augmented birth on infants and children (especially those aged 3 to 5)?

2. How would you describe these effects?

3. What effects do you think most parents and caregivers would notice, if any?

4. Do you notice a difference between the effects of Pitocin induction and Pitocin augmentation?

5. Do you see a cluster of effects that is specific to Pitocin induction or augmentation, that is different from effects of other birth events, interventions, or other life events?

6. If yes, then what distinguishes this cluster from those of other events?

7. Have you seen any children who had Pitocin at their births but showed no effects?

8. If so, why do you think they did not?

9. Do you have anything to add?

Questions for clarification were added as needed through the interviews.

I used a content analysis (Holsti, 1969; Krippendorf, 2004; Patton, 2002) approach to the interview transcripts and condensed the resulting groups of descriptions ("dimensions") into survey items while attempting to find descriptors for the various dimensions. After eliminating duplicate statements and other redundancies from the draft survey, it was returned to a "jury" of the original 6 clinicians, in a format that permitted them to vote on each item with one of three choices—(a) *No,* (b) *Yes,* and (c) *Yes, with the following changes*—and to provide their expert feedback as to the survey's effectiveness in discerning Pitocin's effects from other influences on children at age 3. The jury's votes and feedback were then used to eliminate the least effective items and to condense the survey contents into a manageable size. The finalized survey (Appendix C) was intended to serve as an accurate representation of the salient features of the perceptions provided by expert clinicians of the functional correlates of artificial oxytocin use at birth on children at 3 years of age.

Theoretical, Empirical, and Clinical Support for Hypotheses

Hypothesis 1

There is a relationship between the use of Pitocin at birth and the psychochosocial functioning of children at age 3.

Theoretical support. As stated in chapter 2, the field of prenatal and perinatal psychology posits that "Our earliest experiences in the womb, at birth, and during infancy establish a foundational blueprint for life. This blueprint becomes the infrastructure from which we grow and experience life physically, emotionally, mentally, relationally, and spiritually" (McCarty, 2002b, p. 11). This tenet has been supported by the experience of clinicians working with infants and young children who display various forms of recall or imprinting effects of birth events (Chamberlain, 1998; Cheek, 1986; Emerson, 1998).

Empirical support. A significant cluster of studies has examined relationships between the use of pain medications at birth and later amphetamine addictions (Jacobson et al., 1988), between opiate and barbiturate use at birth and later opiate addiction (Jacobson et al., 1990), and relationships between types of birth trauma and means of suicide (Jacobson et al., 1987), such as the association between asphyxia at birth and suicides involving asphyxiation or between mechanical birth trauma and suicides by violent mechanical means. Other studies have demonstrated a relationship between perinatal risk factors and adolescent suicide (Salk et al., 1985) and between birth complications coupled with maternal rejection during the first year and violent crime by age 18 (Raine et al., 1994). More recently, Blasco (2007) demonstrated that trained observers can reliably identify birth events reenacted by young children during their play. Together, these studies provide persuasive support for the theory that an early experience as significant as birth leaves lasting imprints, and related clinical data.

There are remarkably few studies that specifically explore the possibility of a relationship between artificial oxytocin use at birth and later functioning of the child, and most of those making the attempt included labor induction, by any means, as one of a group of birth complications and interventions that, together, might represent risk factors for autism (Fein et al., 1997; Hollander, 1996), schizophrenia (Bakan & Peterson, 1994), or attention-deficit/hyperactivity disorder (Claycomb et al., 2004).

One study (Eishima, 1992), using Prechtl's (1977) neonatal neurological examination and the Neonatal Behavioral Assessment Scale (Brazelton, 1984) on Day 5 postpartum, suggested that a group of conditions that included labor induction, anesthesia, previous spontaneous abortion, previous induced abortion, and maternal alcohol consumption appeared to affect lability of states, alertness, orientation, habituation, activity, hand-to-mouth activity, defensive movements, head control, and resistance to cuddle. Labor induction with oxytocin, specifically, was significantly correlated with inferior hand-to-mouth activity ($p < .05$), suppressed alertness ($p < .005$), and increased resistance to cuddle ($p < .005$). Eishima (1992) also found a weaker animate visual orientation among the induced group ($p < .01$). She suggested that "even a small difference in low-risk obstetric conditions is related to differences in neonatal neurological status and neonatal behavior" (p. 262). It is unfortunate that no study has apparently followed the infants in this study to determine whether the effects identified 5 days after birth endure beyond this time, and if so, for how long and in what form.

Clinical support. Castellino et al. (1997) reported their clinical observation:

> The rhythm or tempo in which labor and birth progress is . . . a significant factor. Changes in the rhythm of labor may or may not have traumatic impacts on the baby. However, the natural rhythms of labor may change spontaneously, or from intended interventions. These changes may have adverse effects on the labor that lead to adverse imprinting in the baby. . . . Examples of intended interventions that can cause adverse imprinting are labor induction and labor mediating agents such as Pitocin (synoxytocin in Europe) or different forms of anesthesia. (p. 12)

Cheek (1986) described hypnosis clients who spontaneously and accurately replicated their head and shoulder movements during delivery, whereas Emerson (1998) provides an example from a case study of how a Pitocin experience at birth appeared in the artwork of a child as a "rocket blasting off from the earth into the atmosphere. In effect, he felt overly energized and propelled, in a very frightening way, by the Pitocin. As a child and as an adult, he perpetually avoided intense and activating energies" (p. 18).

Describing the Pitocin induction–related problems presented by another adult client, Emerson (1998) wrote,

> During his birth, he experienced the bliss of being in his mother and beginning a long journey to the world, and was just about to start pushing when he was "hit with a blanket of cold water" (the effect of the Pitocin). He felt deeply betrayed by life and his mother (for allowing the Pitocin) and deeply interfered with. Through his regressions, he came to understand that he was constantly interrupting others as he had been traumatically interrupted during his birth. (p. 30)

Rebirthers Ray and Mandel (1987) reported an extensive list of everyday challenges typically faced by adult clients who were induced at birth.

Finally, the experienced clinicians interviewed for the preliminary study that preceded the dissertation research provided a consensus picture of a cluster of individual and interpersonal behaviors and functional challenges typically presented in prenatal and perinatal therapies by young children who were exposed to Pitocin at birth.

Hypothesis 2

There is a significant relationship between Pitocin use at birth and sensory processing at age 3, as measured by the following survey items (see Appendix C):

Q1: My child is easily distressed by/reacts to one or more of the following: light, sound, touch/texture.

Q2: My child is easily distressed by/reacts to one or more of the following: food textures, smells, sensations.

Q3: As an infant, my child was hypersensitive to movement or position changes (e.g., if she/he fell asleep in your arms she/he would cry when moved or put down).

Q4: As a baby, my child protested strongly (screamed, cried, or stiffened) when thrown or lifted up in the air, or when being tipped or held at certain angles or positions.

Q5: My child craves firm pressure and intense contact (crashing, tumbling, bear hugs, being in a "sandwich").

Q6: My child loves to cuddle and show affection to others.

Q7: My child resists holding and contact.

Hypothesis 3

There is a significant relationship between Pitocin use at birth and coordination/motor skills at age 3, as measured by the following survey items (see Appendix C):

Q8: My child had or has problems with coordinating his/her body movements (e.g., crawling on belly, creeping on hands and knees cross-laterally [left arm/right leg; right arm/left leg], walking, running, climbing).

Q9: My child has trouble with puzzles and putting things together.

Q10: My child appears clumsy and tends to bump into objects and people.

Theoretical support for hypotheses 2 and 3. Prenatal and perinatal pioneering clinicians/writers/teachers (Castellino et al., 1997; Cheek, 1986; Emerson, 1998; McCarty, 2002a; Verny & Weintraub, 2002) are in consensus that birth experiences leave lasting somatic imprints that manifest themselves in psychosocial and neurobiological functioning.

Empirical support for hypotheses 2 and 3. In a study in Japan (Eishima, 1992) that employed Prechtl's (1977) neonatal neurological examination and the Neonatal Behavioral Assessment Scale (Brazelton, 1984) on the fifth day after birth, the use of artificial oxytocin at birth was significantly correlated with suppressed alertness and increased resistance to cuddle. Eishima (1992) suggested that "even a small difference in low-risk obstetric conditions is related to differences in neonatal neurological status and neonatal behavior" (p. 262). Because the capacity to process sensory input effectively is an aspect of neurological status and affects overt behavior, Eishima's study implicitly supports the hypothesis that there is a relationship between neonatal neurological status and behavior resulting from artificial oxytocin use at birth, and sensory processing issues at age 3.

Clinical support for hypotheses 2 and 3. The clinicians interviewed for the preliminary study specifically identified issues with physical contact as one of the possible enduring effects of Pitocin use at birth on 3-year-olds, thus corroborating Eishima's (1992) findings.

Hypothesis 4

There is a significant relationship between Pitocin use at birth and affect/mood regulation at age 3, as measured by the following survey items (Appendix C):

Q11: My child reacts intensely (startling, crying, yelling, hitting, retreating) to many things.

Q12: My child is easily overwhelmed.

Q13: When my child gets upset, it's difficult to help him/her calm down.

Q14: My child's moods shift quickly from one extreme to another.

Q15: My child gets easily irritated/upset if not responded to immediately.

Theoretical support. Emotion regulation involves the maintenance or modification of physiological arousal or internal feeling states. Emotion-related behavioral regulation refers to modulation of the overt expression of emotion (i.e., the frequency, intensity, or duration of the facial expressions, vocalizations, and actions that serve as external signals of internal states) (Zeanah, 2000).

Clinical support. Clinicians participating in the preliminary study were in consensus that many children exposed to Pitocin at birth experience challenges to affect (emotion) reactivity, expression, and self-regulation.

Hypothesis 5

There is a significant relationship between Pitocin use at birth and a child's self-esteem/sense of self at age 3, as measured by the following survey items (Appendix C):

Q16: My child tends to be confident and happy.

Q17: My child handles frustration and changes well.

Clinical support. Clinicians participating in the preliminary interview study observed that exposure to Pitocin at birth appears to affect the child's capacity to be "in tune" with him- or herself because the drug seems to have the effect of disconnecting the child from a sense of his or her internal rhythms, suggesting that self-confidence and thereby self-esteem and sense of self may be affected.

Hypothesis 6

There is a significant relationship between Pitocin use at birth and various aspects of autonomic nervous system regulation in the child at age 3, as measured by the following survey items (Appendix C):

Q18: My child is constantly in motion.

Q19: My child has/has had a pattern of self-harming behaviors.

Q20: My child is aggressive (biting, kicking, hitting, pushing).

Q21: My child can focus on something that interests her/him for a long time.

Q22: My child has attention and focusing problems only in specific types of situations or with certain types of triggers.

Q23: My child is hyper and unable to focus under most circumstances.

Q24: My child has difficulty handling situations in which others are directing or setting the pace (e.g., "We have to go to school now").

Q25: My child responds well to being allowed to self-pace within reasonable limits.

Q26: My child seems out of sync with me (too fast or too slow).

Q27: As an infant, my child had ear infections.

Q28: As an infant, my child was "colicky" or fussy and hard to soothe.

Q29: My child has digestive problems (e.g., diarrhea, constipation, tummy ache complaints).

Q30: My child is a fussy or "picky" eater.

Q31: My child has problems with sleeping (falling asleep, staying asleep, or waking) at night.

Theoretical support. Schore (2005) noted that the self develops through repeated episodes of "affect synchrony" between mother and infant: "Psychobiological attunement and the interactive mutual entrainment of physiologic rhythms are fundamental processes that mediate attachment. Thus, throughout the life span, attachment is a primary mechanism for the regulation of biologic synchronicity within and between organisms" (p. 207)

Clinical support. Clinicians contributing to the preliminary study identified a wide variety of challenging functions and behaviors they had observed in children exposed to Pitocin at birth, which appear to represent challenges to this entrainment of physiologic rhythms and hence to the regulation of the autonomic nervous system. They theorized that a mother's and child's exposure to Pitocin at birth disrupts the attunement between mother and child, which in turn affects autonomic nervous system regulation, and thereby, those functions it is known to govern.

Hypothesis 7

There is a significant relationship between Pitocin use at birth and 3-year-olds' functioning in interpersonal situations as reported by their mothers on the following survey items (Appendix C):

Q32: My child is timid or tentative.

Q33: My child has difficulty in structured settings in which others are in control of timing and transitions (e.g., preschool/daycare, activities with other children).

Q34: My child resists receiving help from others.

Q35: My child strongly resists pressure, directions, being hurried.

Q36: When given directions or a demand is made on her/him, my child reacts strongly (e.g., protest, resistance, glazed eyes, "freezes," tears).

Q37: My child does what I ask him/her to do (e.g., coming to the table or helping to clean up toys when asked) without a huge struggle.

Q38: I feel as though my child is the one in charge in our family.

Q39: When things don't go his/her way, my child gets extremely upset (screaming, hitting, pushing, biting).

Q40: In his/her relationships with others my child tends to let others lead and is more of a follower.

Q41: My child has a strong need to be in control.

Q42: My child dominates other children.

Q43: My child plays cooperatively with others.

Q44: My child plays games in which the theme is entrapping others or being trapped.

Q45: My child plays games in which the theme is rescuing or being rescued.

Q46: My child is sensitive to any type of intrusion into his/her physical or mental space.

Q47: My child is really good at communicating "yes" and "no" when he/she needs to.

Q48: My child tends to be intrusive (is really "pushy") and doesn't seem to recognize appropriate boundaries with others.

Hypothesis 8

There is a significant relationship between Pitocin use at birth and attunement between mother and child in infancy and at age 3, as measured by the following survey items (Appendix C):

Q49: I feel as though I can never satisfy my child.

Q50: I feel like I don't know how to connect with my child.

Q51: When my child speeds up, it's hard to connect with him/her; it's like he/she is in his/her own world.

Q52: I would describe my relationship with my child as easy and cooperative, with good rapport.

Q53: As an infant, my child had extreme emotional responses (cried, screamed, struggled, or shut down) to transitions (e.g., sudden shifts in position, attention, activity; diaper changes; baths; new places/people).

Q54: My child has difficulties orienting himself/herself in new situations or places (looking around, noticing events, checking in with me).

Q55: My child has difficulties with transitions (e.g., waking, going to sleep, dressing, new places, changing activities at preschool).

Q56: When things change quickly or unexpectedly, my child reacts strongly (withdraws, cries, becomes aggressive).

Q57: My child copes with transitions better if he/she is involved in how they happen and has some control over them.

Theoretical support for hypotheses 7 and 8. Schore (2005) noted that the self develops through repeated episodes of "affect synchrony" between mother and infant: "Psychobiological attunement and the interactive mutual entrainment of physiologic rhythms are fundamental processes that mediate attachment. Thus, throughout the life span, attachment is a primary mechanism for the regulation of biologic synchronicity within and between organisms" (p. 207)

Clinical support for hypotheses 7 and 8. Clinicians contributing to the preliminary study identified a number of problematic interpersonal behaviors they had observed in children exposed to Pitocin at birth and theorized that the mother's and child's exposure to Pitocin at birth disrupts the attunement between mother and child, which in turn affects the child's capacity to function effectively in interpersonal relationships. In addition, clinicians described a variety of forms of recapitulation or repeated reenactment of birth themes in the lives of these children, which also affects how they engage with others.

Hypothesis 9

There is no significant relationship between timing of Pitocin administration and psychosocial functioning in sequencing activities at age 3, as measured by the following survey items (Appendix C):

Q58: My child has problems with beginning tasks.

Q59: My child procrastinates on starting things.

Q60: My child has a tendency to rush from one thing to the next and rarely slows down.

Q61: My child seeks help with starting things.

Q62: My child can get things started, but in the middle of something will become agitated or distracted, or lose focus.

Q63: My child seeks help from others with finishing activities.

Clinical support. The majority of clinicians interviewed for the preliminary study either identified specific instances or agreed that the timing of administration of Pitocin appeared to correlate with how children moved through sequences in daily life.

Hypothesis 10

There is a significant relationship between the context of the child's birth and the child's psychosocial functioning at age 3, as measured by the following survey items (Appendix C):

Q64: During your pregnancy with this child you experienced extreme stress.

Q65: During your pregnancy with this child you felt well supported.

Q66: Overall, you experienced the birth of this child as: Easy/Difficult.

Q67: Reflecting on the birth, you feel mostly: Positive/Negative.

Q68: There are aspects of this birth that are still troubling or unresolved to you.

Q69: During labor I felt that my birth team and I worked well together to meet both my needs and those of my baby.

Q70: Others took over control of my birth, leaving me feeling powerless and out of control.

Q71: My experience of labor and delivery was more intense than I expected, but I could cope.

Q72: During labor and delivery I felt overwhelmed, out of control, scared.

Q73: My experience of labor and delivery was that it was excruciating, unbearable, far beyond my coping ability.

Q74: I feel that during my pregnancy with this child I developed a strong relationship with him/her.

Q75: Before and during the birth I felt aware of/connected to my baby.

Q76: Given my own experience, I now wonder if during labor my baby may have felt disconnected from me, overwhelmed, unable to cope, in pain, frightened, traumatized.

Q77: In retrospect, I believe that any intervention(s) that took place during my child's birth were medically necessary.

Q78: Your labor began: Spontaneously/With intravenous Pitocin/With the help of something other than Pitocin (Cervidil, Cytotec, castor oil, herbs, sex, nipple stimulation, etc.).

Q79: During your labor you had (select one): No IV (intravenous line in your arm or hand)/An IV providing intravenous fluids/A "heplock" (intravenous line "just in case") but no intravenous fluids throughout labor/Other (describe).

Q80: Was Pitocin used at any time during your labor?

Q81: If Pitocin was used, when was it used?

Q82: In retrospect, do you feel satisfied with the decision to use Pitocin?

Q83: The effect of Pitocin on your labor was helpful.

Q84: You experienced Pitocin-induced contractions as stressful or overwhelming.

Q85: In retrospect, do you believe that your consent for Pitocin was fully informed regarding both the benefits and risks of its use?

Q86: Did you have medication for pain?

Q87: Did you have anesthesia?

Q88: Did you have an epidural?

Q89: If you had an epidural (combination pain medication and anesthetic by catheter into your back), it was started: Early in labor/Toward the middle of labor/Toward the end (within 2 hours of birth)/Throughout labor/I'm not sure *when* it was used but I know that it was used during my labor.

Q90: Your baby was with you for most or all of the hour following the birth.

Q91: Your baby was with you for most or all of the day following the birth.

Q92: In the day following the birth, the baby's father was present most or all of the time.

Q93: The baby's father was/has been involved with you and the baby in a positive and supportive way during the child's life to date.

Q94: During the first 6 months your baby was: Fed entirely at the breast/Fed entirely by bottle/Fed with combination of breast and bottle/Other (describe).

Theoretical support. Schore (2005) emphasized the "affect synchrony" between mother and infant: "psychobiological attunement and the interactive mutual entrainment of physiologic rhythms" (p. 207). Extrapolated backward through pregnancy, labor, and birth, it would seem that the degree to which mother and baby are supported to remain attuned and entrained through the birthing process might serve to minimize the disrupting effects of Pitocin hypothesized by the clinicians to result in enduring misattunement between mother and child and to result in psychosocial dysfunction in the child.

Clinical support. All clinicians interviewed for the preliminary study strongly emphasized the importance of the entire context of the child's birth when viewing the relationship between Pitocin use and the child's psychosocial functioning at age 3, and suggested that context could contribute to minimizing or expanding the apparent effects of Pitocin on the child.

Hypothesis 11

There is no significant relationship between the child's sex and the age and education of the child's parents and the effects of Pitocin on the child's psychosocial functioning at age 3, as measured by the following survey items (Appendix C):

Q95: Your 3-year-old is a: Boy/Girl

Q96: Your current age.

Q97: Child's father's current age.

Q98: Your current level of education is: Did not graduate from high school/High school graduate/GED/Some college/Associate's degree or equivalent/4-year degree or equivalent/Graduate degree or equivalent.

Q99: Father's current level of education is: Did not graduate from high school/High school graduate/GED/Some college/Associate's degree or equivalent/4-year degree or equivalent/Graduate degree or equivalent.

Clinical support. Because the use of Pitocin has become so commonplace as part of the active labor-management policies implemented in the majority of hospital births in the United States, and because the percentage of induced or augmented labors is now between 40% and 50%, it seems unlikely that age or level of education of parents can be considered a significant factor in whether Pitocin is used at birth. It seems equally unlikely that these demographic factors will correlate significantly with any psychosocial functioning found to be associated with its use.

Furthermore, because the 6 clinicians interviewed in the preliminary study observed what they perceived to be effects of Pitocin on psychosocial functioning of children at age 3 and did not provide any consistent observations concerning age or level of education of parents or the sex of the child, it seems unlikely that these variables will be found to bear a significant relationship to the dependent variables.

Chapter 4. Research Methodology and Data Analysis

Research Methods

The present study employed an online survey of mothers of 3-year-olds (Appendix C) to obtain both current and retrospective data related to their birth experience and the development of their child. The intent was to relate information about the birth process, particularly the use of artificial oxytocin (Pitocin), to the psychosocial functioning of children at age 3. The study attempted to answer the following questions:

1.   Is there a relationship between Pitocin use at birth and children's psychosocial functioning at age 3, and if so, what characterizes that relationship?

2.   Is there a relationship between when Pitocin was administered and how children move through sequences in daily life (i.e., an imprinting effect)?

3.   Does the overall context of the child's birth, meaning the mother's experience of the birth (support, stress, ease, satisfaction, etc.), bear any relationship to the child's psychosocial functioning at age 3, when born with or without the use of Pitocin?

4.   Is there a relationship between the age and education level of either parent, or the sex of the child, and psychosocial functioning at age 3, with or without Pitocin at birth?

To date, quantitative and mixed-methods research studies have been inconclusive when seeking to link induction of labor—either alone or as one of a group of obstetrical interventions or birth complications—with later functioning, whereas the findings of an admittedly small interview study (i.e., using qualitative methodology) of the observations of 6 experienced clinicians using a prenatal and perinatal psychology focus suggest that a relationship does exist, albeit possibly at more subtle levels than might be detected by measures used to date or in different domains from those previously examined. It seemed reasonable, therefore, to explore a slightly different approach to the research question: to utilize the clinical observations in survey form to gather data from a relatively large sample of mothers who gave birth with the use of Pitocin and thereby to access their maternal expertise about their own children at age 3, to examine whether these mothers' experience supports the clinical observations and thus indicates a significant relationship between Pitocin use at birth and the psychosocial functioning of their 3-year-olds.

Although Pitocin is employed as an obstetrical intervention in 40% to 50% of births in the United States (Declercq et al., 2006; Zhang et al., 2002), few studies have examined its possible effects, and most of those have reported finding no statistically significant relationship between Pitocin use and subsequent functioning, according to the measures each employed. Because one study (Eishima, 1992) identified some significant relationships, apparently by looking at somewhat more subtle levels of functioning, it was determined that a quantitative study capable of exploring similarly subtle levels of psychosocial functioning had the potential to be the most effective and substantive means of addressing the hypotheses. Although a qualitative study such as was preliminarily conducted with the 6 expert clinicians can indicate a possible direction for further research by suggesting a relationship between independent and dependent variables observed by a small group of experts, a quantitative study in this case offers a means to determine whether there are statistically significant relationships between labor induction/augmentation with artificial oxytocin and the psychosocial functioning of 3-year-olds born with its use.

Several of the relevant studies reviewed (Niswander et al., 1960; Out et al., 1985; Zappitelli et al., 2001) called for prospective research as the optimal method of examining the relationship between perinatal events and later functioning, and this would certainly have been the preferred approach for this study. A prospective study would have the advantages of a design completed before any data are gathered. Prospective participants could be identified during prenatal care, and a formal control group could be created based on actual birth events as documented in the medical records, with accurate information concerning dosage and duration not only of Pitocin use but also of any other obstetric medications employed, and the relationship in time between the use of different medications and interventions. The resulting data would have greater accuracy and the researcher(s) would have more accurate information regarding the occurrence of any confounding variables from the prenatal stage and throughout the period of study.

A prospective study also would permit children's functioning to be evaluated at several stages—for example, at birth, age 1, age 3, and age 5—and would allow the researcher to incorporate other perspectives, such as fathers' and teachers', and other forms of study, such as interviews and observations, in addition to completed surveys. In asserting that prospective, longitudinal studies of the possible effects of labor induction that permit detailed follow-up of large numbers of children are very much needed, Niswander et al. (1960) acknowledged the relative lack of planning and the reliance on sometimes incomplete information inherent in retrospective studies. They noted, however, that such studies have the advantage of capturing a more accurate picture of how inductions are conducted in routine obstetrical practice, whereas prospective studies may result in unusually meticulous efforts to avoid less-than-favorable experiences in study participants, presenting a potential confounding factor. Other disadvantages of a prospective study include significantly greater cost, more complicated logistics, the need for access to medical records, and a far longer time period for execution, with considerable delays before data can be gathered and reported.

Ultimately, the constraints on budget and time inherent in doctoral dissertation research resulted in the selection of a retrospective study comparing groups of Pitocin-exposed and -nonexposed mother-child dyads, using information gathered through mothers' responses to a survey. Retrospective studies are known to have significant limitations: the researcher selects the sample, leading to possible sample bias; there is complete reliance upon respondents' ability to recall events up to 4 years earlier, something known to involve possible bias in what is recalled, due to the nature of the recollection; and it is not possible to assume a cause-and-effect relationship between the intervention under study (Pitocin use) and the dependent variable of later psychosocial functioning because of the inability to identify and control for all confounding variables. On the other hand, a retrospective study is relatively inexpensive to conduct; can be completed fairly quickly, with fewer logistical obstacles to overcome (e.g., maintaining contact with participants for follow-up); and any significant findings may encourage future researchers to follow up with better-designed, more rigorous studies (e.g., an improved survey instrument or prospective studies) to investigate further any significant relationships identified.

Development of Survey Instrument

A survey instrument (Appendix C) was designed specifically for the purpose of this study. Its items were derived from preliminary interviews with experienced clinicians who work from a prenatal/perinatal perspective with infants and children who experienced interventions, stressors, or both at birth. The clinicians' responses were analyzed to identify significant dimensions of the psychosocial functioning of children who had been born with the use of artificial oxytocin, based on their observations.

It seemed possible that an instrument more focused on psychosocial (or psychobiological) functioning might reveal factors missed by instruments geared to assess aspects of functioning now understood to be less pertinent and possibly less predictive. The survey instrument developed from the clinician interviews addresses areas of functioning that, in the participants' clinical opinions, might distinguish 3-year-old children born with artificial oxytocin from those born without its use.

The survey was piloted with a small group of mothers recruited at a local preschool, who agreed to complete the survey on paper and provide feedback about the clarity of the wording of items and ease of responding to the survey. Following revisions based on this feedback, the survey was uploaded to the survey Web site (see Appendices C, D, and E for all items uploaded to the Web site) and a further pilot was conducted with another small group of volunteer mothers of 3-year-old children who met the criteria for the survey.

It would have been advantageous to pilot the survey at both stages with larger groups of mothers; however, as stated earlier, time and budget constraints limited the initial piloting phase. Thus, the "live" run of the survey online for this research also should be viewed in part as a pilot study of the survey's effectiveness, with the understanding that future researchers might benefit from modifications based on what was learned.

After all survey responses were downloaded and incomplete surveys were eliminated from the group, Chronbach's alpha was used to establish the reliability of the measure. This is a test for a survey's internal consistency, identifying "good" items, which have the most advantageous item-to-total-score correlation, and "bad" items, which fall outside the preferred range of correlations. Chronbach's alpha assesses the reliability of a rating summarizing a group of survey responses that measure some underlying factor (e.g., some attribute or behavior). A score is computed from each survey item and the overall rating, a scale, is defined by the sum of these scores over all the survey items. The reliability is then defined as the square of the correlation between the measured scale and the underlying factor the scale is supposed to measure. By this means, items that correlate too low or too high to the total score are eliminated. Common practice is to keep items that correlate between .30 and .60.

Chronbach's alpha flagged a total of 10 items to be deleted from the analysis to increase the reliability of the survey. Following the deletions, Chronbach's alpha was rerun and the remaining items in the survey were found to have a reliability of .92, meaning that less than 10% of the variability in the observed score is due to error.

Strengths and Limitations of Using an Online Survey

The major advantage of the use of an online survey to gather the data for this study was the ability to recruit a relatively large number of participants within a relatively short time frame, providing a sufficient number of participants for the type of statistical analysis planned. In the absence of an academic connection to a maternity hospital, this approach appeared to be the most affordable and time-efficient approach available.

The most significant limitations of gathering data with an online survey are the inability to verify participants' adherence to the stated criteria for participation and the unavailability of each participant's medical records, resulting in a lack of accurate information concerning the dose and duration of Pitocin administration and relying only upon the mothers' recall of their birth experience. This method of sampling excluded mothers who were not computer literate or had no access to computers and mothers who did not use electronic message boards, e-mail lists, or electronic bulletins as ways of forming community with, and obtaining support from, like-minded others. As a result, the sample can in no way be considered representative of the entire population of American mothers who gave birth to children who were between 3 and 4 years old at the time of the survey.

Although it is a tenet of prenatal and perinatal psychology that very early experiences have enduring effects, cause and effect cannot be inferred from survey findings, because the design of the study is nonexperimental—only relationships between Pitocin use/nonuse at birth and later psychosocial functioning can be identified retrospectively. Confounding variables such as parenting style; individual temperament; attachment quality and style; socioeconomic status; significant events, experiences, or traumas between birth and age 3; and domestic violence, maternal smoking, or drug/alcohol use during pregnancy, which are widely reported to influence children's psychosocial functioning, will inevitably escape identification.

Recruitment Strategies and Data Collection Materials and Procedures

The survey, with all psychosocial items in a randomized format, was made available on a survey-hosting Web site (www.qualtrics.com). A link to the site and an invitation to participate (Appendix F) were posted to a wide variety of parenting e-lists, bulletin boards, Web sites, and mailing lists (Appendix G). The researcher personally placed many of the invitations and requested the help of owners of e-mail lists, electronic bulletin boards, and Web sites.

Respondents were offered incentives to participate: If they completed the survey and provided an e-mail address they were to receive a summary of the findings, if they wished, and they were entered into a drawing for one of two $25 gift certificates for Amazon.com or one of eight annual subscriptions to *Pathways* magazine, which was offered by one of the organizations contacted with a request to disseminate the survey invitation.

The initial invitation (Appendix F) listed the basic criteria for participation, and these criteria also were listed on the informed consent page (Appendix D) that introduced the survey on the host Web site, where respondents indicated their agreement to participate.

Setting

Survey participants completed the survey wherever they had access to a computer and the Internet.

Criteria for Inclusion and Exclusion of Study Participants

Participants were 514 mothers of 3-year-olds who gave birth vaginally in a U.S. hospital and who experienced no major maternal or infant medical complications. Participants were required to have been living in the United States and over the age of 18 at time of delivery and to have been in a relationship with the father of their child at the time of the birth and up to the time of the survey. Mothers of premature or low-birth-weight infants and of infants with serious medical conditions or disabilities were excluded by the criteria, as were mothers who had had an abortion, who had lost a baby as a fetus or infant prior to the conception of the (now) 3-year-old, or who had used street drugs or alcohol after the pregnancy was confirmed.

All participants had some degree of computer literacy and access, because the survey was only available online. Although some participants found the survey through a link on a Web site they visited or through informal word of mouth, the majority were mothers who participated in at least one discussion board or electronic mailing list focused on some aspect of parenting, or who received regular bulletins from Web sites or organizations.

Ethical Considerations

The informed consent page called the survey The Behaviors of 3-Year-Olds Through the Eyes of Their Mothers. In the invitation to participate (Appendix F), the survey was described as a study of "the behaviors, emotions, coping skills, and interactions with others that you see in your 3-year-old child" in order to mask the specific focus on Pitocin use, because participants who did not receive Pitocin also were needed to serve as the comparison group. The criteria for participation in the survey were included in this document for review by potential respondents, and an e-mail address was included in case mothers had questions about their eligibility or other survey-related concerns. The informed consent to participate (Appendix D) appeared as the first page on the survey hosting Web site, and participants were required to agree to this before accessing the survey.

Potential participants were informed that e-mail addresses would not be connected to responses during the data analysis and that individual responses would not be discussed or published, because any publication based on the findings would show and discuss only the statistical analysis of the results. They were assured that e-mail addresses for the summary of findings would be stored securely and kept confidential, and it was made explicit that authorized faculty members of Santa Barbara Graduate Institute and members of its institutional review board would have the legal right to review the research records and would protect the confidentiality of the documents in question. In addition, participants were informed that their participation was voluntary and that they could discontinue completing the survey at any point and without penalty if they wished to do so.

Participants were provided with an estimate of the length of time required to complete the survey, based on the completion times of pilot respondents, and were informed that they had the option to complete the survey within a 5-day window, during which they would be returned to the point at which they exited the survey on the previous visit to the site. They were told that it would not be possible for them to return to and change previously completed responses.

It seemed possible that recalling the birth of their 3-year-old might elicit either pleasant or unpleasant memories for respondents, and this possibility was made explicit in the consent form, along with the encouragement that their memories and observations would contribute to greater understanding through the findings of the study. Participants were invited to contact the researcher and were to be offered a list of qualified therapists in their area if they felt the need to access such help following participation in the survey. Participants were provided with full contact information for the director of research of Santa Barbara Graduate Institute, should they have any complaint about the project (see Appendix E).

Data Collection and Management

Raw survey data were downloaded from the survey hosting Web site in the form of a Microsoft Excel database. For purposes of confidentiality, all response data were separated from individual respondents' e-mail addresses, and e-mail addresses were stored in separate, password-protected documents for the purposes of the drawing for the incentives and for e-mailing copies of the summary of findings.

Chapter 5. Results

This chapter presents a description of the sample, an examination of the research questions and the initial testing of hypotheses, and further exploratory investigation of additional questions generated by earlier analyses.

Data Retrieval

The survey was open for mothers to respond from Mother's Day, May 13, 2007, to June 15, 2007. After the survey was deactivated, 514 completed surveys were downloaded from the survey host site (www.qualtrics.com). Because the participants were not invited personally but were e-mailed information about the survey by other individuals, found the invitation on a Web site they visited, or received the invitation as a member of an e-mailed list or a bulletin board, it is not possible to estimate the response rate of invitations received relative to surveys completed.

The survey host Web site indicated 268 additional survey "starts" (see Table 5.1). Those who did not go past the introductory pages may have clicked on the survey link out of curiosity after receiving an invitation and then discovered that either they did not meet the survey criteria detailed on the informed consent page or they could not review the entire survey without responding to every item, because it was structured to permit clicking through to the next page only when all items on a page had been completed.

Toward the end of the survey run, an abbreviated invitation was posted to a widely read weekly electronic bulletin (www.mothering.com). Because this invitation did not contain all the details and the criteria for participation, it contained a link to a stand-alone page on Google's Web pages, which provided the full text of the invitation. Having read the full invitation on this page, those who wished to complete the survey could click on a link directly to the survey itself. During the period that this structure was in place, the completion rate of surveys shown on the host site increased from 68% to 82%, although it cannot be ascertained whether the increase was attributable to the additional steps required to access the survey or to the high level of commitment to survey completion on the part of the bulletin's readers . A list of the parenting lists, Web sites, online forums, and professional mailing lists and bulletins in which the survey invitation was posted is provided in Appendix G.

Table 5.1

Surveys Started and Completed

Surveys started/completed	N	% of total
Did not go past introductory pages	183	23
Went past introductory pages but did not complete	85	11
Completed	514	66
Total	782	100

Descriptive Statistics

Demographics

The final sample comprised 514 mothers of 3-year-olds. Participants' ages are shown in Figure 5.1. Table 5.2 indicates participants' level of education. Participants also reported the ages and education levels of the fathers of their 3-year-olds. Fathers' ages are shown in Figure 5.2, and education levels are shown in Table 5.3.

The 3-year-olds described by these mothers included 240 girls (47%) and 274 boys (53%). Further demographic information (ethnicity, socioeconomic status, geographic location, etc.) was not gathered for two reasons: first, it was important to keep the survey as brief as possible to ensure a maximum number of completions, and thus any demographic information not felt to be critical to the topic of study was not requested; second, given the high proportion of Pitocin use at births and the relatively small size of the sample, it seemed unlikely that any information of true statistical significance would be garnered from the addition of these questions, or that such information would be generalizable.

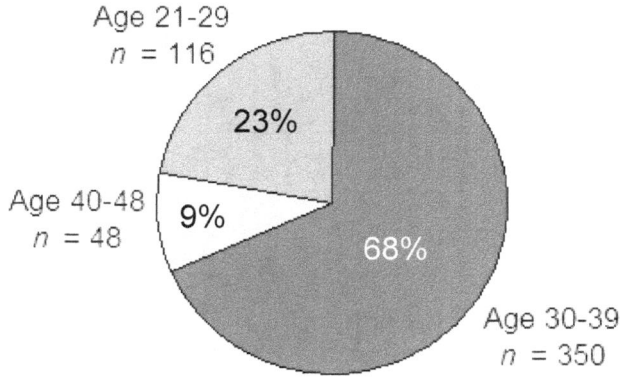

Figure 5.1. Age of mothers (*N* = 514).

Table 5.2

Mother's Education

Mother's education	N	Percentage of total sample
High school, GED or less	15	3
Some college, 2-year degree	135	26
4-year degree	206	40
Master's; doctorate; professional degree	158	31
Total	514	100

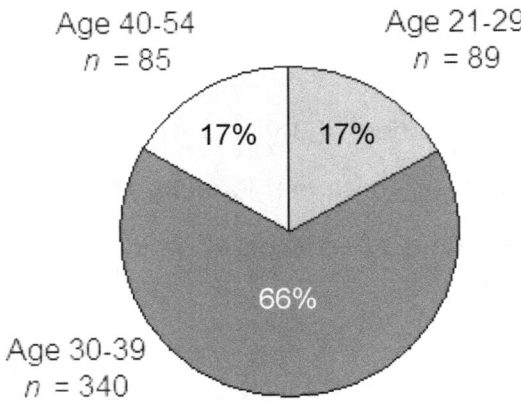

Figure 5.2. Age of fathers (*N* = 514).

Table 5.3

Father's Education

Father's education	N	Percentage of total sample
High school, GED or less	49	10
Some college, 2-year degree	145	28
4-year degree	195	38
Master's; doctorate; professional degree	125	24
Total	514	100

Obstetrical Interventions

Of the 514 respondents, 231 mothers reported having been administered Pitocin at some point during labor with their child, whereas 267 mothers reported no use of Pitocin during labor. Sixteen mothers were unsure whether they had received Pitocin, so these were not included in analyses comparing Pitocin/no Pitocin groups. Information concerning Pitocin administered after the birth of the child for the purpose of preventing postpartum hemorrhage was not gathered, because it was not considered to have had any direct effects on the infant.

Figure 5.3 shows participants' responses to an item stating, "During your labor you had (select one): No IV (intravenous line in your arm or hand)/An IV providing intravenous fluids/A "heplock" (intravenous line "just in case") but no intravenous fluids throughout labor/Other (describe)." Those who checked "Other (describe)" provided a written description of what they received during labor (e.g., antibiotics for group B streptococcus; see Appendix H).

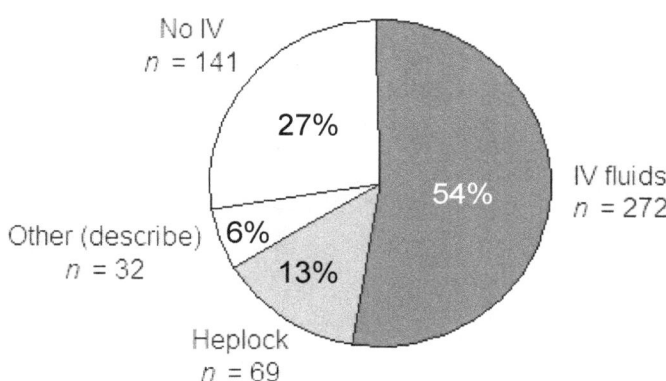

Figure 5.3. IV status and other labor interventions (*N* = 514).

Figure 5.4 indicates women's responses to the survey item about how their labor started. Among these, 65 women reported that their labor began with the help of something other than intravenous Pitocin. This might have included anything from topically applied prostaglandins to nipple stimulation, the use of herbs or castor oil, or intercourse.

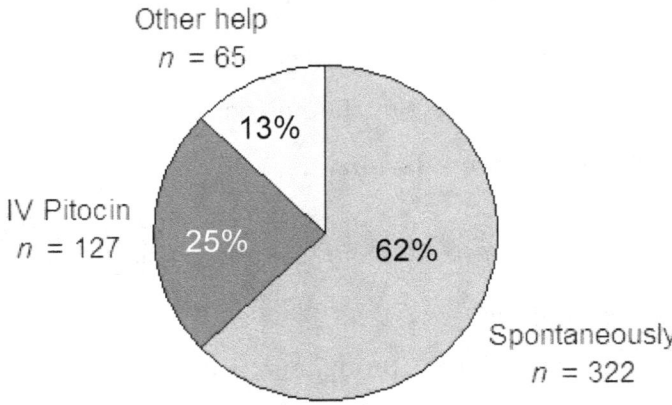

Figure 5.4. Responses to survey item about how labor started (*N* = 514).

Of the 127 women who responded that their labor was induced with Pitocin and the 104 who responded that Pitocin was used during labor other than to start it (augmentation) (Figure 5.5), only 89 women responded to the subsequent question asking when Pitocin was used, saying it was used at the start of labor, suggesting either that some women were not certain about when they received Pitocin, or that the survey questions were not clear. Three women reported having received Pitocin but were unable to remember when it was administered (Table 5.4).

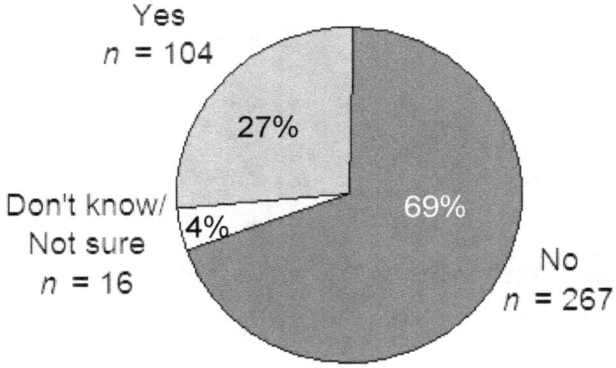

Figure 5.5. Whether or not Pitocin was used at any time in respondents' labors, other than to induce labor (*N* = 387).

Table 5.4

Timing of Pitocin Administration as Recalled by Survey Respondents

Timing of Pitocin administration	*N*	Percentage of respondents
Labor start	89	39
Early/mid Labor	65	28
Late in labor	39	17
Throughout labor	35	15
Don't remember	3	1
Total	231	100

Forty women (17%) were unsure or did not know if they were satisfied or not with their Pitocin experience (Figure 5.6).

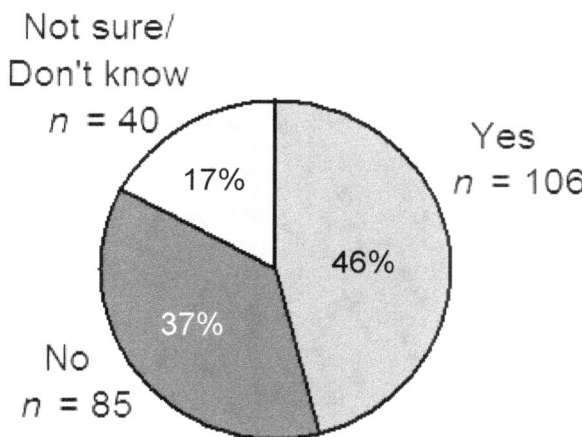

Figure 5.6. Respondents' satisfaction with Pitocin use during labor (*N* = 231).

Figure 5.7 shows that 15% of respondents were unsure as to whether they had been fully informed when giving their consent to be given Pitocin, while over one third reported they consented to Pitocin without being fully informed.

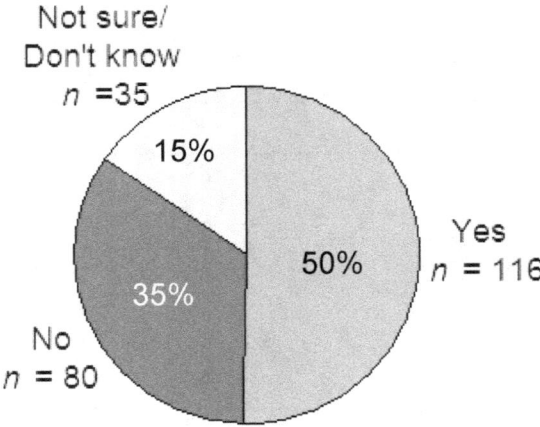

Figure 5.7. Participants' responses to question concerning whether or not their consent for Pitocin use was fully informed (*N* = 231).

Figure 5.8 indicates that more than half of respondents did not use pain medication during labor.

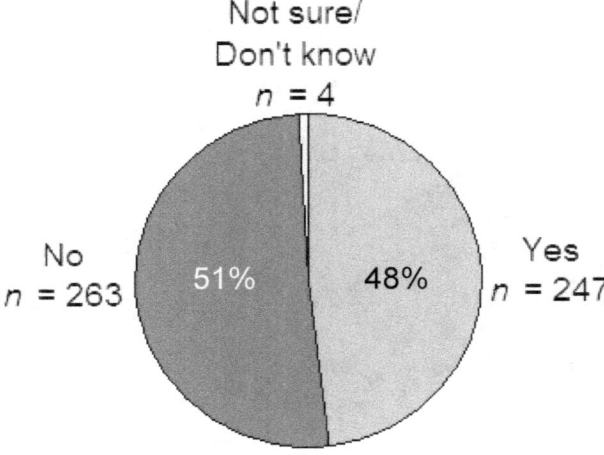

Figure 5.8. Participants' responses to survey item concerning use of pain medication in labor (*N* = 514).

Figure 5.9 provides responses to the question "Did you have anesthesia?" This question may have caused confusion in respondents, who answered the next question, "Did you have an epidural? (combination pain medication and anesthetic by catheter into your back)" (Figure 5.10) in sufficiently discrepant numbers compared to responses to the previous question about anesthesia to suggest a lack of clarity in some mothers' understandings of whether or not receiving an epidural constitutes receiving anesthesia. Of the women surveyed, 229 (45%) reported having had epidural anesthesia during labor and 285 women (55%) reported having no epidural (Figure 5.10). Typically, an epidural contains a "cocktail" that combines anesthesia with an analgesic, effectively numbing sensation from approximately the waist down through the pelvis and upper (and sometimes also lower) legs. Some mothers may have thought anesthesia referred only to general anesthesia typically used for emergency or other major surgeries. Since the use of epidurals became commonplace, other forms of regional anesthesia, typically administered by injection to the site (e.g., a pudendal block), have fallen into disuse.

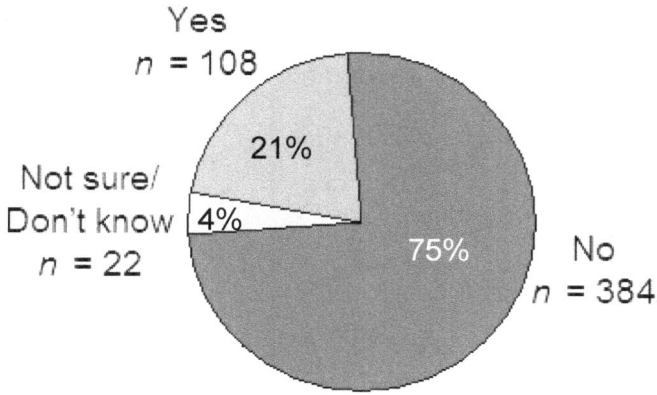

Figure 5.9. Respondents' reports of anesthesia use in labor (*N* = 514).

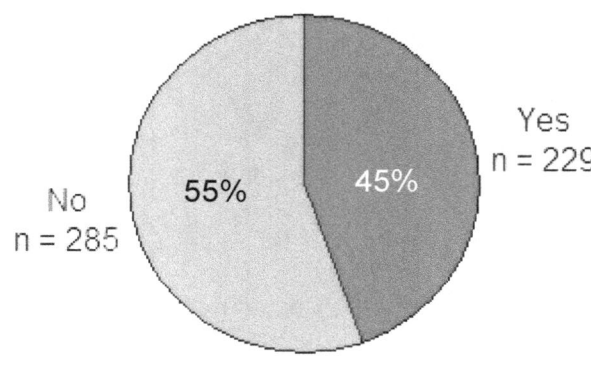

Figure 5.10. Respondents' reports of epidural use in labor (*N* = 514).

Table 5.5 indicates the distribution of responses given by women who received an epidural when asked at what point during labor it had been administered.

Table 5.5

Timing of Epidural Administration as Recalled by Respondents

Timing of epidural administration	N	Percentage
Early	35	15
Toward middle	121	54

Towards end	64	28
Throughout	8	3
Not sure when	1	0
Total	229	100

Figure 5.11 illustrates the relationships between epidural use and Pitocin use as reported by survey participants. Not included in this figure were 4 women who reported having had an epidural but who did not know if they had received Pitocin.

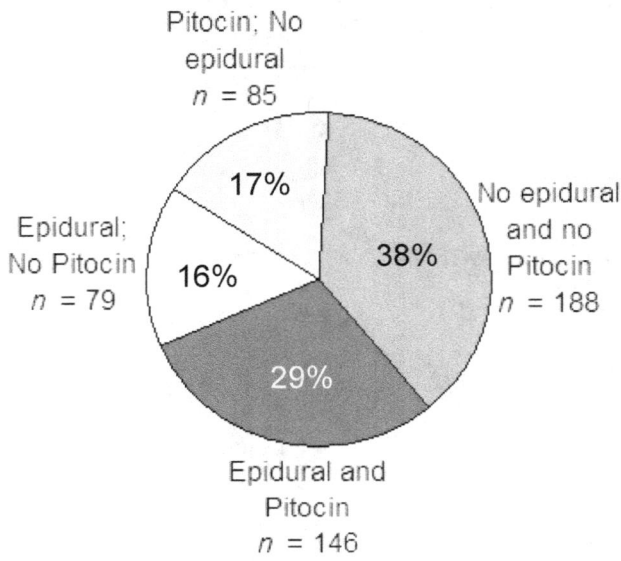

Figure 5.11. Proportions of women who received Pitocin and/or epidural anesthesia (*N* = 498).

Table 5.6 summarizes the distribution of all obstetrical medications employed in the 514 births of 3-year-olds whose mothers participated in this study.

Twenty-two respondents (4%) checked "Other" and provided a written statement describing personal variations in how their child was fed (e.g., "Breast-fed, at 4 months started solid food against my better judgment") (Figure 5.12). It appears from their statements that approximately 18 of these mothers provided breast milk exclusively by breast, bottle, or cup for at least 4 months (see Appendix I for these statements).

Power Analysis

A power analysis was conducted during the course of the survey run, ensuring that the minimum sample size required was obtained so that when the data were subjected to the planned analyses the analyses would be capable of detecting an effect, should the effect exist.

Table 5.6

Use of Obstetrical Medications

Was Pitocin used at any time? (including to start labor)	Did you have medication for pain?	Did you have an epidural?	Did you have anesthesia?	Total
Yes	Yes	Yes	Yes	108
Yes	Yes	Yes	No	24
Yes	Yes	No	No	14
Yes	No	Yes	No	13
Yes	NS/DK[a]	Yes	NS/DK	1
No	Yes	Yes	No	75
No	NS/DK	Yes	NS/DK	2
No	Yes	No	No	20
No	No	Yes	No	2
No	No	No	No	159
No	No	No	NS/DK	8
No	NS/DK	No	NS/DK	1
NS/DK	Yes	Yes	No	4
NS/DK	Yes	No	No	2
NS/DK	No	No	NS/DK	10
				514

[a] Not Sure/Don't Know

The number of survey participants required for adequate statistical power was calculated according to the guidelines for a standard power analysis (Cohen, 1988), and minimum discernible effects levels were determined. Power was calculated under a balanced ANOVA design, even though the data were analyzed in an unbalanced context.

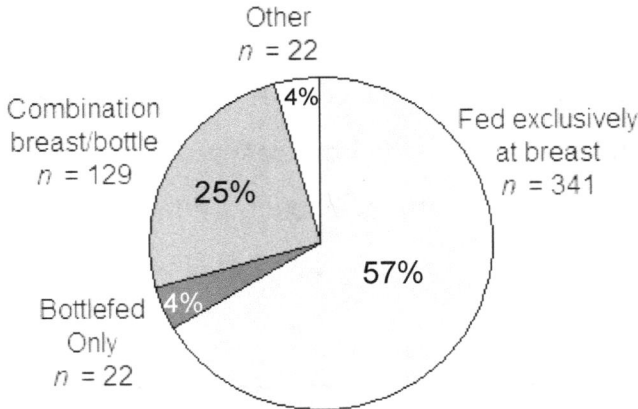

Figure 5.12. How respondents fed their babies for the first 6 months (*N* = 514).

Note. The small discrepancy in "Other" numbers (*n* = 22) shown in Figure 14 above and Table 25 (*n* = 20) (see Post Hoc Analyses) is explained by the fact that in the table are only shown mothers who were sure of whether or not they received Pitocin, and so two of the women who checked "Other" and gave written statements about their feeding method were among those unsure about Pitocin use.

Cell counts for power calculation were based on the smallest number of observations across all the cells, and the corresponding power was taken as a minimum, because any increased observations would only improve the resolution of the analysis. Power calculations were performed for a total of 16 hypotheses.

As shown in Table 5.7, effect size is the minimum difference between the mean values in each cell that will be detectable under the given power and alpha (0.80 and .05, respectively). Sample size represents the minimum number of data points required in each cell to detect the indicated effect size with the given power.

In the absence of estimates for within-factor or between-factor variability, worst-case assumptions (that the responses are uniformly distributed over Level 1 through Level 7 of each scale) were used. Between-factor variances were likewise selected to minimize variance for the given minimal effect and thus to generate worst-case sample sizes for power. Any power indicated is, therefore, a lower bound and may in fact be higher. In addition, the following assumptions were determined to be reasonable within the context of the study, and were employed to simplify the power analysis:

1.   All model terms are fixed effects (i.e., data were collected on the two conditions of Pitocin and no Pitocin).

2.   Different survey responses are uncorrelated.

3.   Responses within different categories on the same survey are uncorrelated.

Table 5.7

Power Analysis: Effect Sizes and Cell Counts

Effect size to detect	Minimum sample size
0.50	253
0.75	112
1.00	64
1.25	42
1.50	29
1.75	22
2.00	17

The power analysis provided estimates for the various hypotheses to be tested, which would permit detection of a reasonably small effect size. For example, for Hypothesis 1 through Hypothesis 8, with a minimum cell count of 231, a difference as small as .75 could be detected. The actual numbers obtained in the sample as they were used in the analyses for hypothesis testing were more than adequate to ensure that the effect sizes would be discerned with a power of .80 and an alpha of .05.

Initial Hypothesis Testing

The following section provides the findings of the hypothesis testing.

Pitocin Use at Birth and Psychosocial Functioning at Age 3

Hypothesis 1 (the main hypothesis) posited that there is a relationship between the use of Pitocin at birth and the psychosocial functioning of children at age 3. This hypothesis encompasses seven subhypotheses (Hypothesis 2 through Hypothesis 8), each of which proposed that a subgroup, or dimension, of psychosocial survey items would show a relationship with Pitocin use at birth.

Table 5.8 lists all psychosocial survey items (measured with 7-point semantic differential–type scales employing polar adjectives). Asterisked items proved to be significant for Pitocin use; that is, Pitocin use made a significant difference in mothers' appraisals of their children on those items.

A two-tailed *t* test compared the two samples: mothers' responses about children born with Pitocin (*n* = 231) and mothers' responses about children born without Pitocin (*n* = 267), on each scaled survey item. Table 5.8 provides the scores for Welch's *t* test for unequal variances, because there was no reason to assume equal variance between the two populations. The power analysis demonstrated that an effect size of 0.75 or smaller (between 0.75 and 0.5, based on numbers per cell) could be detected with a minimum *n* of 231 per cell.

Among the items describing psychosocial functioning in the child, the following items showed a significant difference between Pitocin (P) and no Pitocin (NP) groups:

1. Has/has had a pattern of self-harming behaviors (P: *M* = 1.3550, *SD* = .8966; NP: *M* = 1.2135, *SD* = .7013), *t*(433.031) = 1.940, *p* = .053. (This item was significant in the *t* test for equal variance at *p* = .049, and close to significant in the *t* test for unequal variance; hence, it seemed appropriate to include the item in this list.)

Table 5.8

T test for Independent Samples: Psychosocial Items

Survey item	*t* test	for Equality	of Means
	t	df	Sig. (2-tailed)
Craves firm pressure and intense contact	.996	491.616	.320
Resists holding and contact	1.148	47.032	.252
Trouble with puzzles and putting things together	.112	474.872	.911
Appears clumsy and tends to bump into things and people	1.000	492.583	.318
Easily overwhelmed	.058	488.175	.954
When upset, difficult to help child calm down	-.587	481.695	.557
Easily irritated/upset if not responded to immediately	.161	473.147	.872
Tends to be confident and happy	.132	472.791	.895
Has/has had a pattern of self-harming behaviors	1.940	433.031	.053
Aggressive (biting, kicking, hitting, pushing)	-.016	470.629	.987
Has focusing problems only with specific triggers	-.686	489.957	.493
Has difficulty when others are directing/setting the pace	-.562	474.326	.574
Responds well to being allowed to self-pace	-1.665	471.212	.097

Survey item	t test	for Equality	of Means
	t	df	Sig. (2-tailed)
Child seems out of sync with mother (too fast, too slow)	.518	474.668	.605
Has digestive problems	.707	483.504	.480
Is a fussy or picky eater	1.617	482.875	.106
Has problems with sleeping at night	1.350	472.052	.178
Timid or tentative	-.445	483.553	.657
Difficulties when others control timing and transitions	-.214	459.680	.830
Resists receiving help from others	1.498	471.533	.135
Strongly resists pressure, directions, being hurried	.867	478.217	.387
Reacts strongly to directions, demands	2.281	473.196	.023*
Does what mother asks child to do	.772	475.614	.440
The one in charge in the family	1.665	461.698	.097
Gets extremely upset when things don't go his/her way	-.241	478.337	.810
Lets others lead; is more of a follower	.045	471.338	.965
Strong need to be in control	2.480	478.120	.013*
Dominates other children	2.412	482.352	.016*
Plays cooperatively with others	.621	478.593	.535
Plays entrapping games	-.706	488.698	.480
Plays rescuing games	.879	482.880	.380
Sensitive to intrusion into physical or mental space	.937	470.844	.349
Communicates "yes" and "no" when needs to	-2.327	495.750	.020*
Intrusive/"pushy"; seems not to recognize boundaries	1.263	455.445	.207
Mother feels she can never satisfy her child	1.979	443.229	.048*
Mother feels she doesn't know how to connect with child	.847	470.983	.397
When child speeds up, it's hard to connect with him/her	1.556	477.263	.120
Mother sees relationship as easy and cooperative	2.797	439.243	.005**
Difficulties orienting in new situations/places	.030	486.027	.976
Difficulties with transitions (waking, changing activities)	-.122	485.517	.903
Strong reactions to quick or unexpected changes	-1.010	484.983	.313
Copes better with transitions when involved in how/when	-.245	486.817	.806
Problems with beginning tasks	-.266	480.645	.790
Procrastinates on starting things	.349	469.937	.728

Survey item	t test	for Equality	of Means
	t	df	Sig. (2-tailed)
Rushes from one thing to next and rarely slows down	2.537	467.790	.011*
Seeks help with starting things	.882	492.380	.378
In the middle of things becomes agitated, distracted.	1.779	489.917	.076
Seeks help with finishing activities	-.070	475.970	.944
As an infant, very sensitive to movement/position changes	.307	475.428	.759
As an infant, strongly protested vestibular movement	-.138	482.540	.890
As an infant, had ear infections	2.076	449.952	.038*
As an infant, was "colicky" or fussy and hard to soothe	1.630	470.389	.104
As an infant, extreme emotional responses to transitions	.866	480.223	.387

* $p < .05$; ** $p < .01$; *** $p < .001$

2. Reacts strongly to being given directions or having demands made upon them (P: $M = 3.1082$, $SD = 1.4719$; NP: $M = 2.8165$, $SD = 1.3655$).

3. Strong need to control (P: $M = 4.1991$, $SD = 1.6350$; NP: $M = 3.8427$, $SD = 1.5577$).

4. Dominates other children (P: $M = 3.1169$, $SD = 1.5405$; NP: $M = 2.7865$, $SD = 1.5054$).

5. Good at communicating yes and no when needs to (P: $M = 1.5714$, $SD = .8958$; NP: $M = 1.7753$, $SD = 1.0594$).

6. Mother feels she can never satisfy this child (P: $M = 2.2857$, $SD = 1.4282$; NP: $M = 2.0524$, $SD = 1.1622$).

7. Mother describes her relationship with the child as easy and cooperative (P: $M = 2.7143$, $SD = 1.3007$; NP: $M = 2.4157$, $SD = 1.0421$).

8. Child tends to rush from one thing to the next and rarely slows down (P: $M = 3.2294$, $SD = 1.6190$; NP: $M = 2.8764$, $SD = 1.4625$).

9. Of the five items describing the child as an infant, the item in which the child was described as having had ear infections was also significant for Pitocin (P: $M = 1.9654$, $SD = 1.6833$; NP: $M = 1.6742$, $SD = 1.4071$).

This grouping of psychosocial items found to be significantly related to Pitocin use at birth represents a small proportion of the number of psychosocial items (9 out of 53) and was not a grouping predicted in the dimensions tested in Hypothesis 2 through Hypothesis 8. The total score for psychosocial items (Table 5.8) was not found to be significant for Pitocin use versus no Pitocin use and therefore did not support the main hypothesis (Hypothesis 1).

Pitocin Use at Birth and the Dimensions of Psychosocial Functioning at Age 3

Hypotheses 2 through 8 represent the subgrouping of the 53 psychosocial items into dimensions representing different aspects of functioning. The dimensions employed in the analyses of variance, shown in Table 5.9, are represented by the following hypotheses.

Hypothesis 2: There is a significant relationship between Pitocin use at birth and sensory processing at age 3.

Hypothesis 3: There is a significant relationship between Pitocin use at birth and coordination/motor skills at age 3.

Table 5.9

Analysis of Variance: Total Score and Score for Each Dimension of Psychosocial Functioning

Dimension	Variance	Sum of squares	df	Mean square	F	p
Total score	Between groups	2602.926	1	2602.926	2.205	.138
	Error	585498.771	496	1180.441		
	Total	588101.697	497	1.665		
Sensory processing	Between groups	10.485	1	10.485	.655	.419
	Error	7945.346	496	16.019		
	Total	7955.831	497			
Motor coordination	Between groups	2.516	1	2.516	.597	.440
	Error	2091.501	496	4.217		
	Total	2094.016	497			

Dimension	Variance	Sum of squares	df	Mean square	F	p
Affect/mood regulation	Between groups	.333	1	.333	.027	.871
	Error	6220.486	496	12.541		
	Total	6220.819	497			
Self-esteem	Between groups	1.550E-02	1	1.550E-02	.018	.894
	Error	433.238	496	.873		
	Total	433.253	497			
ANS regulation	Between groups	126.990	1	126.990	2.270	.133
	Error	27751.123	496	55.950		
	Total	27878.112	497			
Interpersonal functioning	Between groups	361.121	1	361.121	2.462	.117
	Error	72764.004	496	146.702		
	Total	73125.124	497			
Mother-child attunement	Between groups	77.174	1	77.174	1.336	.248
	Error	28649.366	496	57.761		
	Total	28726.540	497			

Hypothesis 4: There is a significant relationship between Pitocin use at birth and affect/mood regulation at age 3.

Hypothesis 5: There is a significant relationship between Pitocin use at birth and a child's self-esteem/sense of self at age 3.

Hypothesis 6: There is a significant relationship between Pitocin use at birth and various aspects of autonomic nervous system regulation in the child at age 3.

Hypothesis 7: There is a significant relationship between Pitocin use at birth and 3-year-olds' functioning in interpersonal situations, as reported by their mothers.

Hypothesis 8: There is a significant relationship between Pitocin use at birth and attunement between mother and child in infancy and at age 3.

These hypotheses were intended to explore whether Pitocin correlated with the dimensions of psychosocial functioning into which individual survey items were grouped. Table 5.9 shows the analyses of variance for total score, and between- and within-groups dimensions with and without Pitocin. None of the proposed dimensions differentiated the functioning of Pitocin and no-Pitocin groups to a degree that was statistically significant, and so Hypotheses 2 through 8 were not supported.

As with Hypothesis 1, the power analysis predicted that for these analyses of variance an effect of 0.75 could be detected (power of 0.80, alpha of .05) with an n of 231. This suggests that although psychosocial items were grouped into dimensions that were logically based in theory and clinical practice, the dimensions failed to distinguish between the Pitocin and non-Pitocin groups and any effect not detected would have been too small to be of significance.

Timing of Pitocin Administration and Psychosocial Functioning in Sequencing Activities at Age 3

Hypothesis 9 states that there is no significant relationship between timing of Pitocin administration and psychosocial functioning in sequencing activities at age 3. A series of one-way between-groups analyses of variance was conducted to compare the timing of Pitocin administration with children's psychosocial functioning in sequencing activities.

The ANOVA in Table 5.10 displays the relationship between total score and the independent variable of timing of Pitocin administration. Subsequent rows compare timing of Pitocin administration, comparing three groups of responses—"To start labor," "Early or in the middle of labor," and "Late in labor"—with psychosocial functioning in beginnings, middles, and ends of sequencing activities. A fourth category of responses ("Throughout labor") was excluded from the analysis because many of these responses overlapped with responses to a previous item stating that Pitocin was used to start labor or was administered early in labor.

Table 5.10

Analysis of Variance: Timing of Pitocin Administration and Psychosocial Functioning in Sequencing Activities

Variable	and Source	Sum of squares	df	Mean square	F	p
Total score	Between groups	2827.648	4	706.912	.584	.674
	Error	272265.395	225	121.068		
	Total	275093.043	229			
Sequence beginning	Between groups	7.655	4	1.914	.151	.963

Variable	and Source	Sum of squares	df	Mean square	F	p
	Error	2856.937	225	12.697		
	Total	2864.591	229			
Sequence middle	Between groups	.897	4	.224	.124	.974
	Error	406.794	225	1.808		
	Total	407.691	229			
Sequence ending	Between groups	4.438	4	1.110	.623	.647
	Error	400.710	225	1.781		
	Total	405.148	229			

Based on the power analysis with a power of .80, alpha of .05, and an n of 35 per cell, three different effect sizes were possible. An effect for Pitocin administration time (1.00) answered the question "Do the mean scores in a given level of sequencing (beginning, middle, completing) differ depending on the timing of Pitocin administration?". An effect for sequencing activity (0.75) answered the question "Do the mean scores for different levels of sequencing vary under a particular timing of Pitocin?". An effect for the interaction (1.75) answered the question "Is the effect of the timing of Pitocin administration on the mean score different depending on the specific sequencing item being examined?". In these analyses it was found that the means were statistically indistinguishable across all levels of Pitocin timing for each sequencing item; thus, the null hypothesis was supported.

Context of Birth and Psychosocial Functioning at Age 3

Hypothesis 10 states that there is a significant relationship between the context of the child's birth and the child's psychosocial functioning at age 3. Because all relevant responses from all survey items could be included in testing this hypothesis, the power analysis stated that an effect size as small as .05 could be detected. For the first step in testing this hypothesis, a two-tailed t test for independent samples (Welch's t test for unequal variances) was conducted to compare means on responses to scaled items (as opposed to multiple-choice items) with Pitocin use and no Pitocin use (Table 5.11).

The following items displayed significant differences in the means of mothers' responses for the Pitocin (P) and No Pitocin (NP) groups:

1. Ease of birth (P: $M = 3.4113$, $SD = 2.0086$; NP: $M = 2.5655$, $SD = 1.7511$).

Table 5.11

T test for Independent Means: Pitocin/No Pitocin Use and Scaled Context of Birth Items

Question	t test	For Equality	Of Means
	t	df	Sig. (2-tailed)
Mother felt well supported in pregnancy	-.084	485.554	.933
Mother experienced extreme stress in pregnancy	.304	488.061	.761
Developed strong relationship with child in pregnancy	.011	493.507	.991
Felt aware of/connected to baby before and during birth	1.771	463.157	.077
Ease of birth (Easy/Difficult)	4.971	459.955	.000***
Birth reflections (Positive/Negative)	5.353	406.685	.000***
Aspects of this birth still troubling or unresolved	2.132	469.510	.034*
Mother felt she and birth team worked well together	4.261	45.058	.000***
Others took control of birth: mother felt powerless	6.308	401.393	.000***
Felt overwhelmed, out of control, scared by labor	1.926	465.760	.055
Labor/delivery was excruciating, unbearable	3.406	441.690	.001**
Wonders if in labor baby felt disconnected, scared	4.939	408.202	.000***
Interventions were medically necessary: Agree/Disagree	.968	485.700	.333
Baby with mother most of first hour postpartum	2.793	441.956	.005**
Baby with mother most of first day after birth	1.112	465.457	.267
Father present most or all of day following birth	.196	472.289	.845
Father involved positively and supportively in present	.946	447.811	.344

Note. Pitocin mothers: *n* = 231; no Pitocin mothers: *n* = 267

* *p* < .05; ** *p* < .01; *** *p* < .001

2. Reflections on the birth (Positive/Negative) (P: *M* = 2.2424, *SD* = 1.6049; NP: *M* = 1.5655, *SD* = 1.1365).

3. Aspects of the birth still troubling or unresolved for mother (P: *M* = 2.6320, *SD* = 2.1747; NP: *M* = 2.2322, *SD* = 1.9807).

4. Birth team that worked well together with mother (P: *M* = 2.6017, *SD* = 1.9262; NP: *M* = 1.9176, *SD* = 1.6108).

5. Others took over control of the birth, leaving mother feeling powerless and out of control (P: *M* = 2.7662, *SD* = 2.1803; NP: *M* = 1.6891, *SD* = 1.5133).

6. During labor and delivery mother felt overwhelmed, out of control, scared (P: M = 2.6364, SD = 1.6332; NP: M = 2.3670, SD = 1.4613). (This item was close to significance at p = .055.)

7. Mother's experience of labor was that it was excruciating, unbearable, far beyond her coping ability (P: M = 2.1818, SD = 1.4896; NP: M = 1.7640, SD = 1.2048).

8. Mother reflects that, given her own experience, she now wonders if during labor her baby may have felt disconnected from her, overwhelmed, unable to cope, in pain, frightened, traumatized (P: M = 2.2900, SD = 1.7240; NP: M = 1.6180, SD = 1.2279).

9. Baby was with mother for most or all of first hour after birth (P: M = 2.2251, SD = 2.1672; NP: M = 1.7266, SD = 1.7547).

Of the scaled items pertaining to the context of the birth, almost all those pertaining to the birth itself, through the first hour postpartum, and those pertaining to mothers' reflections upon the birth experience 3 years later proved to be highly statistically significant for Pitocin use. This indicates a significant relationship between Pitocin use and the experience of birth as recalled by the 231 mothers in this study who received Pitocin during labor, as described by these perinatal context items. The significantly higher scores on scaled items for the Pitocin group indicate a more negative rating.

Neither items pertaining to the pregnancy nor those pertaining to the extended postpartum period were shown to be statistically significant for Pitocin. Table 5.12 shows the descriptive statistics on total scores for 17 items for Context of Birth, showing the difference in means between mothers who received Pitocin and those who did not.

Table 5.12

Descriptive Statistics: Pitocin/No Pitocin Use and Context of Birth

	N	Mean	Std. deviation	Std. error	95% Confidence interval for mean		Min.	Max.
					Lower bound	Upper bound		
Pitocin Yes	231	40.8918	17.2640	1.1359	38.6537	43.1298	17.00	91.00
Pitocin	267	34.0861	13.6947	.8381	32.4360	35.7363	17.00	91.00

No							
Total	498	37.2430	15.8065	.7083	35.8513	38.6346	17.00	91.00

A one-way, between-groups analysis of variance using the scaled Context of Birth items found a significant relationship between the use of Pitocin at birth and mothers' descriptions of their birth experiences with their (now) 3-year-olds ($F[1, 496] = 24.023$, $p = .000$). Table 5.13 shows the analysis of variance, comparing total scores summed across all Context of Birth items.

To address further the hypothesis that there is a significant relationship between the context of the child's birth and the child's psychosocial functioning at age 3, mixed effects models were created to test for differences in the relationship between context and psychosocial functioning in the Pitocin and No Pitocin groups. Mixed effects models can be used to investigate how the relationship of one parameter (e.g., context) to another (e.g., psychosocial functioning) varies across pairs of categorical data (e.g., Pitocin/No Pitocin) (Faraway, 2004). This technique was used to determine whether the relationship between Context and total psychosocial score was significantly different for those children exposed to Pitocin and those not exposed to Pitocin.

Table 5.13

Analysis of Variance: Pitocin/No Pitocin Use and Total Score of Context of Birth Items

	Sum of squares	df	Mean square	F	p
Between groups	5736.287	1	5736.287	24.023***	.000
Error	118437.313	496	238.785		
Total	124173.600	497			

$* p < .05; ** p < .01; *** p < .001$

A mixed effects model was developed by taking a simple linear regression of score as a function of context and then introducing grouping categorical variables for Pitocin/no Pitocin in both the constant and linear terms—in effect, adding two parameters to the model. The significance of the added parameters was tested using standard significance tests (F test). A finding of significance for the Pitocin grouping variable would indicate that Pitocin affected either the average value of the score, the relationship between the Context parameter and the score, or both. If neither was significant, it would indicate that Pitocin had no effect on the relationship between Context and score, and that the relationship between Context and score for Pitocin-exposed children and non-Pitocin exposed children was in effect the same.

Context and Total Psychosocial Functioning Score

Analysis of total score indicates that the linear models for the effect of Context on total score are identical for Pitocin and non-Pitocin children—i.e., Context bore a significant relationship to total score but did not differentiate between Pitocin and no Pitocin. The results of these analyses are presented in Table 5.14. Although these results appear to be inconsistent with the conclusion that Pitocin has a significant impact on the context of birth, they indicate that the overall Context and score for Pitocin-exposed children tends to be higher. Thus, any effect of Pitocin on total score is most likely mediated exclusively through the effect of Pitocin on Context.

Table 5.14

Summary of Mixed Model Regression Analysis Regressing Total Score for Psychosocial Functioning on Context and Pitocin

Total score for psychosocial functioning

Predictors	B	SE B	R^2
Constant	123.64***	5.24	14.6%
Pitocin	-0.25	7.53	
Context	0.85***	0.14	
Pitocin x Context	-.023	0.19	

* $p < .05$; ** $p < .01$; *** $p < .001$

Because this first analysis included only the scaled survey items, further analysis was then required to explore the relationships between scaled and unscaled (multiple-choice) context items (e.g., pain medication, anesthesia, or epidural use), Pitocin use, and psychosocial items. Two examples of multiple-choice items follow:

1. Did you have an epidural? (combination pain medication and anesthetic by catheter into your back) (select one) (a) Yes; (b) No; (c) Not sure/Don't know.

2. The epidural was started (select one): (a) Early in labor; (b) Toward the middle of labor; (c) Toward the end (within 2 hours of birth); (d) Throughout labor; (e) I'm not sure when it was used but I know that it was used during my labor.

Because Context was found to have a linear relationship with total score, the following context-related items were examined for their effect on overall Context of Birth:

1.   Whether an epidural was used. In those cases where an epidural was used, the timing of epidural administration.

2.   Whether pain medications were used.

3.   Whether anesthesia was used.

4.   In cases where Pitocin was used, the timing of Pitocin administration (Table 5.15).

Table 5.15

Analysis of Variance: Epidural Use and Overall Context Score

Source	Sum of squares	df	Mean square	F	p
Between groups	5084	1	5084	20.623***	.000
Error	126230	512	247		
Total	131314	513			

$* p < .05; ** p < .01; *** p < .001$

Use of an epidural led to a significant increase in overall Context score (Table 5.16). Considering only cases where an epidural was administered, the timing of an epidural had no effect on Context. (Table 5.17).

Table 5.16

Analysis of Variance: Timing of Epidural Administration, if Epidural was Used, and Overall Context Score

Source	Sum of squares	df	Mean square	F	p
Between groups	955	4	239	0.778	0.5405
Error	68750	224	307		
Total	69705	228			

Table 5.17

Analysis of Variance: Use of Pain Medication and Overall Context Score

Source	Sum of squares	df	Mean square	F	p
Between Groups	2990	1	2990	11.931***	.0005979
Error	128324	512	251		
Total	131314	513			

*$p < .05$; ** $p < .01$; *** $p < .001$

Use of pain medication led to a statistically significant increase in Context score. (Table 5.18). Use of anesthesia led to a statistically significant increase in Context score (Table 5.19).

Considering only cases where Pitocin was administered, the timing of Pitocin had no effect on Context

The overall findings of analyses of variance comparing nonscaled survey items contributing to the experience of the Context of Birth indicate that not only Pitocin but also the administration of other medications—but not the timing of the administration—significantly increased Context scores. Because no direct relationship was found between

Table 5.18

Analysis of Variance Use of Anesthesia and Overall Context Score

Source	Sum of squares	df	Mean square	F	p
Between groups	2206	1	2206	8.7474**	.003244
Error	129108	512	252		
Total	131314	513			

*$p < .05$; ** $p < .01$; *** $p < .001$

Table 5.19

Analysis of Variance: Timing of Pitocin Administration, If Used, and Overall Context Score

Source	Sum of squares	df	Mean square	*F*	*p*
Between groups	1287	5	257	0.8613	0.5079
Error	67263	225	299		
Total	68550	230			

Context and psychosocial functioning at age 3, Hypothesis 10 was not supported. However, it appears that Pitocin use has an additional, indirect relationship to psychosocial functioning at age 3, in bearing a significant relationship to increased Context of Birth scores (i.e., mothers experienced the context of their birth as more challenging or negative). In addition, use of other medications during labor also appears to contribute to a statistically significant increase in Context scores.

Child's Sex, Parents' Ages and Education Levels, and Psychosocial Functioning at Age 3

Hypothesis 11 states that there is no significant relationship between any of the demographic data and the total score on Pitocin/no Pitocin and a child's psychosocial functioning at age 3. The data included child's sex (H12); mother's age (H13); father's age (H14); mother's education level (H15); and father's education level (H16). The power analysis predicted that an effect size of .05 could be detected by the following analyses. This hypothesis was tested with the use of subhypotheses representing the sex of the child, mother's age, father's age, mother's education, and father's education.

Because linearly scaled covariates (mother's and father's age) were included with categorical variables (child's sex, mother's/father's level of education, and Pitocin exposure/no exposure), mixed models were used to investigate the interactions between the various factors and their effects on relevant measurements. Model selection using Schwarz-Bayesian Criteria (SBC) (Kutner, Nachtsheim, & Neter, 2004) was employed to investigate any effects of the above parameters on overall psychosocial score.

SBC is a well-established formula (Kutner et al., 2004) for scoring and comparing models by establishing a trade-off between the error of a model and the number of parameters it requires, adjusted for the size and complexity of the data that the model is trying to fit. SBC rewards the model for fitting the data well but penalizes it for having too many parameters; the penalty is adjusted in such a way that it penalizes each parameter less on average for models that have larger data sets. A lower SBC score means that the model (a) fits the data better, (b) uses fewer parameters, or (c) both. Thus, for any two models, the one with the lower SBC score is generally simpler and more powerful; this provides a robust tool for model selection with only a few distributional assumptions. Final models were developed by parameter elimination via formal significance testing (F test) on models returned by the selection algorithm (Faraway, 2005).

The only significant factor developed for score was father's education, which was tested on the basis of a null hypothesis that all levels of father's education had an identical effect on overall score, $F(1, 496)$ = 10.522, p = .01245. In all cases a value of greater than 1 for father's education resulted in a significant reduction of overall score, a clear but inconsistent effect. This finding suggests that fathers with at least a high school education have some influence on the degree to which their children manifest problems in their psychosocial functioning at age 3.

With the exception of father's education, testing of the child's sex, the ages of the parents, and mother's education in relation to the total score on Pitocin/no Pitocin and the child's psychosocial functioning at age 3 supported the null Hypotheses 11 through 16.

Post Hoc Analyses

Having completed the initial analyses testing the hypotheses for this study, it was clear that the total score on the wide variety of psychosocial items in the survey was an inadequate means to demonstrate any significant distinction between psychosocial functioning in 3-year-old children exposed to Pitocin at birth and those not exposed. In addition, none of the dimensions into which these items were grouped in designing the survey, based on functional domains, differentiated to a statistically significant degree between Pitocin use at birth and no Pitocin use, in terms of the child's psychosocial functioning as described by the mothers. At the same time, nine individual psychosocial items differentiated to a statistically significant degree between children exposed to Pitocin and those not exposed. These items, together with the names of the dimensions in which they were included, are shown in Table 5.20.

Table 5.20

Nine Items Significant for Pitocin

Survey item	Dimension	Significance: 2-tailed
Reacts strongly to directions, demands	Interpersonal dynamics: Responses to structure/support	.023
Strong need to be in control	Interpersonal dynamics: control/co-op'n/ leadership	.013
Dominates other children	Interpersonal dynamics: control/co-op'n/ leadership	.016
Communicates "yes" and "no" when needs to	Interpersonal dynamics: Boundaries	.020
Mother feels she can never satisfy her child	Interpersonal dynamics: Mother's experience of relationship	.048
Mother sees relationship as easy and cooperative	Interpersonal dynamics: Mother's experience of relationship	.005
Rushes from one thing to next and rarely slows down	Sequencing: beginnings	.011
Has/has had a pattern of self-harming behaviors	ANS regulation: Activity level	.053
As an infant, had ear infections	ANS regulation: Physiological	.038

Note. Pitocin mothers: n = 231; no Pitocin mothers: n = 267

The full list of survey items with *t* test results are as follows:

1. Reacts strongly to being given directions or having demands made upon them (P: M = 3.1082, SD = 1.4719; NP: M = 2.8165, SD = 1.3655).

2. Has a strong need to control (P: M = 4.1991, SD = 1.6350; NP: M = 3.8427, SD = 1.5577).

3. Dominates other children (P: M = 3.1169, SD = 1.5405; NP: M = 2.7865, SD = 1.5054).

4. Is good at communicating yes and no when needs to (P: M = 1.5714, SD = .8958; NP: M = 1.7753, SD = 1.0594).

5.   Mother feels she can never satisfy this child (P: M = 2.2857, SD = 1.4282; NP: M = 2.0524, SD = 1.1622).

6.   Mother describes her relationship with the child as easy and cooperative (P: M = 2.7143, SD = 1.3007; NP: M = 2.4157, SD = 1.0421).

7.   Child tends to rush from one thing to the next and rarely slows down (P: M = 3.2294, SD = 1.6190; NP: M = 2.8764, SD = 1.4625).

8.   Has or has had a pattern of self-harming behaviors (P: M = 1.3550, SD = .8966; NP: M = 1.2135, SD = .7013), t(433.031) = 1.940, p = .053 (this item came close to significance).

9.   Of the five items describing the child as an infant, the item in which the child was described as having had ear infections was significant for Pitocin (P: M = 1.9654, SD = 1.6833; NP: M = 1.6742, SD = 1.4071).

As can be seen in Table 5.20, six of the items were grouped in the dimension involving interpersonal dynamics, whereas two pertained to autonomic nervous system regulation and one to the child's capacity to negotiate through sequences.

This finding of a grouping of statistically significant items in similar dimensions suggested the possibility that the survey's psychosocial items might reveal other significant relationships if grouped differently; therefore, a principal component analysis was employed to examine, through the use of a different type of analysis, whether different groups might exist within the data and with significance.

Principle Component Analysis

Dean, Gray, and Anderson (1996) noted that among a number of studies conducted in the 1970s and 1980s, some reported a relationship between perinatal factors and cognitive outcomes, or between perinatal events (e.g., pregnancy factors, gestational age, birth weight, or obstetrical complications) and children's behavioral and educational performance, whereas other studies failed to find such a relationship. The authors noted that perinatal events have a multivariate nature, yet the studies typically used a univariate design. Their remedy was to employ a principal component analysis (PCA) to examine the underlying factor structure of perinatal events for children in their study.

In the case of the present research, a group of 6 expert clinicians described a broad range of aspects of psychosocial functioning they believed to be associated with a specific perinatal event, yet a single, total score was initially used to test the hypotheses, together with a group of dimensions to which survey items were assigned on the basis of relatively standard categories of psychosocial functioning. Because neither total score nor the separate dimensions were able to distinguish the functioning of children born with Pitocin from that of those born without Pitocin, two conclusions were possible: (a) that the expert clinicians are wrong about the relationship with psychosocial functioning at age 3 or (b) that the way the survey responses were tested, as a single score, and the dimensions to which items were assigned by the researcher might not be the most effective means to discern any statistically significant relationships that might exist in the data.

Principal component analysis is a technique for data reduction, explaining the variance-covariance structure of a set of variables in terms of a smaller number of linear combinations of those variables. In addition, PCA often allows (due to its close relationship with factor analysis) the identification of linear relationships that were not previously suspected, potentially identifying additional avenues for investigation or providing additional explanatory power to an analysis (Johnson & Wichern, 2002). PCA is typically used (as it is here) as an intermediate step, preparing data for further analysis.

To identify additional relationships potentially present in the responses from the survey data, a principal component analysis was run on the scale responses from all 53 psychosocial items. Components were recovered via eigenvalue extraction and potential rotations to increase the significance of loadings and were evaluated using both varimax and likelihood criteria (Johnson & Wichern, 2002). Neither method of rotation yielded significant improvements; therefore, no rotations were included in the final PCA. Examination of the component-by-component and cumulative variances indicated a large degree of independence among the various survey items.

A scree plot shows the components sorted by decreasing fraction of the total variance explained, so that Principal Component 1 accounts for the largest fraction of the variance, with each succeeding component accounting for as much of the remaining variability as possible. The scree plot in Figure 5.13, in which eigenvalues are plotted against 19 of the principal components, and visual examination of the cumulative proportion of variance suggested cutoffs at 3, 5, or 12 components. Twelve components accounted for 59.66% of the total data variance (compared with 33.81% for 3 components and 41.64% for 5 components).

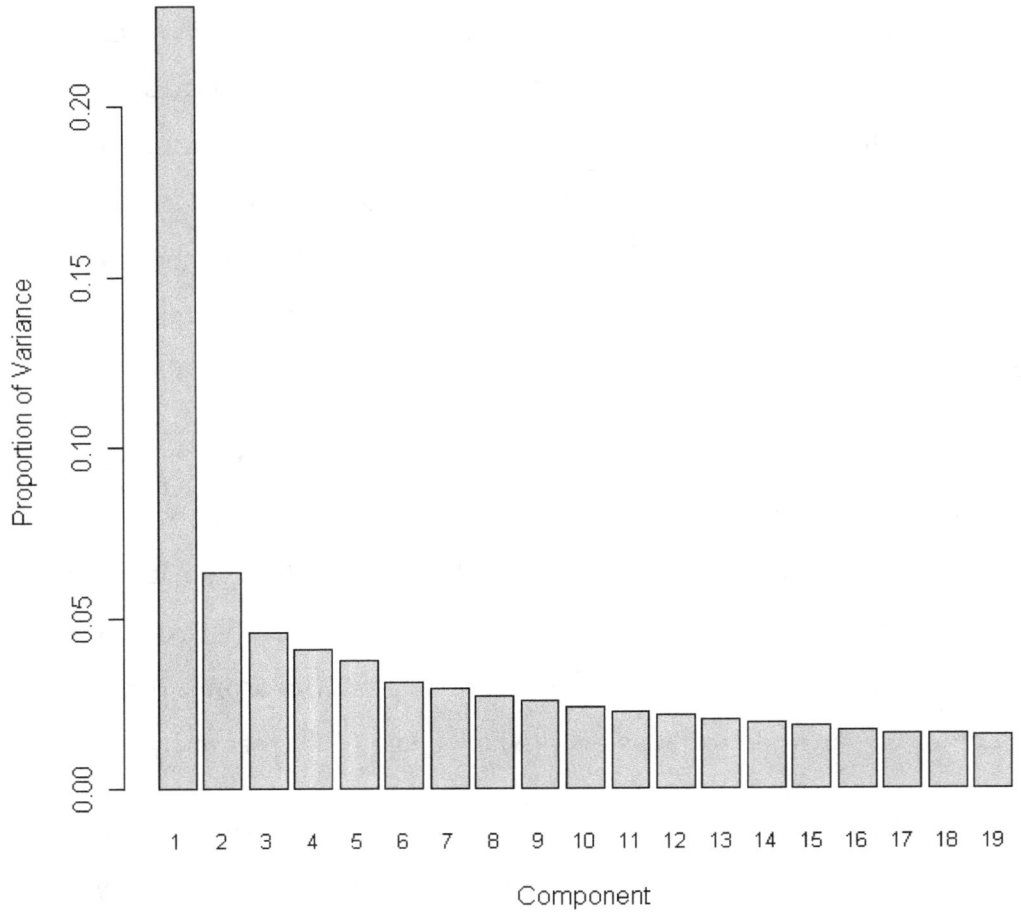

Figure 5.13. Scree plot for principal component analysis.

Furthermore, beyond the 12th component, the proportion of variance explained dropped below 2%, roughly that which would be expected if all survey items were linearly independent (Table 5.21). Accordingly, the first 12 components were selected for further study, with the acknowledgment that 12 components do not completely describe the data but rather simply represent the most significant contributors to the overall variance and identify strong relationships within the data that might potentially be linked to Pitocin use.

Identification of the underlying factors accounting for the components was arrived at in consultation with 4 of the original clinician interviewees participating in the preliminary study (Jennifer Absey, Ray

Castellino, Wendy Anne McCarty, and Jean Weitensteiner), because their clinical expertise qualifies them as subject-matter experts in the psychosocial functioning of young children. With the assistance of these experts, each of whom offered to participate in this phase of the analysis, the items contained in each component and their relationships to each other in the groupings were discussed, and descriptors were identified for each of the underlying factors. In all but the case of Component 1, in which all 20 items were negatively loaded, items in each component formed two groups, one comprising positively loaded items and another comprising negatively loaded items. What was required was to interpret each component, or factor, to identify a psychosocial attribute that might be responsible for increasing the positive scores while decreasing the negative scores in each factor. If no psychosocial attribute could be identified for each factor, there would be no value in testing them for significance for Pitocin, because there would be no way to explain any statistically significant findings.

Table 5.21

PCA Components Showing # of Items, Standard Deviations, Proportions of Variance, and p Values

Component	# of items	SD	Proportion of variance	Cumulative proportion	p value
Comp. 1	20	5.1479671	0.2293934	0.2293934	.1313
Comp. 2	10	2.69833957	0.06302352	0.29241695	.3957
Comp. 3	10	2.29743926	0.04568751	0.33810446	.2289
Comp. 4	3	2.16965847	0.04074668	0.37885114	.3828
Comp. 5	7	2.08291899	0.03755383	0.03087234	.6712
Comp. 6	11	1.88855666	0.03087234	0.44727730	.7442
Comp. 7	5	1.84388084	0.02942898	0.47670628	.4166
Comp. 8	9	1.76335874	0.02691478	0.50362106	.0012**
Comp. 9	13	1.71644289	0.02550164	0.52912270	.3557
Comp. 10	11	1.65764673	0.02378447	0.55290717	.3908
Comp. 11	12	1.60396470	0.02226892	0.57517608	.1425
Comp. 12	15	1.57266200	0.02140820	0.59658429	.02789*
Comp. 13	7	1.52353925	0.02009170	0.61667599	-
Comp. 14	14	1.48450591	0.01907539	0.63575137	-
Comp. 15	15	1.44366382	0.01804021	0.65379158	-
Comp. 16	8	1.39115968	0.01675187	0.67054346	-
Comp. 17	14	1.35958754	0.01600014	0.68654360	-

Component	# of items	SD	Proportion of variance	Cumulative proportion	p value
Comp. 18	12	1.35337440	0.01585424	0.70239784	-
Comp. 19	17	1.33208716	0.01535942	0.71775725	-

$* p < .05; ** p < .01; *** p < .001$

PCA Factors Found to Be Significant for Pitocin

One-way between-groups analyses of variance performed on the 12 components of the PCA (Table 5.21) resulted in two components being found to bear statistically significant relationships to Pitocin use at birth: Component 8, for which the underlying factor was interpreted as Assertiveness, and Component 12, for which the underlying factor was interpreted as Need to Control Environment (Table 5.22). It should be noted that although Component 1 accounted for the largest fraction of the variance, it failed to discriminate to a statistically significant degree between Pitocin use and no Pitocin use.

Table 5.22

Analysis of Variance: Pitocin/No Pitocin and Components 8 and 12 of Principal Component Analysis

Component		Sum of squares	df	Mean square	F	p
Factor 8: Assertiveness	Between groups	32.53	1	32.53	10.544***	.001245
	Error	1530.41	496	3.09		
	Total	1562.94	497			
Factor 12: Need to control environment	Between groups	12.03	1	12.03	4.8633*	.02789
	Error	1226.71	496	2.47		
	Total	1250.77	497			

$* p < .05; ** p < .01; *** p < .001$

Table 5.23 shows the abbreviated descriptors of individual survey items grouped into each factor, with positively loaded items grouped first and negatively loaded items grouped below them. The loadings are small because there were a total of 53 items and 53 components in the principal component analysis, resulting in smaller values than would be expected with a smaller number of components. To clarify how the factors were interpreted and the subsequent discussion of the results, the dimension into which that item was originally grouped is provided beside each item.

In Welch's two-sample t test, the means for Factor 8 were 1.346381 for the group that received Pitocin (n = 231), and 1.858906 for the group that did not (n = 267), $t(464.977)$ = 3.2204, p = .00137, meaning a lower average score for the Pitocin group than for the non-Pitocin group, implying that Pitocin resulted in the children being less assertive than children who did not receive Pitocin.

Table 5.23

PCA Components Significant for Pitocin: Factors and Loadings

Item #	Factor	Dimension in which item was grouped	Factor Loading
	Factor 8: attribute Assertiveness		
Q46	Sensitive to intrusion	Interpersonal dynamics: boundaries	0.2
Q56	Reacts strongly when things change quickly	Mother-child attunement: transitions	0.19
Q57	Copes with transitions better when involved	Mother-child attunement: transitions	0.25
Q25	Responds well to self-pace	ANS regulation: Timing/pacing/tempo	0.23
Q29	Digestive problems	ANS regulation: Physiological	-0.16
Q30	Picky eater	ANS regulation: Physiological	-0.55
Q31	Problems with sleeping	ANS regulation: Physiological	-0.18
Q27	Baby ear infections	ANS regulation: Physiological	-0.42
Q28	Baby colicky, fussy, hard to soothe	ANS regulation: Physiological	-0.25
	Factor 12: attribute: Need to Control Environment		
Q5	Craves firm pressure	Sensory processing: Tactile/proprioceptive	0.32
Q59	Procrastinates on starting things	Sequencing	0.3
Q62	Loses focus in the middle	Sequencing	0.15
Q25	Responds well to self-pace	ANS regulation: Timing/pacing/tempo	0.16
Q28	Baby colicky, fussy, hard to soothe	ANS Regulation: Physiological	0.23
Q57	Copes with transitions better when involved	Mother-child attunement: transitions	0.26
Q34	Resists receiving help from others	Interpersonal dynamics: Responses to structure/support	0.15
Q35	Strongly resists pressure; being hurried	interpersonal dynamics:	0.18

Item #	Factor	Dimension in which item was grouped	Factor Loading
Q41	Strong need to be in control	Responses to structure/support Interpersonal dynamics: Control/cooperation/leadership	0.33
Q20	Aggressive	ANS Regulation: Activity Level	-0.19
Q29	Digestive problems	ANS Regulation: Physiological	-0.25
Q3	Baby hypersensitive to movement/position	Sensory processing: Vestibular	-0.23
Q61	Reacts strongly when things change quickly	Mother-child attunement: Transitions	-0.18
Q33	Difficulty with others' timing/transitions	Interpersonal dynamics: Responses to structure/support	-0.18
Q39	Gets upset when things don't go their way	Interpersonal dynamics: Control/cooperation/leadership	-0.16

The mean for the Pitocin group (n = 231) in Factor 12 was 2.481183, $t(464.513)$ = 2.1868, p = .02926, and the mean for the non-Pitocin group (n = 267) was 2.169549, resulting in a higher average score for the former group. In this case, Pitocin appears to result in functioning that implies a greater need to control the environment. Together, the findings of the principal component analysis support the main hypothesis (Hypothesis 1) that there is a relationship between the use of Pitocin at birth and certain aspects of psychosocial functioning of children at age 3, as represented in Factor 8 and Factor 12.

Because the principal component analysis resulted in a finding of two significant factors for Pitocin, the remaining hypotheses originally tested using the total score on psychosocial items were retested using Factors 8 and 12.

For Hypothesis 10 (There is a significant relationship between the context of a child's birth and the child's psychosocial functioning at age 3), as with the testing of total psychosocial score with Context items, a mixed effects model was used to investigate (a) the score obtained via Factor 8 of the PCA (Assertiveness) and (b) the score obtained via Factor 12 of the PCA (Need to Control Environment).

Context and Factor 8 (Assertiveness) scores. Results for the regression of Factor 8 (Assertiveness) on Context and Pitocin are presented in Table 5.24. Analysis of Component 8 indicates that the effect of Context on Assertiveness is likely negligible for non-Pitocin children. However, introduction of Pitocin appears to reduce Assertiveness scores while simultaneously introducing a positive linear relationship between

Table 5.24

Summary of Mixed Model Regression Analysis Regressing Factor 8 (Assertiveness) Scores on Context and Pitocin

Factor 8: Assertiveness

Predictors	B	SE B	R^2
Constant	2.28***	0.29	.03%
Pitocin	-1.34**	0.41	
Context	-.01	.01	
Pitocin x Context	.02*	0.10	

*$p < .05$; ** $p < .01$; *** $p < .001$

Assertiveness scores and Context. This means that as Context scores increase, Assertiveness scores also increase.

Context and Factor 12 (Need to Control Environment) scores. Results for the regression of Factor 12 (Need to Control Environment) on Context and Pitocin are presented in Table 5.25. Analysis of Factor 12 indicates that Context, whether in the absence or presence of Pitocin, plays no significant role in scoring for that component. This indicates that there is no relationship between Need to Control Environment and Context for this group in either the presence or the absence of Pitocin.

Pitocin Use at Birth and Method of Feeding in First 6 Months

Finally, examination of the responses to the survey question about how the survey participants fed their infants in the first 6 months after birth revealed some apparently large discrepancies in numbers between the children who did and those who did not receive Pitocin at birth, with regard to those fed exclusively at the breast compared with those who were fed by combined methods. This survey item was included because the intervention under study, Pitocin use at birth, is believed to interfere with the normal oxytocin systems operating within and between mother and baby at and immediately following birth and is both a significant facilitator and an outcome of the breast-feeding relationship. Several previous studies (Crost & Kaminski, 1998; Out et al., 1985; Palmer, Avery, & Taylor, 1979; Zuppa,

Vignetti, Romagnoli, & Tortorolo, 1984) found similar statistically significant differences in breast-feeding rates between mothers who had induced labors and those who did not. Given the size of the discrepancy found in this study, it seemed valuable to subject the data to analysis for statistical significance.

Table 5.25

Summary of Mixed Model Regression Analysis Regressing Factor 12 (Need to Control Environment) Scores on Context and Pitocin

Component 12: Need to Control Environment

Predictors	B	$SE\ B$	R^2
Constant	2.23***	0.26	.01%
Pitocin	.04	0.37	
Context	-.00	.01	
Pitocin x Context	.01	.01	

* $p < .05$; ** $p < .01$; *** $p < .001$

An initial cross-tabulation was performed on how the method of feeding in the first 6 months related to Pitocin or no Pitocin use at birth (Table 5.26). Within the combined-feeding-method group no distinctions were made regarding proportions of breast- or bottle-feeding.

Table 5.26

Cross-tabulation: Method of Feeding in First 6 Months by Pitocin/No Pitocin at Birth

	Baby Fed Entirely at Breast	Baby Fed with Combination of Breast and Bottle	Baby Fed Entirely by Bottle	Other (text responses)	Total
Pitocin	96	129	6	0	231
No Pitocin	231	0	16	20	267
Total	327	129	22	20	498

To prepare the data for testing, text responses by women who checked the "Other" box for method of feeding were excluded, because they constituted exceptions to the designated groups that respondents selected by checking the appropriate box. Because the question of interest is whether Pitocin, as a manifestation of a hormonal relationship between mother and infant, may interfere with breast-feeding, the cells containing the numbers of exclusively bottle-feeding mothers and those containing numbers of combination-feeding mothers were combined to form a two-by-two table (Table 5.27).

A null hypothesis would state that there is no relationship between Pitocin use at birth and method of feeding in the first 6 months, and therefore, given that the total numbers in the Pitocin and no Pitocin groups are close to equal, an equal distribution of infants fed exclusively at the breast and combination-fed infants would be expected if there was no relationship between Pitocin use and feeding method.

Fisher's exact test (Casella & Berger, 2002; Fisher, 1922) was selected as a procedure that can be used for data in a two-by-two contingency table. It is an alternative to the chi-square test that can be used when the numbers in the table's cells are highly imbalanced, as is true in this case. It is based on exact probabilities from a specific distribution, whereas the chi-square test relies on a large-sample approximation. Fisher's exact test was used to test the bivariate relationships between feeding methods (exclusively at the breast or combination feeding) and exposure/nonexposure to Pitocin at birth.

Table 5.27

Comparison between Exclusive Breastfeeding and Other Forms of Feeding with Pitocin and No Pitocin at Birth

	Baby Fed Entirely at Breast	Combination Breast/Bottle-feeding Plus Exclusive Bottle-feeding	Totals
Pitocin	96	135	231
No Pitocin	231	16	247
Total	327	151	478

The result of this analysis indicates that infants exposed to Pitocin at birth were significantly less likely to be exclusively fed at the breast during the first 6 months than were those infants not exposed to Pitocin (95% C.I., Fisher's $p < .000$). Further discussion of this finding appears in chapter 6.

Chapter 6. Discussion

This study employed a pilot survey instrument to explore mothers' recollections of giving birth and their perceptions of their children, in order to investigate the possibility that Pitocin use at birth to induce or augment labor might bear a relationship to the psychosocial functioning of children born with its use. The age range between 3 and 4 years old was selected as the period to be studied.

To examine this question, a group of 6 prenatal and perinatal clinicians experienced in working with infants and children was interviewed in a preliminary study to gather their perceptions about how Pitocin use at birth might influence children in an enduring way through the age of 3. The descriptions of these clinicians were subjected to content analysis and ultimately served in the construction of the survey. To pilot the instrument, the survey was posted at an online survey hosting Web site and made available to mothers of 3-year-old children who met the research criteria. Hypotheses were tested through analysis of the data from the resulting 514 completed surveys. This discussion brings to bear not only the empirical data available, to evaluate the findings of the study, but also the clinical and theoretical support provided by the field of prenatal and perinatal psychology, as a means of understanding these findings.

Overview and Discussion of Results

The main hypothesis (Hypothesis 1) proposed that there is a relationship between the use of Pitocin at birth and the psychosocial functioning of children at age 3. The results of the initial statistical analysis failed to support the main hypothesis, in that the total score for psychosocial items on the survey did not show a significant relationship to Pitocin use, based on mothers' perceptions.

The subhypotheses, Hypotheses 2 through 8, each examined the possibility of a relationship between seven dimensions of psychosocial functioning into which survey items were grouped: sensory processing (Hypothesis 2), coordination/motor skills (Hypothesis 3), affect/mood regulation (Hypothesis 4), self-esteem (Hypothesis 5), autonomic nervous system regulation (Hypothesis 6), functioning in interpersonal situations (Hypothesis 7), and mother-child attunement (Hypothesis 8).

These hypotheses were tested with analyses of variance for total scores in each dimension and none of them was found to be significant for Pitocin use. However, a group of 9 of the 53 psychosocial items was found to distinguish, to a statistically significant level, mean scores for children born with Pitocin use from those born without its use at birth, as perceived by their mothers in their survey responses. Table 6.1 provides a list of these items, together with the dimensions into which they were originally grouped, with the significance levels for each item from the original *t* test.

These results suggest that if birth events may leave enduring imprints, as previous studies (Csaba, 2008; Csaba et al., 2004; Jacobson & Bygdeman, 1998; Jacobson et al., 1987; Jacobson et al., 1988; Jacobson et al., 1990) have proposed, such imprints, in the form of the psychosocial functioning reflected by the survey items, were not sufficiently reported in respondents' descriptions of their 3-year-olds to demonstrate significance either on overall psychosocial score or the scores for each dimension. Nevertheless, that these nine items were significant for Pitocin suggests that the psychosocial functioning of the 3-year-olds described in the survey who were born with Pitocin's use differs to some degree from that of the children born without Pitocin and that, together, the items describe functional challenges involving interpersonal dynamics, timing/pacing, and autonomic nervous system regulation, along the lines described by the clinicians in the original interview study.

Table 6.1

Survey Items Significant for Pitocin, with Original Dimensions

Survey item	Dimension	Significance: 2-tailed
Reacts strongly to directions demands	Interpersonal dynamics: Responses to structure/support	.023*
Strong need to be in control	Interpersonal dynamics: Control/ cooperation/ leadership	.013*
Dominates other children	Interpersonal dynamics: Control/ cooperation/ leadership	.016*
Mother feels she can never satisfy her child	Interpersonal dynamics: Mother's experience of relationship	.048*
Mother sees relationship as easy and cooperative	Interpersonal dynamics: Mother's experience of relationship	.005**[a]
Communicates "yes" and "no" when needs to	Interpersonal dynamics: Boundaries	.020*
Rushes from one thing to next and rarely slows down	Sequencing: Beginnings	.011*

Survey item	Dimension	Significance: 2-tailed
As an infant, had ear infections	ANS regulation: Physiological	.038*
Has/has had a pattern of self-harming behaviors	ANS regulation: Activity Level	.053[b]

Note. Pitocin group: $n = 231$; no Pitocin group: $n = 267$

[a] This item was reverse-scored, so mothers of Pitocin-born children reported their relationships to be *less* easy and cooperative to a statistically significant degree than mothers describing relationships with their children born without Pitocin. [b] This item tested significant in the *t* test for equal variances ($p = 0.049$) and so could arguably be considered very close to significant.

* $p < .05$; ** $p < .01$; *** $p < .001$

Similarly, Eishima's (1992) research, using Prechtl's (1977) neonatal neurological examination and the Neonatal Behavioral Assessment Scale (Brazelton, 1984) on the fifth day after birth, found a cluster of behaviors in infants that correlated significantly with labor induction with oxytocin: inferior hand-to-mouth activity, suppressed alertness, weaker animate visual orientation, and increased resistance to cuddle. Although no specific item of the nine found significant for Pitocin in this study exactly parallels those found by Eishima (1992) to be significant for labor induction with oxytocin, Eishima's perception that "even a small difference in low-risk obstetric conditions is related to differences in neonatal neurological status and neonatal behavior" (p. 262) appears to be supported in general terms 3 to 4 years after birth, judging by the type of psychosocial functioning challenges described in the present study. This seems to reflect a degree of failure of a sort in the process described by Schore (2005) and referred to in chapter 3 as the development of "psychobiological attunement and the interactive mutual entrainment of physiologic rhythms [that] are fundamental processes that mediate attachment. Thus, throughout the life span, attachment is a primary mechanism for the regulation of biologic synchronicity within and between organisms" (p. 207). It also pertains to the observations of the 6 clinicians interviewed that Pitocin use appears to disrupt the entrainment of physiologic rhythms and hence both autonomic nervous system regulation and interpersonal attunement.

Principal Component Analysis

A principal component analysis was utilized to determine how the 53 psychosocial survey items might load on dimensions other than those to which they had originally been assigned, and whether the factors thus formed might discriminate more successfully between children born with and those born without Pitocin use at birth. A total of 12 factors, accounting for 59.66% of the total data variance, were considered worthy of further examination. Analyses of variance revealed two factors (Factor 8 and Factor 12) significant for Pitocin use. These factors were interpreted as Assertiveness (Factor 8) and Need to Control Environment (Factor 12). The findings of this secondary analysis appear to support the main hypothesis (Hypothesis 1) of a relationship between Pitocin use at birth and psychosocial functioning at age 3.

What these findings appear to suggest is that Pitocin use at birth may have some degree of effect on internal regulation systems and that a child's interaction with his or her environment may be in service to managing internal dysregulation or discomfort. The factor named Assertiveness suggests situations in which the child is able to use age-appropriate social skills to engage with others, to communicate needs, and to obtain help in coping with challenges to self-regulation. The interaction between Pitocin and this factor, or psychosocial attribute, of Assertiveness has the effect of reducing its power in comparison with results for the non-Pitocin group.

The items comprising the factor (or psychosocial attribute) named Need to Control Environment seem to portray circumstances in which the child is struggling to attain some control over his or her environment, but without the social niceties displayed in Factor 8. In this case, the child seems to be taking a "my way or the highway" stance and is experiencing significant internal dysregulation, which seems to drive the child's efforts to gain external control; the child is attempting to gain control because of feeling out of control. Here it seems that the interaction with Pitocin increases the strength of the factor—that is, the need to control the environment and its attendant behaviors—in the Pitocin group more than in the non-Pitocin group.

With both factors, it seems that the child experiences difficulties in relation to their internal and external worlds (negative scores) and responds to these difficulties behaviorally—in Factor 8 by engaging with others to communicate problems and needs, and in Factor 12, apparently, by attempting to gain or regain control of what they feel they can control in the face of what they feel they cannot. What both factors appear to have in common is the child's experience of being challenged predominantly by "outside-in" experiences: problems with digesting food, intrusions on boundaries, being pressured, transitions, rapid changes, being physically moved (as an infant), starting and persisting in activities or sequences, other people's timing and pacing, and even receiving help from others. Because endogenous oxytocin is known to play a significant role in digestion and the absorption of nutrients via activation of the vagus nerve (Uvnäs-Moberg, 2003), this finding lends credence to the possibility that Pitocin use at birth may have enduring effects on the oxytocin system.

Furthermore, as noted, Csaba (2008) asserted that "Perinatally, the first encounter between the maturing receptor and its target hormone results in hormonal imprinting, which adjusts the binding capacity of the receptor for life" (p. 9) and that "excess of the target hormones or presence of foreign molecules which are able to bind to the receptors, provoke faulty imprinting in the critical periods with life-long morphological, biochemical, functional or behavioural consequence" (p. 7). As Buckley (2007) pointed out, the number of oxytocin receptors in the uterus increases dramatically toward the point of initiation of spontaneous labor, and because mothers who receive Pitocin for inducing labor are not yet in labor, one must assume that to varying degrees they do not yet have their full complement of oxytocin receptors. As typically administered, Pitocin use is quite likely to constitute an "excess of the target hormones" for the available number of receptors.

The effect of exogenous oxytocin on the offspring has been little studied, and less appears to be known about oxytocin receptors in human infants during and following birth than in their mothers. However, in light of the type of survey items composing Factors 8 and 12, a variety of autonomic nervous system regulation items (including several involving digestion), and other items related to mother-child attunement and interpersonal dynamics, the PCA findings suggest the possibility that the binding of exogenous oxytocin (Pitocin) to oxytocin receptors during labor and birth may, indeed, result in faulty imprinting, affecting aspects of autonomic nervous system regulation and interpersonal dynamics. In addition, because both mother and baby are subjected to Pitocin during labor and birth, and because both experience this same postulated faulty imprinting in the oxytocin system, one might speculate that both may contribute to a relative lack of attunement within their relationship, reflected in the significant difference in scores between Pitocin-exposed and -nonexposed dyads on Factor 8 and Factor 12, as reported by the mothers.

Some similarity exists between the descriptions of behaviors apparently intended as means to cope with internal dysregulation and Emerson's (1998) portrayal of a therapy client whose birth had been induced with Pitocin who felt "overly energized and propelled, in a very frightening way, by the Pitocin"

(p. 18). The clinicians interviewed in the preliminary study described the infusion of Pitocin as confusing to the baby because it is externally administered (i.e., intravenously to the mother) but is experienced internally as it travels via the umbilical cord into the circulating blood of the baby, while also influencing the duration and intensity of uterine contractions moving the baby through the birth canal.

It is speculated that the behaviors described in Factor 8 and Factor 12 are symptomatic of similar confusion regarding "outside-in" experiences, such as the ingestion of food or being subjected to other people's timing and needs, and that normal interpersonal interactions may thus be colored by the overall imprint effect of the experience of Pitocin at birth. This interpretation is also supported by the theorizing of the 6 prenatal/perinatal clinicians that the dual exposure of mother and child to Pitocin during the birth process disrupts the attunement between them, which in turn affects the child's capacity to function effectively in interpersonal relationships.

It is worth noting that, of the 53 psychosocial items on the survey, 5 items described the child as an infant:

1. As an infant, my child had ear infections.

2. As an infant, my child was extremely sensitive to movement or position changes (e.g., if she/he fell asleep in my arms she/he would become upset and cry when moved or put down, rather than sleeping through such changes).

3. As an infant, my child protested strongly (screamed, cried, or stiffened) when thrown or lifted up in the air, or when being tipped or held at certain angles or positions.

4. As an infant, my child had extreme emotional responses (cried, screamed, struggled, or "shut down") to transitions (e.g., sudden shifts in position, attention, or activity; diaper changes; baths; or new places/people).

5. As an infant, my child was "colicky" or fussy and hard to soothe.

These five items appeared, in groups of two or more, in the majority of PCA factors studied (13 out of a total of 19 initially reviewed, and 7 out of the 12 examined more closely), including the two found to be significant for Pitocin, suggesting that there is some continuity in disturbance of functioning, and its nature, between infancy and age 3. Csaba's (2008) assertion concerning faulty hormonal imprinting provides a reasonable, if at this point purely speculative, explanation for this continuity.

The strongest theoretical support for the finding of significance of Pitocin for these two factors and the prevalence of the relatively small number of infant items among the factors was not identified prior to the execution of the study but rather emerged in the process of interpreting the meaning of the two factors.

Polyvagal Theory

The polyvagal theory of Stephen Porges (1995) offers a way of interpreting the meanings of Factor 8 (Assertiveness) and Factor 12 (Need to Control Environment) from the principal component analysis. This theory proposes that "physiological state limits the range of behavior and psychological experience" and that "the evolution of the mammalian autonomic nervous system provides the neurophysiological substrates for the emotional experiences and affective processes that are major components of social behavior" (p. 35).

The autonomic nervous system is the neuron-endocrine-immune structure that enables survival (Chitty, 2001). Traditionally, it was considered to have two branches: the parasympathetic, responsible for rest and rebuilding, and the sympathetic, responsible for the mobilization into fight or flight. Porges' (1995) polyvagal theory proposes that the autonomic nervous system has not two branches but three and is based in three phylogenetic stages of the development of the mammalian autonomic nervous system. Each state is associated with a distinct autonomic subsystem that is retained in mammals. These autonomic subsystems are phylogenetically ordered and behaviorally linked to social communication (e.g., facial expression, vocalization, listening), mobilization (e.g., fight-flight behaviors) and immobilization (e.g., feigning death, vaso-vagal syncope, and behavioral shutdown). The social communication system (i.e., Social Engagement System . . .) is dependent upon the myelinated vagus, which serves to foster calm behavioral states by inhibiting the sympathetic influences to the heart and dampening the HPA [hypothalamic-pituitary-adrenal] axis. The mobilization system is dependent on the functioning of the sympathetic nervous system. The most phylogenetically primitive component, the immobilization system, is dependent on the unmyelinated or "vegetative" vagus, which is shared with most vertebrates. With increased neural complexity due to phylogenetic development, the organism's behavioral and affective repertoire is enriched. The theory emphasizes the functional aspect of neural control of both the striated muscles of the face and the smooth muscles of the viscera, since their functions rely on common brainstem structures. (p. 36)

For a visual representation of this construct, see Appendix J. The theory outlines a neurobiological model of how social behavior is linked to regulation of both visceral state and facial expressivity, and how social behavior can function as a regulator of physiological activity. This is how the healthy infant, who has limited mobility, is capable from birth of eliciting bonding responses from the primary caregiver, activating the biochemical interactions involving oxytocin and prolactin that ensure nourishment, bonding, and attachment.

Porges (2001) used Jackson's (1958) theory of dissolution to demonstrate that, when stressed, humans first attempt to utilize the phylogenetically newest of the three systems—social engagement, or the social nervous system—to elicit the needed response to alleviate the stress. If this fails, the system defaults to the fight/flight, or sympathetic, system; and finally, if fighting or fleeing are unsuccessful or not available options, to the immobilization or "freeze" response. (It should be pointed out that these defaults become increasingly costly, healthwise, if they are repeatedly employed over the life span because the individual has become accustomed to a perception of his or her environment as unsafe.) Porges (2004) coined the term *neuroception* to describe "how neural circuits distinguish whether situations or people are safe, dangerous, or life threatening . . . without our conscious awareness" (p. 19).

The polyvagal theory can be applied to the psychosocial attributes identified in Factor 8 (Assertiveness) and Factor 12 (Need to Control Environment) by scrutinizing the items clustered in these factors. In Factor 8, the child is experiencing some degree of discomfort or distress and appears to be employing social engagement, or the social nervous system, to communicate distress and the need for help. In Factor 12, the cluster of items portrays a situation in which the child is again experiencing discomfort or distress but either has failed to achieve help that alleviates these or does not expect to receive such help and so defaults to mobilization utilizing the sympathetic branch of the autonomic nervous system.

In the case of Factor 8, Pitocin reduced scores, suggesting that the child was less effective in employing social engagement as a first strategy. In the case of Factor 12, Pitocin increased scores, implying that fight/flight strategies were exaggerated in comparison to those of children who were not exposed to Pitocin. Carter et al. (2007) note that "oxytocin . . . sits at the center of a neuroendocrine network that coordinates social behaviors and concurrent responses to various stressors, generally acting to reduce reactivity to stressors" (p. 11), suggesting that Pitocin may disrupt the role of endogenous oxytocin in these children's responses to stressors.

The clinicians in the original interview study suggested that because Pitocin is administered, in essence, to both mother and baby, it may have the effect of causing both parties to become disconnected from their endogenous rhythms and their rhythmic interaction during the process of labor, and this lack or loss of attunement, or disharmonious imprint, may continue into their later relationship without the awareness of either party. Given Jacobson et al.'s (1987) argument that, as in many other species, humans are more likely than not to have a sensitive period immediately after birth in which a mechanism such as imprinting might operate to enhance survival, Csaba's (2008) hormonal imprinting theory provides a possible description of such a mechanism and lends empirical support to the clinicians' observations.

These mechanisms might be particularly applicable if the Pitocin use took place at the birth of a first child, because the mother would have no prior maternal experience of mother-child relating with which to compare her experience of the relationship with her 3-year-old. This relative lack of attunement, very likely mediated by the postulated faulty oxytocin system, holds the possibility of resulting in the child having an ongoing experience, or neuroception, of feeling unsafe, especially if, as the clinicians suggested, the Pitocin experience forms an imprint involving "outside-in" intrusion. If the mother is not attuned to the child (whether on an ongoing basis or on a particular occasion), social engagement strategies are less likely to be effective and the child's system would then default to the fight/flight response. Polyvagal theory will be addressed further during discussion of implications for theory and future research.

The prevalence of infant items in the two significant PCA factors and elsewhere in the PCA may then be explained by a history of dysregulation from infancy that continues into the present, resulting in social engagement strategies and then defaulting to sympathetic activation, in attempts to alleviate discomfort and obtain help with internal regulation. Here, Schore's (2005) description of mutual regulation between mother and child pertains, because the absence of such attunement might be expected in the Pitocin-exposed mother-child dyads, resulting in the type of internal dysregulation (problems with eating, sleeping, movement, and intrusion) described in the infant items. Given that oxytocin plays a role in activating the vagal nerve, which in turn increases the activity of the gut hormones that facilitate digestion, it is interesting that the symptoms of internal dysregulation in Factor 8 and Factor 12 include problems with digestion both in infancy and at age 3, lending additional credence to the theory of hormonal imprinting affecting oxytocin systems (Csaba, 2008).

Hypothesis 9 proposed that there was no relationship between the timing of Pitocin administration and children's psychosocial functioning in sequencing activities at age 3. This hypothesis was supported by the data, contradicting the perceptions of the expert clinicians. It is possible that mothers, lacking the specific prenatal/perinatal perspective and experience guiding the clinicians in their observations of children's functioning, might not perceive what may be subtle signs of a challenge in a sequencing activity. It is also possible that the small number of items in this survey dimension were inadequate to discern to a statistically significant degree challenges in sequencing activities among Pitocin-exposed and -nonexposed children.

Two items from the sequencing dimension on the survey appeared in PCA Factor 12, and a number of items concerning difficulties with transitions (assigned to the dimension of mother-child attunement) and timing/pacing/tempo appeared in both Factor 8 and Factor 12, suggesting that problems with transitions, problems with timing/pacing/tempo, and problems with sequencing might have some degree of overlap. Indeed, these items are found clustered in three other components of the 12 PCA components that were scrutinized.

Disruptions to "psychobiological attunement and the interactive mutual entrainment of physiologic rhythms" (Schore, 2005, p. 207) and the process of "contingent responsivity" (p. 206) between mother and infant may be what underlies responses to these survey items, which represent an appreciable proportion of the two significant factors in the PCA.

Hypothesis 10 was based on the clinicians' emphasis that an obstetrical intervention such as Pitocin use could not possibly be investigated in isolation from the context in which it was administered. Such context includes the mother's experience of her pregnancy and the degree of support she felt from others, how much control she felt she had over decisions made about her labor and any complications or interventions made, the course of the labor itself and her capacity to cope, and the personalities and attitudes of all those present during labor and the birth of her baby. The hypothesis assumed a significant relationship between the overall context of the child's birth, from the perspective of the mother, and the child's psychosocial functioning at age 3.

In the first stage of analysis, a *t* test found statistically significant differences in the means on 8 of 12 scaled survey items relating to the birth itself, depending upon whether Pitocin was used. This finding indicated that mothers' experiences of the birth of their now 3-year-olds was less positive and more challenging with Pitocin use. The following are the items that were statistically significant for Pitocin (with an additional item that was close to significance), as reported by the 231 mothers whose labors involved use of Pitocin:

1. Ease of birth.

2. Reflections on the birth positive/negative.

3. Aspects of the birth still troubling or unresolved for mother.

4. Birth team that worked well together with mother.

5. Others took over control of the birth, leaving mother feeling powerless and out of control.

6. During labor and delivery mother felt overwhelmed, out of control, scared. (This item was close to significance, at $p = .055$.)

7. Mother's experience of labor was that it was excruciating, unbearable, far beyond her coping ability.

8. Mother reflects that, given her own experience, she now wonders if during labor her baby may have felt disconnected from her, overwhelmed, unable to cope, in pain, frightened, traumatized.

9. Baby was with mother for most or all of first hour after birth.

With reference to this last item, Cartwright (1977) compared induced and spontaneous labors in 2,182 live births and determined that there was no difference in the number of mothers who held their babies immediately after their birth. In contrast, the present study found a statistically significant difference between Pitocin and non-Pitocin births in responses to the survey item asking how much of the first hour postpartum babies spent with their mothers. Although this item did not specify holding the baby as opposed to the baby being "with the mother," Pitocin nevertheless appeared to differentiate the two populations on this item. However, the reasons for the difference cannot be assumed without further information, and the relationship cannot be assumed to be causal.

A one-way, between-groups analysis of variance using total score summed across the scaled Context of Birth items was found to be significant for Pitocin (p = .000), suggesting that Pitocin significantly affected in a negative direction the mothers' experience of the birth. A mixed effects model analysis was then employed to explore whether the relationships between the context of birth, as measured by the scaled survey items, and psychosocial functioning at age 3 were significantly different for Pitocin-exposed children and those not exposed to Pitocin at birth, using, in turn, the total score for psychosocial survey items and then the scores for Factor 8 (Assertiveness) and Factor 12 (Need to Control Environment) from the principal component analysis.

Analysis of total score indicated that the linear models for the effect of Context on total score were identical for Pitocin and non-Pitocin children; however, examination of the data (Table 5.14) indicated that overall context and psychosocial score for Pitocin-exposed children tended to be higher, so that any effect of Pitocin on score was probably an effect of the impact of Pitocin on Context. This is consistent with the finding that Pitocin did not result in significantly different total scores on all psychosocial survey items.

The regression analysis of Factor 8 (Assertiveness) on Context and Pitocin found that the effect of the context of birth on total score appeared to be negligible; however, introducing Pitocin appeared to reduce Assertiveness scores while displaying a positive linear relationship between Assertiveness scores and Context: as Context scores increased, so did scores on Assertiveness. What this suggests is that the more negative the birth experience was for the mother, the higher the child's scores on the Assertiveness factor, whereas the use of Pitocin is associated with decreased Assertiveness scores.

Taken together with the understanding of the findings of the principal component analysis of the significance of Factors 8 and 12 for Pitocin use, and because the composition of both factors suggests that they describe psychosocial functioning in the service of alleviating discomfort and internal dysregulation, this finding implies that the need for Assertiveness, or social engagement, as a coping strategy is increased by higher Context scores but that the child's ability to employ this strategy is reduced in relation to Pitocin use, resulting in a default to fight/flight strategies. This, in turn, would suggest that the more challenging the birth experience was perceived to be by the mother, the more likely her child would be to display symptoms of internal dysregulation. Whether this is attributable to a relative lack of mother-child attunement as a result of mother's and child's experiences of birth or is purely due to the child's experience of dysregulation and discomfort is a matter of speculation, and again, causality cannot be inferred.

The results of the regression analysis of Factor 12 (Need to Control Environment) on Context and Pitocin showed no such relationship, and indicated that with or without Pitocin, Context was not significant in the scoring of Factor 12.

Individual analyses of variance were run to examine the relationships between overall Context score and various interventions that were presented in multiple-choice format on the survey. All the interventions presented involved the use of medications other than Pitocin, or the timing of their administration. These analyses found that the use of epidural anesthesia, other anesthesia, and pain medication all appeared to contribute to significant increases in overall Context score; however, the timing of their administration did not show a relationship to Context score.

One must naturally conclude, therefore, that Pitocin was not the only chemical intervention that bore a significant relationship to increased overall Context scores. However, given that 272 participants reported having had an IV transfusing fluids, 247 reported use of pain medication, 108 reported use of anesthesia, and 229 reported use of an epidural (Table 5.6), it is clear that many of the participants received not just one but a combination of medications.

Hypothesis 11 was a summary hypothesis postulating that the demographic information gathered from participants would not bear any statistical relationship to psychosocial functioning at age 3. Hypothesis 12 concerned the sex of the 3-year-old, and Hypotheses 13 through 16 concerned the ages and levels of education attained by each parent. Because the variables included both linear and categorical types, these analyses used mixed models in which all variables were compared with each other and with Pitocin/no Pitocin scores on psychosocial functioning. Only the father's education, in cases when fathers had at least a high school education/GED, was found to have significance. In this case, it was associated with a reduction in overall psychosocial score—the degree to which children manifested difficulties in psychosocial functioning at age 3. All of the null hypotheses 11 through 16 except that concerning the father's education were thus supported by the findings.

The finding of a statistically significant positive influence of father's education on the child's psychosocial functioning is consistent with a substantial body of research, the findings of which include that more-educated fathers are more likely to display interest in their children's education (Flouri & Buchanan, 2003) and to have a positive influence on the language and cognitive development and emotional regulation of young children (Cabrera, Shannon, & Tamis-Lemonda, 2007). Fathers' education is a consistent predictor of the quality of mother-child interactions (Tamis-Lemonda, Shannon, Cabrera, & Lamb, 2004) and is related to externalizing problems in their children (McKee et al., 2007), and fathers' parenting practices play a critical role in child development (McKee et al.; Phares, 1996).

Feldman (2000, as cited in Flouri & Buchanan, 2003) suggested a possible explanation why fathers' (but not mothers') level of education was found to bear a significant relationship to a reduction in the child's psychosocial score: "Whereas the mother-child relationship is biologically based, the father-child attachment may be less evolutionarily programmed and therefore requires a supportive marriage and actual involvement to emerge" (p. 82). Flouri and Buchanan also referenced the work of Hosley and Montemayor (1997), reporting that "many men believe that involvement with children is a voluntary activity" (p. 83), which may serve as an explanation for more-educated fathers making the choice to be involved with their children. It is hoped that future research will attempt to elucidate the interaction among parental characteristics, parenting practices, the status of the marital relationship, and children's psychosocial functioning in the context of the use of artificial oxytocin at birth.

Although the relationship between Pitocin use at birth and subsequent feeding methods was not a direct focus of this research, it is worth noting the finding (Out et al., 1985) that the number of mothers who breast-fed was significantly larger among a group of mothers who experienced spontaneous labor than among an induced-labor group. This finding was replicated in the present study, in the post hoc analysis of the responses to the survey item asking respondents about how they fed their babies during the first 6 months. The result of this analysis indicated that infants exposed to Pitocin at birth were significantly less likely than infants not exposed to Pitocin to be exclusively fed at the breast during the first 6 months. A similar analysis with the axes reversed would have produced the same significant relationship but would suggest that, conversely, infants who were fed exclusively at the breast were significantly less likely to have been exposed to Pitocin at birth than those who were not. Because no survey items were designed to identify specific reasons for respondents' use of feeding exclusively at the breast or of combined feeding methods, no conclusions can be drawn about reasons for the above findings and no causal relationship can be assumed between Pitocin and feeding method.

Several other studies have found an association between induction of labor and lower breast-feeding rates at hospital discharge (Crost & Kaminski, 1998; Ounsted et al., 1978; Palmer et al., 1979) and between oxytocin use for labor induction, among other obstetrical interventions, and lower breast-feeding rates at discharge (Zuppa et al., 1984).

The present study found that Pitocin use resulted in statistically significant differences in scores (p = .005) on the Context item concerning whether the baby was with his or her mother for most of the first hour postpartum, which could possibly contribute to the lower rates of breast-feeding or perhaps could play an additional role in disrupting the nursing relationship and early mother-child attunement. However, the survey did not specifically ask mothers when breast-feeding was initiated, so no conclusions can be drawn about whether the time they spent with their infants during the first hour after birth included the initiation of breast-feeding.

Delay in initiating breast-feeding in the period following birth has been found to be a significant factor in weaning before 6 weeks (DiGirolamo, Grummer-Strawn, & Fein, 2001). In the present study, 231 mothers who did not receive Pitocin at all during labor reported feeding their child exclusively at the breast during the first 6 months, and none used combined feeding methods. In the Pitocin group, 96 mothers reported feeding their infants exclusively at the breast and 129 reported combined feeding methods. Only a very small number of mothers in either group reported exclusive bottle-feeding (6 in the Pitocin group and 16 in the non-Pitocin group). An additional 20 mothers, all in the no-Pitocin group, checked "Other" and provided written descriptions of their feeding methods (see Appendix I).

This item was worded to differentiate mother-infant dyads that experienced a relationship that is both facilitated by oxytocin production and results in its increase. Lifestyle information was not gathered in this survey; therefore, no assumptions can be made from the findings about the possibility that the mothers receiving Pitocin induction or augmentation may, as a group, differ in personality characteristics or lifestyle choices from mothers who did not receive Pitocin, in ways that correspond to eventual infant feeding method, as suggested by Out et al. (1985, 1986).

Out et al. (1985) cited studies during the 1970s in which researchers theorized that induction of labor might have deleterious psychological effects on women's experience of labor and early mother-infant interaction. The authors pointed out that distinctions had not been made between elective inductions and inductions as a result of a complication, which in itself might result in any effects observed. They speculated that differences in experience of labor also might be explained in part by differences in personal characteristics between women choosing induction of labor and those preferring labor to begin spontaneously.

Although this may have been an accurate appraisal of the situation in the 1970s and 1980s in the Netherlands, the climate of hospital birth in the United States in the 21st century is now predominantly one of active management of labor. It is likely that personal characteristics distinguishing induced mothers from those experiencing spontaneous labor no longer carry as much weight as the current practice of "daylight obstetrics," as discussed in chapter 2.

Out et al. (1985, 1986) also concluded that differences in outcomes between women whose labors were induced and those whose labors were spontaneous could not be entirely explained by personal characteristics, although in their study it appeared that mothers choosing induction of labor were less anxious and more self-confident but also less emotionally involved with their newborns. The present study did not gather data concerning how many of the respondents chose elective induction as opposed to receiving Pitocin for medical indications; however, such information would appear to be of value in a future study.

It must be stated here that both reduced time spent by the newborn with the mother in the hour following birth and reduced numbers of infants fed exclusively at the breast in the Pitocin group may nonetheless not be related exclusively, or at all, to Pitocin use at birth. In the present study, 146 mothers reported receiving epidural anesthesia as well as Pitocin, whereas 24 reported a combination of Pitocin use, pain medication, and epidurals, and an additional 14 mothers reported the use of Pitocin and pain medication. In a review of the literature on the effects of birthing practices on the breast-feeding dyad, Smith (2007) cited a study suggesting that many babies exposed to epidural anesthesia were unable to latch and suck effectively (Baumgarder, Muehl, Fischer, & Pribbenow, 2003) and another finding that 67% of mothers receiving epidural analgesia, as opposed to 29% who labored without epidurals, reported partial breast-feeding or formula-feeding at 12 weeks (Volmanen, Valanne, & Alahuhta, 2004).

An Australian prospective cohort study investigated whether the addition of the opioid fentanyl to epidural analgesia resulted in difficulties with establishing breast-feeding and found that women "who had epidurals were less likely to fully breastfeed their infant in the few days after birth and more likely to stop breastfeeding in the first 24 weeks" (Torvaldsen, Roberts, Simpson, Thompson, & Elwood, 2006, p. 1), although the relationship could not be assumed to be causal. Nonetheless, it is known that "all drugs administered for pain relief to the laboring woman cross the placenta" (Smith, 2007, p. 625). Smith also notes that "lactation professionals have observed that prolonged intravenous hydration seems to increase edema in breast tissue" (p. 626), possibly inhibiting "the expansion of milk ducts and consequent release of milk during the milk-ejection reflex" (p. 626), causing latch and breast problems. Intravenous hydration is an intrinsic factor in the current mode of delivery of Pitocin and is virtually universal prior to epidural administration, to prevent a drop in blood pressure and deterioration in fetal heart rate (Kinsella, Pirlet, Mills, Tuckey, & Thomas, 2000).

In addition, the more painful labor reported by many women receiving Pitocin for induction or augmentation may be a contributing factor in the use of epidural anesthesia, so that Pitocin may be directly (or indirectly, through accompanying epidural use) related to reduced numbers of mothers feeding their infants exclusively at the breast. At the same time, some of the women in the present study who received epidural anesthesia for pain relief during labor may also have received Pitocin augmentation in order to improve the quality of contractions, because labor can be slowed by the administration of an epidural. Hence, it is equally possible that either Pitocin or epidural use, or the combination, could be responsible for more mother-infant separation during the first hour or for problems with initiation of breast-feeding, or both, and it would clearly be of value to tease out these different factors in future research.

In light of the present study's finding of a significant relationship between Pitocin use and reduced numbers of mothers feeding their infants at the breast during the first 6 months, further investigation is warranted. The relationship between Pitocin use at birth, the contribution of the use of epidural anesthesia that frequently either precedes or results from Pitocin administration, and subsequent feeding methods represents a possible influence of Pitocin use upon an intervening variable (infant feeding method) that may influence later psychosocial functioning in the child. Such an investigation could lend support to Schore's (2005) assertions concerning the importance of attunement in the early mother-infant relationship.

Because oxytocin plays a significant role in lactation and attachment behaviors, the findings of the present study may lend support to the theory that exogenous oxytocin (Pitocin) use may result in faulty endogenous oxytocin systems, which may then affect the success of or the motivation for the breast-feeding relationship.

Although the present study did not explicitly examine the mother's emotional involvement with her newborn, the survey items that represent the two PCA factors significant for Pitocin portray a relationship in which mothers' scores suggested that they experienced difficulties in their relationships with their 3-year-olds to a significantly higher degree than did mothers who did not receive Pitocin. This appears to corroborate Buckley's (2007) assertion that disruption of hormonal systems in the perinatal period may "disrupt social [and reproductive] behaviors later in life" (p. 4), and the growing evidence in research from a wide variety of disciplines that supports such a theory. Buckley speculates that the peaks of oxytocin present in mother and baby in the hour or so following birth "are also involved in switching on immediate and appropriate mothering behavior in all mammalian species, and that this time (when other hormones . . . are also at peak levels) represents a 'sensitive period' for mother-infant interactions and attachment" (p. 5).

Among the findings of an Australian prospective longitudinal study (Rowe-Murray & Fisher, 2001) of 203 first-time mothers, examining the effects of mode and place of delivery on first mother-infant contact and maternal emotional well-being as assessed by the profile of mood scores and Edinburgh postnatal depression score, was that mothers who delivered their babies by cesarean section had compromised first contact with their babies compared with mothers who had vaginal births, with or without instrument delivery. Furthermore, the researchers found that when first contact was delayed it was associated with greater maternal mood disturbance through 8 months postpartum (the length of the study) in both the cesarean birth group and the group who delivered vaginally. The authors note that, given the evidence that newborns are capable of sophisticated levels of perception and that their brains are organized at least in part by early relational experiences, particularly during the period of high arousal resulting from elevated oxytocin levels in the hour following birth, delayed first contact with the mother, together with the persistent effect of this delay on the mother's emotional state, could have as yet unknown consequences for both parties. "Early mother-infant contact may be a psychosocial casualty of medically managed delivery" (p. 1073).

Because Rowe-Murray and Fisher (2001) compared only three modes of delivery—spontaneous vaginal births, instrumental vaginal births, and cesarean births—without reference to how labor began, their study cannot contribute directly to the examination of the relationship between Pitocin-induced or -augmented births and delayed mother-infant contact, success of breast-feeding, or the quality of the subsequent relationship between mother and infant, with the possibly contributing factor of the effects of the delayed contact on the mother's emotional well-being. Nonetheless, these findings support the concerns raised by the present study.

The present study's findings suggest that mother-child relationships may be affected by the use of Pitocin at birth, and although further study is needed to disprove or verify these findings, mothers planning to give birth in a hospital in the United States, and those who support them, at least need to know that there is now some question about the long-term relationship between Pitocin-induced or -augmented labors and children's later psychosocial functioning. Along with the known medical risks of induction and augmentation, the psychosocial ramifications need to be carefully weighed.

Implications for Theory

Although the findings of this study did not reveal a statistically significant difference between Pitocin and non-Pitocin groups in total score for psychosocial functioning items on the survey, there were several statistically significant findings supporting the main hypothesis. A group of individual psychosocial items, the two factors in the principal component analysis (Assertiveness and Need to Control Environment), the role played by Pitocin and other medications in the mother's perceptions of her birth experience, and the relationship between this birth context and her child's functioning, as demonstrated in Factor 8 (Assertiveness), all suggest that there is substance to the clinicians' reports of psychosocial functioning challenges in children born with the use of Pitocin. This study substantiates theory in the field of prenatal and perinatal psychology by proposing that obstetrical interventions may create some form of enduring, hormonally mediated imprint that mothers can observe in their child's later psychosocial functioning.

It would seem imperative that any future theoretical considerations of Pitocin use at birth incorporate the perspective of polyvagal theory (Porges, 1995), because this provides a plausible and much-tested neurobiological model that served to provide some insight into the significant findings in this study. Prenatal and perinatal psychology theory greatly benefits from the neurobiological explanations provided by polyvagal theory for what has been observed clinically but is only now beginning to be researched. Additionally, longitudinal human studies into the effects of exogenous oxytocin binding with oxytocin receptors in the perinatal period may serve to clarify how Csaba's (2008) hormonal imprinting theory may pertain in mother-baby dyads and, if the postulated faulty imprinting exists in humans, whether it persists in the child or within the mother-child relationship.

Implications for Practice

Psychotherapists and other clinicians working with children or with the resolution of issues relating to birth need to understand polyvagal theory in order to use a neurobiological framework both for their understanding of the presenting problems and to educate family members about how to interpret and respond to symptoms. Clinicians should be aware that clusters of behaviors and issues resembling those described in Factor 8 and Factor 12 may signify a child who experiences a subjective lack of safety in his or her environment, and possibly also experiences environmental intrusion, and should further explore this possibility with the child and the parent. Clinicians should be informed about the possibility that very early experiences, such as those from birth, may have imprinting effects that manifest themselves in challenges to psychosocial functioning such as those described here. Although oxytocin abnormalities have been implicated in schizophrenia, autism, and other mental health problems, it is possible that oxytocin abnormalities also underlie other, less severe, psychosocial issues.

Moving beyond the realm of psychotherapy to professionals involved in birth, it is important that these professionals stay current with the literature. A number of recent studies and articles call for greater attention to be paid to the thoughts, feelings, and needs of mothers throughout pregnancy and birth and suggest that these be weighed more carefully against protocol and routine practices.

The need to reconsider carefully much of what has become standard practice and to refocus on the individual mother's and baby's needs is articulated in studies such as the two Listening to Mothers studies (Corry, 2004; Declercq et al., 2002; Declercq et al., 2006) and is being increasingly expressed by obstetricians and other physicians, in articles such as those by Lyerly et al. (2007) and a commentary on that article that states, among other things,

> Before the ascent of randomized controlled trials and clinical practice guidelines, obstetrics earned Archie Cochrane's "wooden spoon" as the least evidence-based

specialty in medicine. In our rush to incorporate "hard" evidence into obstetric practice, we have lost sight of the softer art of medicine, coercing patients into accepting increasing levels of intervention for decreasing amounts of narrowly quantifiable benefit. Maternity practitioners may soon deserve the "wooden club" for their keen ability to overestimate risk and undervalue patient autonomy. (Klein et al., 2007, p. 266)

The importance of reviewing and taking seriously research into the interaction of exogenous oxytocin (Pitocin) with maternal and fetal oxytocin receptors and the possible long-term consequences cannot be overstated. Researchers into obstetrical practices, traditionally divorced from postpartum follow-up of offspring, must ensure that they are fully aware of the possibility of such consequences.

It is hoped that the findings of this study will constitute a first step toward reexamination of the risks of Pitocin use to induce or augment labor, which has become such an entrenched aspect of the active management of labor, and that research into relationships between Pitocin use and later psychosocial functioning in children born with its use will resume, after what has been something of a hiatus of more than 20 years.

Limitations of the Study

One of the major limitations of this study is that there was no way to verify participants' adherence to the stated criteria for participation. Although I responded to well over 100 e-mails—many of them requests to participate despite not meeting one or more of the criteria, or requesting clarification regarding eligibility—other potential participants may have elected not to check on concerns about their eligibility and completed the survey anyway. Others may have completed the survey out of curiosity, without considering eligibility at all. In addition, invitations to participate in the research were placed in two widely read e-mail bulletins, but it was not possible to estimate how many participants were drawn from these bulletins as opposed to those responding to invitations disseminated by other means, and if doing so created a specific bias in the sample. That the number of completed surveys doubled during the last week of the survey run suggests that a considerable number of participants were readers of the bulletins; however, readers also might have passed the invitation along to friends, as had been taking place earlier during the month the survey was online.

Fortunately, in observing survey completions over this period, it was clear that the proportion of mothers who experienced Pitocin use in their birth and those who did not varied little throughout the month of the survey, suggesting that there was not a preponderance of unmedicated births among the bulletin readers. This also suggests that obstetrical interventions took place even among mothers who may be strongly committed to a more attachment-parenting, natural birthing approach.

Although the sample is representative of women who are sufficiently computer-literate to access and complete the survey, no information was gathered about geographical location within the United States, socioeconomic status, or ethnicity. No generalizations can be made from the sample studied to the general population of mothers of 3-year-olds who gave birth in hospitals in the United States.

The criteria did not exclude children with developmental diagnoses such as pervasive developmental delay, autism spectrum disorders, or sensory integration dysfunction, all of which can be diagnosed before the age of 3, and there was no survey item allowing parents to identify their 3-year-olds as such. Collecting this information might have added value to the study in identifying any relationships between Pitocin use at birth and these diagnoses, something of considerable interest to the fields of psychology and education. Regrettably, there also were no survey items asking about instrument deliveries (forceps and vacuum extraction), episiotomies, birth order of the 3-year-olds under study, or whether breast-feeding was successfully initiated during the first hour postpartum.

It is also important to acknowledge that any relationships found between Pitocin use at birth and psychosocial functioning at age 3 may have been confounded by lifestyle and other experiences during the intervening years (e.g., parenting style, philosophy, and means of discipline; child's temperament; individual characteristics of the mother/parents and the interactions between these and the child's temperament; time of first contact between mother and child after birth and the nature and quality of their attachment; emotional or physical traumas, including surgeries and other difficult medical procedures; domestic violence; or parental smoking or drug/alcohol use). Such experiences might result in the functioning of the children reported by their mothers, or might affect mothers' perceptions of their child's functioning. It should be noted here, however, that one study cited earlier (Kirsch, 1997) failed to find a relationship between individual factors among a group of perinatal risk factors, including induction of labor, and temperament as measured by the Temperament Assessment Battery for Children—Revised. Naturally, such possibly confounding variables would warrant closer attention in any future study; in particular, the role played by oxytocin in the attachment relationship seems worthy of closer scrutiny.

No medical records for the birth were collected from the mothers who participated in this study, so that dose- and duration-related relationships between Pitocin and psychosocial functioning could not be examined. The same was true of other medications, although combinations of medications may have contributed significantly to different outcomes for different children. In addition, the criteria did not specify which types of problems constituted "serious medical complications for mother or baby," so mothers used their own judgment about what qualified or disqualified them from participating in response to this criterion. No Apgar scores were obtained, so mothers' reports concerning the child's status at birth had to be relied upon. No information was gathered from the mothers about whether their babies had required resuscitation at birth. In any case, in the absence of medical records, this information would have been unreliable because such procedures typically take place on a warming bed and cannot always be observed by the mother.

Because statistical analysis did not result in Pitocin differentiating significantly between means for Pitocin use and no Pitocin use, it was not possible to use a total score on psychosocial items to examine further the relationships between drug interactions and psychosocial functioning. In addition, it is conceivable that other obstetrical medications might have had the same or other significant relationships to scores on psychosocial functioning, because the analyses of the survey data were conducted only to distinguish between Pitocin and no-Pitocin groups.

The same is true of the baby being with the mother during the first hour. Although there was a statistically significant difference in responses to this item between Pitocin and non-Pitocin mothers, it is possible that other medications might have resulted in the same outcome. It would require further and more detailed examination of the relationships between the different medications and combinations of medications to tease out which are most likely to affect what takes place during the first hour and possibly also the initiating and ongoing success of breast-feeding.

The survey did not ask mothers whether they received Pitocin at delivery to prevent postpartum hemorrhage. As Buckley (2007) states, "Pitocin is now administered to almost every woman birthing under obstetric care, either during labor (to speed contractions) or following birth (to prevent hemorrhage) and so 'induction' may be an inaccurate marker for Pitocin exposure" (p. 23). It is not known how many of the mothers in this study received Pitocin at delivery and which of them received it after having had none for labor induction or augmentation. Although postpartum Pitocin administration would not affect the newborn systemically, how this administration might interact with bonding and breast-feeding in the first hour postpartum could not be explored with the data gathered in the survey.

The survey would have benefited from more extensive piloting of the original large number of survey items to ensure that all the postulated dimensions of psychosocial functioning were adequately represented with the most effective items.

Choices on the survey item involving method of feeding did not make a clear distinction between bottle-feeding pumped breast milk and formula-feeding and did not provide mothers with an option to clarify the duration of exclusive breast milk feeding (as opposed to formula-feeding) and when solid foods were introduced. It might have been valuable to invite mothers to report on how soon after birth breast-feeding was initiated, if it was, and the amount of skin-to-skin contact during feeding of any type, because this experience is known to optimize lactation and oxytocin production in both mother and infant.

There may have been limitations inherent in exploring the relationship between Pitocin use at birth and 3-year-old psychosocial functioning by asking mothers to report on the functioning of their 3-year-olds. In general, parents are more likely to see their child as similar to, rather than different from, other children, unless the difference is physically obvious. Many parents are unaware of their child having difficulties with, for example, hyperactivity or negotiating transitions, especially in the case of a firstborn, until the child is attending school and is expected to function in concordance with a group of children — to sit and focus for periods of time, to follow directions, to transition from one activity to another, and to get along with peers.

In addition, it is possible that the mother's own experience of Pitocin while giving birth may result in a propensity to be less able to attune to the child, though the child, rather than the quality of attunement in the mother-child relationship, would typically be seen as the source of any psychosocial problem. This is something that the clinicians interviewed for this study have observed, and I have observed this in my own clinical practice, although the findings for Context showed only a linear relationship with Factor 8 (Assertiveness) in the present study.

Finally, the survey required mothers to report on their experiences of giving birth 3 years earlier, and memories are known to become increasingly unreliable over time and may be colored by intervening experiences.

Implications and Directions for Future Research

The significant research findings presented in this dissertation and the theories that stand to explain them should form a stepping stone for future researchers to investigate further the relationship between Pitocin (artificial oxytocin) use at birth and psychosocial functioning in children born with its use.

This study began with a preliminary interview study from which over 300 possible survey items ultimately were derived. A future study that sought to improve upon the present study would benefit from more extensive piloting of this type of large group of items and the subsequent use of principal component analysis with which to tease out the factors into which items loaded. Such an analysis might eliminate redundancies rather than anticipating even apparently logical groupings of items.

As indicated above, future research also might prove more effective by studying children at age 5, when they are attending school, are learning to function within structured situations and social groups, and are having expectations placed upon them by teachers and peers. Having both mothers and teachers complete a similar survey (with the mother, naturally, being the respondent providing information about the child's birth) would provide a more complete picture of each child's psychosocial functioning, although by age 5 it is possible that additional intervening circumstances could confound data supposedly relating to the child's birth experience with Pitocin.

The opportunity to verify through medical records a mother's recollections of the birth would increase the level of accuracy of birth-related information. An alternative approach might be to employ specifically trained, skilled interviewers to interview a sample of mothers (and another of teachers) of children who were or were not exposed to Pitocin at birth, without discussion of the birth history, so that the interviewer is unaware of which children were exposed. The resulting interviews would be analyzed on dimensions of psychosocial functioning and then correlated with separately gathered information about each child's Pitocin exposure.

In the present study, Pitocin use did not differentiate to a statistically significant degree the psychosocial functioning of 3-year-olds based on the timing of Pitocin administration—whether to induce labor or, later on, to augment labor. Given the oxytocin research that suggests that faulty hormonal imprinting may result from an excess of hormones flooding the receptors, it would be valuable to compare the mother-infant relationships or psychosocial functioning of children born with Pitocin for induction with that of children born with Pitocin for augmentation of labor. Such research could test the assumption that oxytocin used to augment a labor that began spontaneously would be targeting a full complement of oxytocin receptors, whereas oxytocin used to induce labor may target an insufficient number of receptors.

To date, studies have not examined the infant's psychosocial functioning through the first year of life or sought to identify whether there is any form of continuity from infancy to later years. The present study suggests some continuity between psychosocial functioning in infancy and in childhood. Exploring this possibility might be accomplished by videotaped observation of infants and infant-mother interactions, because so much of later development and regulation builds upon early emotional development in the context of the mother-infant relationship. With the addition of interviews to explore in greater depth mothers' perceptions of the birth and their interpersonal relationships with their infant, analyzed by trained observers and then followed up in childhood with a second round of observation and interviews, this additional approach might contribute qualitatively to the current climate of greater interest in women's experiences of birth.

Because the two significant-for-Pitocin factors in the PCA appeared to be differentiating the Pitocin-exposed children's responses to a neuroception of lack of safety, which seemed to relate directly to the first two levels of responses delineated in Porges' (1995, 2001, 2007) polyvagal theory, it is possible that a survey designed to elicit descriptions of all three levels of response—social engagement (ventral vagal system), fight/flight (sympathetic nervous system activation), and freeze (parasympathetic nervous system activation or dorsal/vegetative vagal system)—might prove effective in describing children's responses to environments and experiences they perceive as unsafe, plausibly based on very early experiences such as obstetrical interventions. Such a survey also might be usefully applied when investigating further possible imprinting effects from prenatal and birth experiences as well as other early stressors.

An alternative approach to exploring the relationship between Pitocin use at birth and later psychosocial functioning might use the measures being evaluated by Porges and his colleagues in their exploration of applications of polyvagal theory, such as respiratory sinus arrhythmia, heart period reactivity, and cortisol levels (Doussard-Roosevelt, Montgomery, & Porges, 2003) or by "evaluating the relation between spontaneous social engagement behavior measured by eye gaze behaviors and the visceromotor (e.g., respiratory sinus arrhythmia) and somatomotor (e.g., right tympanic membrane compliance) components of the Social Engagement System" (Heilman, Bal, Bazhenova, & Porges, 2007, p. 531). Similar approaches might have value in performing a comparison between Pitocin-exposed and non-Pitocin-exposed children, although Doussard-Roosevelt et al. (2003) caution researchers about limitations of the methodologies employed with the children in these studies. This approach may serve to distinguish on a neurobiological level children who are relaxed and well-regulated from those whose subjective experience, or neuroception, is of a lack of safety, resulting in the types of functioning challenges described in Factor 8 (Assertiveness) and Factor 12 (Need to Control Environment) of this study and the internal correlates of these challenges.

Finally, in the study of newborns cited earlier in this dissertation as one of the few previous studies to consider the possible relationship between obstetrical interventions and infant functioning and to attempt to tease out the various interventions and effects, Eishima (1992) stated,

> It is uncertain which factor affects the babies, the drug, the induction itself or the reason for the induction. Maternal stress resulting from drug administration should also be studied as these effects may be mediated by common factors of this kind. (p. 261)

Like Eishima (1992), I find that it is as yet unclear whether any of the significant relationships found in this study between Pitocin use at birth and later psychosocial functioning in the child are directly attributable to the effects of Pitocin in the infant's or the mother's body during the perinatal period, to the interaction of both, or more indirectly, to the changes wrought during labor and the postpartum period by the use of Pitocin as an intervention. Examples of such changes found in this study are the significant differences reported in the time the newborn spent with the mother during the first hour and the difference in numbers of mothers who exclusively breast-fed their infant for the first 6 months.

Because one intervention so frequently begets others, multiple interventions appear to have become the rule rather than the exception for births in the United States. As a result, it will continue to be challenging to isolate the effects of one intervention (e.g., Pitocin) from those of another (e.g., epidural anesthesia) and to evaluate the nature of such effects, or to recognize when interventions arise out of medical necessity and when they are employed for other reasons—and whose reasons these are.

Conclusions

The findings of this study suggest that there is a relationship between Pitocin use at birth and certain aspects of psychosocial functioning at age 3, for which polyvagal theory provides a reasonable explanation. In this sample, children exposed to Pitocin scored significantly differently from children not born with Pitocin on two factors. Pitocin reduced scores on the first factor, Assertiveness, which might be viewed as an aspect of social engagement in polyvagal theory, as a functional way of coping with internal discomfort and dysregulation, suggesting a less effective use of social engagement strategies. Pitocin had the opposite effect on the second factor, increasing scores on Need to Control Environment, which appears to be a manifestation of the activation of the sympathetic nervous system to mobilize fight or flight responses, again as a coping mechanism for experiences of dysregulation, apparently resulting in a neuroception of lack of safety.

What remains less clear is whether psychosocial functioning at age 3 is affected directly by the baby's experience of Pitocin in the bloodstream, by the effects of Pitocin on his or her experience of labor, by the mother's experience of Pitocin-induced/augmented labor, or by the effects on the mother of losing the biological initiation of labor and its natural rhythm. Psychosocial functioning might be equally affected by a similar experience in the baby or by some combination of all these, resulting in a relative lack of attunement in the mother-child dyad. This, in turn, may influence the perceptions of the child reflected in survey responses.

It is also unclear whether a combination of effects is responsible for or an outcome of less time spent together during the first hour after birth, relatively less exclusive breast-feeding, and thus a different experience of early interactions between mother and infant. The theory of hormonal imprinting (Csaba, 2008) suggests a possible mechanism by which the perinatal binding of exogenous oxytocin (Pitocin) to oxytocin receptors in mother and child may contribute to the differences between Pitocin-exposed and non-Pitocin-exposed children (as reported by their mothers) found in the study.

In a recent study of the relationship between epidural use, oxytocin infusion, and newborn skin temperature during breast-feeding at 2 days postpartum, researchers at the Karolinska Institute in Sweden, known for its extensive research into birth and mother-infant interactions during the newborn period, asserted that "since these interventions have become widely accepted, there is an increasingly important need to investigate whether these interventions influence the physiology of the mother and infant immediately following birth and/or in the long-term" (Jonas, Wiklund, Nissen, Ransjö-Arvidson, & Uvnäs-Moberg, 2007, p. 56). From a prenatal and perinatal psychology perspective, one might add that we also need to understand the influences on neurobiological (including hormonal) and psychosocial development.

Csaba (2008), Porges (1995, 2003, 2007), and Schore (2005), among others, have provided us with a substantial theoretical basis, and considerable research has been and is being conducted to test and implement their theories. We are continuing to learn about the exquisite orchestration of parturition, and our understanding of how intervention affects this organization is in its infancy. Prenatal and perinatal psychology brings to the table a sensitivity to the very early environments and experiences that are thought to contribute to the architecture of the brain, the organization of our neurobiology, and our interpersonal relationships, which can only inform and enhance this new knowledge.

The practice of obstetrics is now coming under considerable scrutiny from within the field, and a decade or more of active management of labor and drastically reduced choices for mothers has resulted in a flurry of recent publications—*Pushed* (Block, 2007); *Birth: The Surprising History of How We Are Born* (Cassidy, 2006a); "The Mommy Uprising" (Cassidy, 2006b); *Birth Crisis* (Kitzinger, 2006); *Reading Birth and Death: A History of Obstetric Thinking* (Murphy-Lawless, 1998); *Born in the USA: How a Broken Maternity System Must be Fixed to Put Women and Children First* (Wagner, 2006). These publications express concern about women's loss of autonomy in deciding where and how they give birth, note the psychosocial effects of these losses, and advocate the delicate task of including the individual beliefs, needs, and circumstances of mothers and babies when managing risk.

The present study should serve as a small but significant contribution to this dialogue and to the current climate of questioning what has become routine and unquestionably accepted about the way birth is conducted in the United States, sometimes in the face of scientific evidence. The study strongly suggests that the use of Pitocin is not a benign intervention without psychosocial and very likely neurobiological consequences for both mother and child. The subject warrants further research to examine more deeply the question of whether such interventions should continue electively and without verifiable medical indications, and to identify and weigh the risks of such interventions against the perceived benefits to individual mothers and infants.

Young children today are presenting in ever greater numbers psychosocial problems that once were considered comparatively rare. Even when problem behaviors do not meet the criteria for mental health or developmental diagnoses, they may signal a relative lack of capacity for attunement in relationships or high levels of internal dysregulation that may have lifelong consequences. We have an obligation to examine carefully any factors that may contribute to these challenges, including current obstetrical practices such as the use of artificial oxytocin during labor. Further, we must ensure that issues resulting from unexamined and possibly unnecessary interventions at birth are identified, and that mothers are provided an opportunity to give a fully informed consent for such interventions, in order to optimize the first hours, weeks, and months of mothers' relationships with their infants.

Appendix A: Operational Definitions of Independent and Dependent Variables

These are the dimensions and subgroups of items within those dimensions that together, either may influence, or comprise, the "psychosocial functioning" of the child. Where there was a source in the literature that defined a term in a way congruent with its use in this study or by the clinicians participating in the preliminary study, it has been quoted with the relevant citation. Where no consensual definition could be accessed, I have provided my own definition, meeting the same criteria.

Affect/Emotion/Mood Regulation: According to Zeanah (2000), "Thompson (1994) defined emotion regulation as individuals' attempts to monitor, evaluate, and modify their emotional reactions, particularly in pursuit of a goal. These regulation attempts may involve internal or external processes, distinctions Eisenberg (1997) labeled emotion regulation and emotion-related behavior regulation. Emotion regulation involves the maintenance or modification of physiological arousal or internal feeling states. Emotion-related behavioral regulation refers to modulation of the overt expression of emotion (i.e., the frequency, intensity, or duration of the facial expressions, vocalizations, and actions that serve as external signals of internal states). These regulatory behaviors are typically goal-directed and, hence, may involve attempts to modify the context in which the emotion was elicited. . . maintaining proximity to mother is a primary goal during the second half of the first year of life, and emotion-related behavioral regulation is undertaken in its service" (pp. 62-63).

Attunement (Mother-Child): According to Schore (2005), how the self develops is through repeated episodes of "affect synchrony" between mother and infant: ". . . psychobiological attunement and the interactive mutual entrainment of physiologic rhythms are fundamental processes that mediate attachment." (p. 207), and ". . . the spontaneous emotional communication that occurs within the attachment relationship has been described as 'a conversation between limbic systems'" (p. 208). He states: ". . . the empathic caregiver's sensory stimulation coincides with the infant's endogenous rhythms, allowing the mother to appraise the nonverbal expressions of her infant's internal arousal and psychobiological states, regulate them, and communicate them back to the infant. In this process of 'contingent responsivity,' the tempo of their engagement, disengagement, and reengagement is coordinated. In such interactions the mother must be attuned not so much to the child's overt behavior as to the reflections of the rhythms of his or her internal state, enabling the dyad to create 'mutual regulatory systems of arousal'" (p. 206). ". . . . Thus, throughout the life span, attachment is a primary mechanism for the regulation of biologic synchronicity within and between organisms" (p. 207).

Autonomic Nervous System Regulation/Organization: "The ANS is the part of the central nervous system that governs the functions of digestion, assimilation, elimination, heart rate, breathing rate, and metabolic rates. . . . . The ANS is strongly influenced by the person's emotional system" (Castellino, 1997, p. 32). Effective ANS regulation involves maintaining the homeostasis between the parasympathetic and sympathetic nervous systems of the child so that arousal levels are commensurate with whatever stimuli are present.

Birth (difficulty of): The mother's subjective experience of the difficulty of the birth of her child as rated on a 7-point semantic differential-type scale.

Birth Team: Those present during labor and delivery: some individuals may be chosen by the mother, others about whom mother has little choice. In this study, how these individuals cooperate among themselves and with the mother may define the mother's experience of her labor and delivery. The team contributes to the context of the birth.

Boundaries (interpersonal): "Interpersonal Boundaries define and protect the physical, emotional and psychological territory between two people" (K Squared Enterprises, 2007). The term is used in this dissertation to mean how the child relates to his or her own boundaries and those of others.

Context: The state of the mother's primary relationship and relationships with other family and extended family members (e.g., in-laws), her preparedness for birthing and sense of empowerment (or lack of it), her support system in life and at the birth, her choice of hospital and caregivers, preexisting conditions/complications, persons present and unfolding events during labor and delivery.

Control/ Cooperation/Leadership: This term refers to how the child interacts with peers, siblings and groups.

Coordination/Motor Skills: This refers to the skill that requires an individual to utilize their skeletal muscles effectively. Motor skills and motor control depend upon the coordinated functioning of the brain, skeleton, joints, and nervous system. Most motor skills are learned in early childhood, although disabilities or trauma can affect motor skills development. Motor development is the development of action and coordination of one's limbs, as well as the development of posture control, strength, balance, and perceptual skills.

Distractibility/Focusing: "The distractible child notices every thing that is going on around her. Not only is she distracted by external stimuli, but she also will be distracted from a task by her own thoughts, daydreams, and internal stimuli" (Keith, 2004). The term is used in this dissertation to describe the child's ability to focus on activities and whether any distractibility is global or trigger- or situation-specific.

Emotional Reactivity: Used here to describe the degree to which a child responds emotionally to situations/stimuli.

Epidural Anesthesia: According to Brochert (2000), "epidural anesthesia is a method used to eliminate pain during certain procedures or surgeries. In this form of anesthesia, medication is injected inside the spinal column with a needle or thin tube. An epidural, as the procedure is commonly called, is usually used for procedures performed below the rib cage. It is often the preferred way to reduce pain during childbirth. It can also be used for pain control after surgery or childbirth" (¶ 1-2). ". . . A needle or special tube is inserted through the skin of the back into the spinal column until it touches, but not pierces, the sac that contains the spinal cord, then withdrawn slightly before the medication is injected. Thus, the medicine is delivered just outside the sac that contains the spinal cord. The medication acts on nerves that come from the spinal cord and carry pain messages to the brain. An epidural is different from spinal anesthesia, a procedure in which the medication is injected inside the sac that contains the spinal cord. Epidurals are usually preferred for childbirth and are often better for pain control. An epidural requires more medication and takes longer to work than a spinal, but is less likely to cause headaches and low blood pressure" (¶ 4-5).

Jacobson and Uretsky (2007) elaborate: "An epidural is a local (regional) anesthetic delivered through a catheter (small tube) into a vacant space outside the spinal cord called the epidural space. The drugs commonly used in epidural anesthesia are bupivicaine (Marcaine, Sensorcaine); chloroprocaine (Nesacaine); and lidocaine (Xylocaine). The solutions of anesthetic should be preservative-free. The anesthetic agents that are infused through the small catheter block spinal nerve roots in the epidural space and the sympathetic nerve fibers adjacent to them. Epidural anesthesia can block most of the pain of labor and birth for vaginal and surgical deliveries. Epidural analgesia is also used after cesarean sections to help control postoperative pain" (¶ 1-3).

Hyperactivity/Activity Level: *The American Heritage® Science Dictionary* offers this definition: "An abnormally high level of activity or excitement shown by a person, especially a child, that interferes with the ability to concentrate or interact with others" ("Hyperactivity," n.d.).

Interpersonal Dynamics: Used here to describe the mother's perceptions of how her child typically interacts with others in his/her life including parents, other adults, siblings and peers.

Mother's Experience with Child and Parenting Style: Mothers' perceptions of their relationship with their child and their role as parent in that relationship.

Mother's Experience of Labor/birth: The mother's recollections of her subjective experience of labor and delivery of her child.

Mother's Experience of her Relationship with Baby Before and During Birth: Mothers' perceptions of their relationship with their child through the pregnancy, labor and delivery of the child, used here to contribute to her perspective on the context of the birth of her child.

Psychosocial Functioning (at Age 3): The *McGraw-Hill Concise Dictionary of Modern Medicine* defines this term as follows: "The development of the personality, and the acquisition of social attitudes and skills, from infancy through maturity" ("Psychosocial Development," 2002). "Psychosocial functioning describes a person's ability to perform the tasks of daily life and to engage in mutual relationships with other people in ways that are gratifying to self and others and that meet the needs of the organized community in which the person lives" ("Clinical Social Work Service," 2007, ¶ 3).

Recapitulations: The ways in which an individual unconsciously plays out a significant past event, for example, an infant who became stuck in the birth canal repeatedly wedging himself/herself into "tight corners."

Regulatory/Physiological Effects: Used here to refer to any issues with eating, sleeping or overall health that result from how the child's body, in the past or the present, functions in everyday life.

Responses to Structure/Support: How the child responds to structured situations and structure and support offered to them by others, particularly authority figures.

Rhythm: (See attunement [Mother-Child] above). This term is typically used colloquially by prenatal and perinatal clinicians without a single, precise, consensual definition; however, Schore's description above (attunement) appears to capture the essence of the term as it is used and so stands as the definition for this dissertation.

Self-esteem/Sense of Self (child's): According to the *Random House Unabridged Dictionary* this refers to "a realistic respect for or favorable impression of oneself; self-respect" ("Self-Esteem," 2006). The term is used in this dissertation to mean how the child feels about and sees himself or herself, as understood by the child's mother.

Self-regulation: Schore (2005) offers this description: "The process of development itself is believed to represent a progression of stages in which adaptive self-regulatory structures and functions enable new interactions between the individual and the social environment. It now is established that emotions are the highest order direct expressions of bioregulation in complex organisms, that the maturation of the neural mechanisms involved in self-regulation is experience-dependent, and that these critical affective experiences are embedded in the attachment relationship. In other words, attachment relationships are essential because they facilitate the development of the brain's self-regulatory mechanism. Studies reveal that these essential self-regulatory structures are located in the right (and not left) brain. Consensus now indicates that attachment can be defined as the dyadic regulation of emotion, that the attainment of the self-regulation of affect is a major developmental achievement, and that normal development represents the enhancement of self-regulation" (p. 206).

Sensory Integration Dysfunction: Also known as Dysfunction of Sensory Integration, defined by Mauro as "a neurological disability in which the brain is unable to accurately process the information coming in from the senses. Individuals may be *oversensitive* to some sensations, wildly overreacting to touch or movement or loss of balance; *undersensitive* to some sensations, needing crashing or banging or sharp sounds and flavors to register anything; or a combination of both. Sensory integration problems can affect the five traditional senses—particularly touch and hearing, but also taste, sight and smell—as well as two additional senses: the *vestibular* sense, which tells us where our body is in space, and the *proprioceptive* sense, which tells us what position our body is in. Children with Dysfunction of Sensory

Integration may appear hyperactive, oppositional, obsessive-compulsive, or attachment disordered, when in fact they are just reacting to and compensating for their unreliable and unpredictable view of the world" (Mauro, n.d.).

Sequencing: How an individual moves through a sequence of steps in an activity that involves a sequence of beginning, middle, and end, for example, getting ready to go out, getting ready for bed, selecting toys to play with, playing with them, then putting the toys away. Here attention is paid to whether the child can move smoothly through such sequences or has difficulty at random points in sequences or repeatedly at specific points.

Social Support (for mother during labor): Used here to describe the mother's perceptions of how she was supported socially and emotionally during the labor and delivery of her child. Supporters could include family members, hospital staff, or paid labor support personnel ("doulas").

Speech/Language Development: Used here to describe the combination of receptive language (understanding what is said, written or signed) and expressive language (speaking, writing or signing) that comprises speech and language development. These skills are partly innate and partly learned, as children interact with other people and the environment.

Tactile (Proprioceptive): According to *The American Heritage Dictionary* (2003), proprioception is "the unconscious perception of movement and spatial orientation arising from stimuli within the body itself. In humans, these stimuli are detected by nerves within the body itself, as well as by the semicircular canals of the inner ear."

Timing/Pacing/Tempo: In relation to birth, Castellino (1997) asserts, "the rhythm or tempo in which labor and birth progress is . . . a significant factor. Changes in the rhythm of labor may or may not have traumatic impacts on the baby. However, the natural rhythms of labor may change spontaneously, or from intended interventions. These changes may have adverse effects on the labor that lead to adverse imprinting in the baby" (p. 12). The term is used in this dissertation to mean how the child relates to the tempo and timing of others and how capable the child is of pacing their own activities or internal rhythms in harmony with those of others, for example, a parent.

Transitions: Used here to refer both to daily transition situations such as moving from one activity to another in daycare/preschool or at home, leaving home, getting ready for bed, stopping play activity prior to a meal, etc. and also to life transitions: moving from crib to toddler bed, starting preschool, etc.

Vestibular: "Vestibular—The sensory system located in the inner ear that allows us to maintain balance and enjoy movements such as swinging" ("Vestibular," n.d.). "Vestibular sense - a sensory system located in structures of the inner ear that registers the orientation of the head" ("Vestibular Sense," 2003-2008).

References

Boundaries (interpersonal). (2007). K Squared Enterprises. Retrieved February 18, 2007, from http://www.ksquaredenterprises.com/ service_workshops.htm

Brochert, A. (2000). *Epidural anesthesia*. University of Illinois Medical Center. Retrieved November 11, 2007, from http://uimc.discoveryhospital.com/ main.php?id=2949

Clinical social work service. (2007). University of Iowa Hospitals and Clinics: Department of Social Service. Retrieved February 11, 2007, from http://www.uihealthcare.com/depts/socialservice/department/services/ socialwork.html

Hyperactivity. (n.d.). In *the American Heritage science dictionary*. Retrieved March 4, 2007, from http://dictionary.reference.com/browse/hyperactivity

Jacobson, N. M., & Uretsky, S. D. (2007). Epidural therapy. In *Encyclopedia of surgery: A guide for patients and caregivers.* Retrieved November 11, 2007, from http://www.surgeryencyclopedia.com/Ce-Fi/Epidural-Therapy.html

Keith, K. (2004). *Children's temperament styles: Implications for elementary school adjustment.* Retrieved February 18, 2007, from http://childparenting.about.com/cs/childdevelopment/a/temperament_2.htm

Mauro, T. (n.d.). *Getting a diagnosis: The first step toward helping your child.* Retrieved February 11, 2007, from http://specialchildren.about.com/od/ gettingadiagnosis/g/DSI.htm

Proprioception. (2003). In *The American Heritage® dictionary of the English language,* (4th ed.). Retrieved February 11, 2007, from http://www.thefreedictionary.com/proprioception

Psychosocial development. (2002). In *McGraw-Hill concise dictionary of modern medicine.* Retrieved February 11, 2007, from http://medical-dictionary.thefreedictionary.com/psychosocial+development

Self-esteem. (2006). In *Random House unabridged dictionary.* Retrieved March 4, 2007, from http://dictionary.reference.com/browse/self-esteem

Vestibular. (n.d.). *Diagnostic definitions.* Retrieved February 11, 2007, from http://kid-power.org/definitions.html

Vestibular sense. (2007). *WordNet 3.0, Farlex clipart collection*. Retrieved February 11, 2007, from http://www.thefreedictionary.com/vestibular+sense

Appendix B: Glossary of Terms

Forceps: According to Ross, Beall, and Bonni (2007), "forceps are instruments designed to aid in the delivery of the fetus by applying traction to the fetal head. Many different types of forceps have been described and developed throughout time. Generally, forceps consist of 2 mirror image metal instruments that are maneuvered to cradle the fetal head and are articulated, after which traction is applied to effect delivery."

Labor: MedicineNet ("Definition of labor," 2002) defines labor as follows: "Childbirth, the aptly-named experience of delivering the baby and placenta from the uterus to the vagina to the outside world. There are two stages of labor. During the first stage (called the stage of dilatation), the cervix dilates fully to a diameter of about 10 cm. In the second stage (called the stage of expulsion), the baby moves out through the cervix and vagina to be born . . . Parturition is another term for 'labor.' It comes from the Latin *parturire*, 'to be ready to bear young' and is related to *partus*, 'to produce.' To labor in this sense is to produce."

Labor Augmentation: The use of artificial oxytocin to stimulate or augment uterine contractions that are considered inefficient in effecting cervical dilation, (i.e., irregular, or insufficiently powerful or frequent).

Labor Induction: "Inducing labor is the act of starting labor mechanically or medically" (American Medical Association, 2004).

Obstetrical Interventions: Used here to describe any action performed by medical personnel that adds to, changes, or diverges from the physiologic birth process.

Obstetrician: "A physician specialist expert in the delivery of total obstetrical care and the diagnosis and treatment of gynaecological disease" ("Obstetrician," 1997).

Obstetrics: "A branch of medicine dealing with the care of women during pregnancy, childbirth, and the period during which they recover from childbirth. Origin: L. Obstetricius" (Online Medical Dictionary, 1997).

Oxytocin: According to *The Columbia Electronic Encyclopedia* (2007) "Oxytocin [is a] hormone released from the posterior lobe of the pituitary gland that facilitates uterine contractions and the milk-ejection reflex. The structure of oxytocin, a cyclic peptide consisting of nine amino acids, was determined in 1953 and in the same year it was synthesized in the laboratory. Both oxytocin and antidiuretic hormone are biosynthesized in the hypothalamus of the brain and travel down neuronal axons to the posterior pituitary, where they accumulate prior to release. Stimuli that elicit the release of oxytocin include childbirth, suckling, and coitus; the uterine contractions that result may facilitate either childbirth or the ascent of spermatozoa through the fallopian tubes. Oxytocin may also play a role in the initiation of labor. The milk-ejection response occurs only in females immediately after childbirth. The role of oxytocin in males is unknown."

Pitocin: According to the package insert for Pitocin (Monarch Pharmaceuticals, 2004, p. 1), "Pitocin . . . is a sterile, clear, colorless aqueous solution of synthetic oxytocin, for intravenous infusion or intramuscular injection. Pitocin is a nonapeptide found in pituitary extracts from mammals. It is standardized to contain 10 units of oxytocic hormone/mL and contains 0.5% Chlorobutanol, a chloroform derivative as a preservative, with the pH adjusted with acetic acid. Pitocin may contain up to 16% of total impurities. The hormone is prepared synthetically to avoid possible contamination with vasopressin (ADH) and other small polypeptides with biologic activity. . . . Oxytocin is distributed throughout the extracellular fluid. Small amounts of the drug probably reach the fetal circulation. . . .

Antepartum: Pitocin is indicated for the initiation or improvement of uterine contractions, where this is desirable and considered suitable for reasons of fetal or maternal concern, in order to achieve vaginal delivery. It is indicated for (1) induction of labor in patients with a medical indication for the initiation of labor, such as Rh problems, maternal diabetes, preeclampsia at or near term, when delivery is in the best interests of mother and fetus or when membranes are prematurely ruptured and delivery is indicated; (2) stimulation or reinforcement of labor, as in selected cases of uterine intertia; (3) as adjunctive therapy in the management of incomplete or inevitable abortion. . . .

Postpartum: Pitocin is indicated to produce uterine contractions during the third stage of labor and to control postpartum bleeding or hemorrhage."

Perinatal: Pertaining to the period immediately before and after birth. MedicineNet ("Definition of Perinatal," 1998) states: "the perinatal period is defined in diverse ways. Depending on the definition, it starts at the 20th to 28th week of gestation and ends 1 to 4 weeks after birth. The word 'perinatal' is a hybrid of the Greek 'peri'- meaning 'around or about' and 'natal' from the Latin 'natus' meaning 'born.'" As used in this dissertation, the term refers to the period immediately before, during, and after birth.

Prenatal: "Occurring or existing before birth. . . . The word 'prenatal' comes from the Latin 'pre-,' before + '(g)natus,' birth = before birth. 'Antenatal' is often used in lieu of 'prenatal' in the UK, Australia, etc." ("Definition of Prenatal," 2000). As used in this dissertation the term refers to the period from conception until the beginning of labor.

Prenatal and Perinatal Psychology: As used in this dissertation, the field of prenatal and perinatal psychology is viewed as integrating the empirical research of fetal psychology (DiPietro et al., 2004; DiPietro et al., 2006; Hepper, 1992, 2005; Nijhuis, 1992; Piontelli, 1992, 2002) with the cumulative body of knowledge amassed by clinicians whose clients—adults, children and infants—have indicated in their process the influence of prenatal and birth experiences on their current lives. The field stands on a foundation drawn from cell biology, embryology, developmental neuroscience, obstetrics, midwifery and maternal-child nursing, perinatology, neonatology, social neurobiology, attachment and trauma theories and infant mental health, among others, and expands the time-frame encompassed by fetal psychology on a continuum through birth and the first year of life. Prenatal and perinatal psychology seeks to explain the experiences of babies from conception through the first year of life and to study the psychosocial impact of these experiences across the lifespan.

References

American Medical Association. (2004). Techniques used to aid delivery. In *Family Medical Guide* (4th ed.). Retrieved February 11, 2007, from http://www.medem.com

DiPietro, J. A., Caulfield, L. E., Irizarry, R. A., Chen, P., Merialdi, M., & Zavaleta, N. (2006). Prenatal development of intrafetal and maternal-fetal synchrony. *Behavioral Neuroscience, 120*(3), 687–701.

DiPietro, J. A., Irizarry, R. A., Costigan, K. A., & Gurewitsch, E. D. (2004). The psychophysiology of the maternal-fetal relationship. *Psychophysiology, 41*(4), 510–520.

Hepper, P. G. (1992). Fetal psychology: An embryonic science. In J. G. Nijhuis (Ed.), *Fetal behaviour: Developmental and perinatal aspects* (pp. 129–156). Oxford, England: Oxford University Press.

Hepper, P. G. (2005). Unraveling our beginnings. *The Psychologist, 18*(8), 474–477.

Labor. (2002). In *Medterms online medical dictionary*. Retrieved February 12, 2007, from http://www.medterms.com/script/main/art.asp?articlekey=6194

Nijhuis, J. G. (Ed.). (1992). *Fetal behaviour: Developmental and perinatal aspects.* Oxford, England: Oxford University Press.

Obstetrician. (1997). In *Online medical dictionary*. Retrieved April 7, 2007, from http://cancerweb.ncl.ac.uk/cgi-bin/omd?obstetrician

Obstetrics. (1997). In *Online medical dictionary*. Retrieved April 7, 2007, from http://cancerweb.ncl.ac.uk/cgi-bin/omd?obstetrics

Oxytocin. (n.d.). In *The Columbia electronic encyclopedia* (6th ed.). Retrieved November 12, 2007, from http://www.answers.com/topic/oxytocin

Perinatal. (1998). In *Medterms online medical dictionary*. Retrieved February 12, 2007, from http://www.medterms.com/script/main/art.asp?articlekey=7898

Piontelli, A. (1992). *From fetus to child: An observational and psychoanalytic study.* New York: Tavistock/Routledge.

Piontelli, A. (2002). *Twins: From fetus to child.* New York: Routledge.

Prenatal. (2000). In *Medterms online medical dictionary*. Retrieved February 12, 2007, from http://www.medterms.com/script/main/art.asp?articlekey=10694

Ross, M. G., Beall, M. H., & Bonni, A. (2007). *Forceps delivery.* Retrieved February 11, 2007, from http://www.emedicine.com/med/topic3284.htm

Appendix C: Survey

	Survey Items
	MAIN SURVEY
	Sensory Processing
1.	My child is easily distressed by/reacts to one or more of the following: light, sound, touch/texture: Never ☐ ☐ ☐ ☐ ☐ ☐ Always
2.	My child is easily distressed by/reacts to one or more of the following: food textures, smells, sensations: Never ☐ ☐ ☐ ☐ ☐ ☐ Always
	Vestibular:
3.	As an infant, my child was hypersensitive to movement or position changes (e.g., if she/he fell asleep in your arms she/he would cry when moved or put down): Never ☐ ☐ ☐ ☐ ☐ ☐ Always
4.	As a baby, my child protested strongly (screamed, cried or stiffened) when thrown or lifted up in the air, or when being tipped or held at certain angles or positions: Never ☐ ☐ ☐ ☐ ☐ ☐ Always
	Tactile (Proprioceptive):
5.	My child craves firm pressure and intense contact (crashing, tumbling, bear-hugs, being in a "sandwich"): Never ☐ ☐ ☐ ☐ ☐ ☐ Always
6.	My child loves to cuddle and show affection to others: Never ☐ ☐ ☐ ☐ ☐ ☐ Always
7.	My child resists holding and contact: Never ☐ ☐ ☐ ☐ ☐ ☐ Always
	Coordination/Motor Skills: ***In relationship to self***
8.	My child had or has problems with coordinating his/her body movements (e.g., crawling on belly, creeping on hands and knees cross-laterally [left arm/right leg; right arm/left leg], walking, running, climbing): Never ☐ ☐ ☐ ☐ ☐ ☐ Always
9.	My child has trouble with puzzles and putting things together:

	Never ☐ ☐ ☐ ☐ ☐ ☐ Always
	In relationship to others
10.	My child appears clumsy and tends to bump into objects and people: Never ☐ ☐ ☐ ☐ ☐ ☐ Always
	Affect/Emotion/Mood Regulation ***Emotional Reactivity:***
11.	My child reacts intensely(startling, crying, yelling, hitting, retreating) to many things: Never ☐ ☐ ☐ ☐ ☐ ☐ Always
12.	My child is easily overwhelmed: Never ☐ ☐ ☐ ☐ ☐ ☐ Always
13.	When my child gets upset, it's difficult to help him/her calm down: Never ☐ ☐ ☐ ☐ ☐ ☐ Always
14.	My child's moods shift quickly from one extreme to another: Never ☐ ☐ ☐ ☐ ☐ ☐ Always
15.	My child gets easily irritated/upset if not responded to immediately: Never ☐ ☐ ☐ ☐ ☐ ☐ Always
	Self-esteem:
16.	My child tends to be confident and happy: Never ☐ ☐ ☐ ☐ ☐ ☐ Always
17.	My child handles frustration and changes well: Never ☐ ☐ ☐ ☐ ☐ ☐ Always
	ANS Regulation ***Hyperactivity/Activity Level:***
18.	My child is constantly in motion: Never ☐ ☐ ☐ ☐ ☐ ☐ Always
19.	My child has/has had a pattern of self-harming behaviors: Never ☐ ☐ ☐ ☐ ☐ ☐ Always
20.	My child is aggressive (biting, kicking, hitting, pushing): Never ☐ ☐ ☐ ☐ ☐ ☐ Always
	Distractibility/Focusing:
21.	My child can focus on something that interests her/him for a long time: Never ☐ ☐ ☐ ☐ ☐ ☐ Always

22.	My child has attention and focusing problems only in specific types of situations or with certain types of triggers: Never ☐ ☐ ☐ ☐ ☐ ☐ Always
23.	My child is hyper and unable to focus under most circumstances: Disagree ☐ ☐ ☐ ☐ ☐ ☐ Agree
	Timing/Pacing/Tempo:
24.	My child has difficulty handling situations in which others are directing or setting the pace, e.g., "we have to go to school now": Never ☐ ☐ ☐ ☐ ☐ ☐ Always
25.	My child responds well to being allowed to self-pace within reasonable limits: Never ☐ ☐ ☐ ☐ ☐ ☐ Always
26.	My child seems out-of-sync. with me (too fast or too slow): Never ☐ ☐ ☐ ☐ ☐ ☐ Always
	Regulatory/Physiological Effects:
27.	As an infant, my child had ear infections: Never ☐ ☐ ☐ ☐ ☐ ☐ Always
28.	As an infant, my child was "colicky" or fussy and hard to soothe: Never ☐ ☐ ☐ ☐ ☐ ☐ Always
29.	My child has digestive problems (e.g., diarrhea, constipation, tummy ache complaints): Never ☐ ☐ ☐ ☐ ☐ ☐ Always
30.	My child is a fussy or "picky" eater: Never ☐ ☐ ☐ ☐ ☐ ☐ Always
31.	My child has problems with sleeping (falling asleep, staying asleep, or waking) at night: Never ☐ ☐ ☐ ☐ ☐ ☐ Always Describe any sleeping problem(s): _____
	Interpersonal Dynamics **Responses to Structure/Support:**
32.	My child is timid or tentative: Never ☐ ☐ ☐ ☐ ☐ ☐ Always
33.	My child has difficulty in structured settings in which others are in control of timing and transitions: Never ☐ ☐ ☐ ☐ ☐ ☐ Always
34.	My child resists receiving help from others:

	Never ☐ ☐ ☐ ☐ ☐ ☐ Always
35.	My child strongly resists pressure, directions, being hurried: Never ☐ ☐ ☐ ☐ ☐ ☐ Always
36.	When given directions or a demand is made on her/him, my child reacts strongly (e.g., protest, resistance, glazed eyes, "freezes", tears): Never ☐ ☐ ☐ ☐ ☐ ☐ Always
37.	My child does what I ask him/her to do (e.g., coming to the table or helping to clean up toys when asked) without a huge struggle: Never ☐ ☐ ☐ ☐ ☐ ☐ Always
	Control/ Cooperation/ Leadership:
38.	I feel as though my child is the one in charge in our family: Never ☐ ☐ ☐ ☐ ☐ ☐ Always
39.	When things don't go his/her way, my child gets extremely upset (screaming, hitting, pushing, biting): Never ☐ ☐ ☐ ☐ ☐ ☐ Always
40.	In his/her relationships with others my child tends to let others lead and is more of a follower: Never ☐ ☐ ☐ ☐ ☐ ☐ Always
41.	My child has a strong need to be in control: Never ☐ ☐ ☐ ☐ ☐ ☐ Always
42.	My child dominates other children: Never ☐ ☐ ☐ ☐ ☐ ☐ Always
43.	My child plays cooperatively with others: Never ☐ ☐ ☐ ☐ ☐ ☐ Always
	Recapitulations:
44.	My child plays games in which the theme is entrapping others or being trapped: Never ☐ ☐ ☐ ☐ ☐ ☐ Always
45.	My child plays games in which the theme is rescuing or being rescued: Never ☐ ☐ ☐ ☐ ☐ ☐ Always
	Boundaries (interpersonal):
46.	My child is sensitive to any type of intrusion into his/her physical or mental space: Never ☐ ☐ ☐ ☐ ☐ ☐ Always
47.	My child is really good at communicating "yes" and "no" when he/she needs to:

	Never ☐ ☐ ☐ ☐ ☐ ☐ Always
48.	My child tends to be intrusive (is really "pushy") and doesn't seem to recognize appropriate boundaries with others: Never ☐ ☐ ☐ ☐ ☐ ☐ Always
	Mother's Experience of Relationship with Child:
49.	I feel as though I can never satisfy my child: Never ☐ ☐ ☐ ☐ ☐ ☐ Always
50.	I feel like I don't know how to connect with my child: Never ☐ ☐ ☐ ☐ ☐ ☐ Always
51.	When my child speeds up, it's hard to connect with him/her, it's like he/she is in his/her own world: Never ☐ ☐ ☐ ☐ ☐ ☐ Always
52.	I would describe my relationship with my child as easy and cooperative, with good rapport: Never ☐ ☐ ☐ ☐ ☐ ☐ Always
	Transitions ***Baby:***
53.	As an infant, my child had extreme emotional responses (cried, screamed, struggled, or shut down) to transitions, e.g., sudden shifts in position, attention, activity; diaper changes; baths; new places/people: Never ☐ ☐ ☐ ☐ ☐ ☐ Always
	Child:
54.	My child has difficulties orienting him/herself in new situations or places (looking around, noticing events, checking in with me): Never ☐ ☐ ☐ ☐ ☐ ☐ Always
55.	My child has difficulties with transitions (e.g., waking, going to sleep, dressing, new places, changing activities at preschool): Never ☐ ☐ ☐ ☐ ☐ ☐ Always
56.	When things change quickly or unexpectedly, my child reacts strongly (withdraws, cries, becomes aggressive): Never ☐ ☐ ☐ ☐ ☐ ☐ Always
57.	My child copes with transitions better if he/she is involved in how they happen and has some control over them: Never ☐ ☐ ☐ ☐ ☐ ☐ Always
	Sequencing ***Beginnings:***

58.	My child has problems with beginning tasks: Never ☐ ☐ ☐ ☐ ☐ ☐ Always
59.	My child procrastinates on starting things: Never ☐ ☐ ☐ ☐ ☐ ☐ Always
60.	My child has a tendency to rush from one thing to the next and rarely slows down: Never ☐ ☐ ☐ ☐ ☐ ☐ Always
61.	My child seeks help with starting things: Never ☐ ☐ ☐ ☐ ☐ ☐ Always
	Middles of Sequences:
62.	My child can get things started, but in the middle of something will become agitated or distracted, or lose focus: Never ☐ ☐ ☐ ☐ ☐ ☐ Always
	Endings:
63.	My child seeks help from others with finishing activities: Never ☐ ☐ ☐ ☐ ☐ ☐ Always
	CONTEXTUAL ITEMS **Pregnancy:**
64.	During your pregnancy with this child you experienced extreme stress: Never ☐ ☐ ☐ ☐ ☐ ☐ Always
65.	During your pregnancy with this child you felt well supported: Never ☐ ☐ ☐ ☐ ☐ ☐ Always
	Birth:
66.	Overall, you experienced the birth of this child as: Difficult ☐ ☐ ☐ ☐ ☐ ☐ Easy
67.	Reflecting on the birth, you feel mostly: Positive ☐ ☐ ☐ ☐ ☐ ☐ Negative
68.	There are aspects of this birth that are still troubling or unresolved to you: Disagree ☐ ☐ ☐ ☐ ☐ ☐ Agree
	Mother's Experience of the Birth Team
69.	During labor I felt that my birth team and I worked well together to meet both my needs and those of my baby: Agree ☐ ☐ ☐ ☐ ☐ ☐ Disagree

70.	Others took over control of my birth, leaving me feeling powerless and out of control: Agree ☐ ☐ ☐ ☐ ☐ ☐ Disagree
	Mother's Experience of Labor/Birth
71.	My experience of labor and delivery was more intense than I expected, but I could cope: Never ☐ ☐ ☐ ☐ ☐ ☐ Always
72.	During labor and delivery I felt overwhelmed, out of control, scared: Never ☐ ☐ ☐ ☐ ☐ ☐ Always
73.	My experience of labor and delivery was that it was excruciating, unbearable, far beyond my coping ability: Never ☐ ☐ ☐ ☐ ☐ ☐ Always
	Mother's Experience of her Relationship with Baby Before and During Birth
74.	I feel that during my pregnancy with this child I developed a strong relationship with him/her: Agree ☐ ☐ ☐ ☐ ☐ ☐ Disagree
75.	Before and during the birth I felt aware of/connected to my baby: Always ☐ ☐ ☐ ☐ ☐ ☐ Never
76.	Given my own experience, I now wonder if during labor my baby may have felt disconnected from me, overwhelmed, unable to cope, in pain, frightened, traumatized: Never ☐ ☐ ☐ ☐ ☐ ☐ Always
77.	In retrospect, I believe that any intervention(s) that took place during my child's birth were medically necessary: Agree ☐ ☐ ☐ ☐ ☐ ☐ Disagree
	Birth Interventions
78.	Your labor began: ☐ Spontaneously ☐ With intravenous Pitocin ☐ With the help of something other than Pitocin (Cervidil, Cytotec, castor oil, herbs, sex, nipple stimulation, etc.)
79.	During your labor you had (select one): ☐ No IV (intravenous line in your arm or hand) ☐ An IV providing intravenous fluids ☐ A "heplock" (intravenous line "just in case", but no intravenous fluids throughout labor ☐ Other (describe) _____
80.	Was Pitocin used at any time during your labor?

	☐ Yes	
	☐ No	
	☐ Don't Know/Not Sure	
81.	If Pitocin was used, when was it used?	
	☐ To get labor started	
	☐ Early or in the middle of labor	
	☐ Late in labor	
	☐ Throughout labor	
	☐ Don't remember	
82.	In retrospect, do you feel satisfied with the decision to use Pitocin:	
	☐ Yes	
	☐ No	
	☐ Not sure/Don't know	
83.	The effect of Pitocin on your labor was helpful:	
	Agree ☐ ☐ ☐ ☐ ☐ ☐ Disagree	
84.	You experienced Pitocin-induced contractions as stressful or overwhelming:	
	Agree ☐ ☐ ☐ ☐ ☐ ☐ Disagree	
85.	In retrospect, do you believe that your consent for Pitocin was fully informed regarding both the benefits and risks of its use?	
	☐ Yes	
	☐ No	
	☐ Not sure/Don't know	
86.	Did you have medication for pain?	
	☐ Yes	
	☐ No	
	☐ Not sure/Don't know	
87.	Did you have anesthesia?	
	☐ Yes	
	☐ No	
	☐ Not sure/Don't know	
88.	Did you have an epidural?	
	☐ Yes	
	☐ No	

	Not sure/Don't know ☐
89.	If you had an epidural (combination pain medication and anesthetic by catheter into your back) was started: ☐ Early in labor ☐ Towards the middle of labor ☐ Towards the end (within 2 hours of birth) ☐ Throughout labor ☐ I'm not sure when it was used but I know that it was used during my labor
	Postpartum
90.	Your baby was with you for most or all of the hour following the birth: Agree ☐ ☐ ☐ ☐ ☐ ☐ Disagree
91.	Your baby was with you for most or all of the day following the birth: Agree ☐ ☐ ☐ ☐ ☐ ☐ Disagree
92.	In the day following the birth, the baby's father was present most or all of the time: Agree ☐ ☐ ☐ ☐ ☐ ☐ Disagree
93.	The baby's father was/has been involved with you and the baby in a positive and supportive way during the child's life to date: Agree ☐ ☐ ☐ ☐ ☐ ☐ Disagree
94.	During the first 6 months your baby was: ☐ Fed entirely at the breast ☐ Fed entirely by bottle ☐ Fed with combination of breast and bottle ☐ Other (describe) _____
	Demographic Items
95.	Your 3-year-old is a ☐ girl ☐ boy
96.	Your current age:
97.	Child's father's current age:
98.	Your current level of education is: ☐ Less than High School ☐ High School/GED ☐ Some College ☐ 2-year College Degree ☐ Four-year College Degree

	☐ Master's Degree
	☐ Doctoral Degree
	☐ Professional Degree (JD, MD)
99.	Father's current level of education is:
	☐ Less than High School
	☐ High School/GED
	☐ Some College
	☐ 2-year College Degree
	☐ Four-year College Degree
	☐ Master's Degree
	☐ Doctoral Degree
	☐ Professional Degree (JD, MD)

Appendix D: Informed Consent Page

Santa Barbara Graduate Institute

Claire L. Winstone

INFORMED CONSENT

The Behaviors of Three-year-olds Through the Eyes of their Mothers

You are being asked to participate in a research study. This page provides you with information about the study. Please read the information below before deciding whether or not to take part.

The purpose of this study is to gain a better understanding of the behaviors of 3-year-olds as perceived by their mothers.

Eligibility

You are eligible to participate in this study if:

1. You were over 18 at the time of giving birth to this child (Currently 36-47 months of age).

2. Your baby was born vaginally (not by cesarean) in an American hospital.

3. You did not lose a baby (miscarriage/abortion/stillbirth) prior to this child.

4. You did not use street drugs or alcohol following confirmation of the pregnancy.

5. Your child was not born prematurely (under 37 weeks) and/or low birth weight (i.e., less than 5 pounds 8 ounces)

6. There were no significant medical complications for mother or baby.

7. You were in relationship with the father of this child at the time of his/her birth and are still in relationship with him.

Time Commitment: If you agree to be in this study, you will be asked to complete a survey. It should take you approximately 20-30 minutes to complete it.

You may complete the questionnaire all in one sitting, or you may fill it out at different times within a 5-day period. If you exit the survey before finishing it and then open it at a later time, you will be brought to the question where you left off. You will not be able to go back and change your answers once you have completed a page.

<u>Voluntary Participation</u>: Your participation is voluntary. You can stop your participation at any time without penalty. Only those who complete the entire survey will be eligible to win one of two $25.00 gift certificates to Amazon.com and several annual subscriptions to *Pathways* family wellness magazine.

<u>Anonymity, Confidentiality and Privacy Protection</u>:

- I have designed the survey in collaboration with Qualtrics, the site that is hosting the questionnaire, so that your e-mail address is not connected to your responses. There will be no way for me or anyone else to identify who gave a particular response. While any form of communication via the Internet carries a minimal risk of loss of confidentiality, all of the information gathered in this study is intended to be completely anonymous.

- Any publication related to the data will show and discuss the statistical analysis of the results and will never discuss individual examples.

- If you choose to have a summary sent to your e-mail address that information will be stored securely and kept confidential. Authorized persons from Santa Barbara Graduate Institute and members of the Institutional Review Board have the legal right to review these research records and will protect the confidentiality of those records to the extent permitted by law.

<u>Benefits</u>: There are a number of benefits to participating in the study. Participants may find it helpful to review their experiences as they respond to the survey items and may gain valuable new perspectives on their own family dynamics. Some of the results may be published in professional journals and publications in order to serve as a stepping stone for further research in service of children and families. The study will add to the body of knowledge in the field of psychology. It may help parents increase their understanding of family dynamics and explore new ways of parenting.

If you have completed all items on the survey and have provided an e-mail address at the end, you may choose to receive a summary of the findings. Your e-mail address will be entered into a drawing for one of two $25 gift certificates for www.amazon.com and one of several annual subscriptions to *Pathways* family wellness magazine as a gesture of appreciation for your participation in the study.

<u>Risks</u>: There are no known physical risks associated with participating in this research. However, some women may experience mental or emotional discomfort such as sadness, fear, anxiety, depression, loss of self-esteem, shame, guilt, embarrassment, and so forth, when contemplating their responses to survey items. If completing the survey elicits strong concerns or feelings and you would like to talk to a licensed therapist, please feel free to contact me (Claire Winstone: see below) and I will provide you with the names of qualified counselors in your area.

<u>Contact Information</u>: You may also contact me with questions or queries about the project at 661-251-9311 or e-mail me at cwinstone@sbgi.edu. You may register any complaint you may have about the project with Jill Kern, Director of Research, by mail (Santa Barbara Graduate Institute, 525 Micheltorena, Suite 205, Santa Barbara, CA. 93103), by phone (805 963-6896 ext. 106), or by e-mail (<u>jkern@sbgi.edu</u>).

<u>Thank You</u>: As an expression of my appreciation, you will be entered in a drawing for one of two $25.00 gift certificates for Amazon.com and several annual subscriptions to *Pathways* family wellness magazine. In addition, you may choose to receive a summary of key findings from the survey.

Once again, thank you for your participation.

<u>Statement of Consent</u>: If you choose to click on the ">>" button, you are affirming that you have (a) read this page describing what is involved in participating in this study and what potential benefits and risks of participating in this research exist; that you have (b) taken the time to consider the information provided; and that you have (c) voluntarily agreed to participate in the project.

Clicking the ">>" button will take you to the beginning of the survey. Please complete all items in the survey and provide an e-mail address (requested at the end of the survey) if you wish to receive a summary of the findings when the research is complete, and to be entered into the drawing for the gifts described above.

Appendix E: End of Survey Pages

Thank you so much for participating in this survey. I hope that you found it interesting and perhaps gained some new perspectives on your child and your family dynamics.

If you enter your e-mail address in the box provided below, you will be entered into a drawing for one of two $25.00 gift certificates for Amazon.com or one of eight annual subscriptions to *Pathways* family wellness magazine in appreciation for your time and contribution to my research.

Please enter me into the drawing for $25.00 Amazon.com gift certificates and annual subscriptions to *Pathways* magazine.

My e-mail address is: _____

If you would like to be e-mailed a summary of the findings of this research, please click on the circle below.

☐ Yes, I would like to receive a summary of the findings of this study.

If any questions, concerns or strong feelings arise for you either as a result of completing this survey or of reading the summary of findings when you receive it, you are welcome to contact me (Claire Winstone: 661-251-9311; cwinstone@sbgi.edu) to discuss these or to receive contact information for qualified counselors in your area. You may register any complaint you may have about the project with Jill Kern, Director of Research, by mail (Santa Barbara Graduate Institute, 525 Micheltorena, Suite 205, Santa Barbara, CA. 93103), by phone (805 963-6896 ext. 106), or by e-mail (jkern@sbgi.edu).

Appendix F: Invitations to Participate

ASKING THE EXPERTS: MOMS! (V-1)

WHAT IS THIS ABOUT?

Since mothers are the greatest experts in their children, I am sending you this invitation to participate in a study about the behaviors, emotions, coping skills and interactions with others that you see in your 3-year-old child.

WHY SHOULD YOU PARTICIPATE?

1. You will receive a summary of the findings about how children cope in certain situations.

2. Everyone who completes the entire survey will have a chance to win one of two $25.00 gift certificates to Amazon.com or one of several annual subscriptions to *Pathways* family wellness magazine.

3. You will be making a contribution towards expanding our understanding of young children.

4. I hope you will find the survey questions interesting and thought-provoking.

5. You may learn something new as a parent through your participation.

CAN ANY MOTHER OF A 3-YEAR-OLD PARTICIPATE?

If you are (or someone you know is), the mother of a 3-year-old and meet the following criteria:

1. Over 18 at the time of giving birth to this child (Currently 36-47 months of age).

2. Baby was born vaginally (not by cesarean) in an American hospital.

3. Did not lose a baby (miscarriage/abortion/stillbirth) prior to this child.

4. Mother did not use street drugs or alcohol following confirmation of the pregnancy.

5. Child was not born prematurely (under 37 weeks) and/or low birth weight (i.e., less than 5 pounds 8 ounces)

6. There were no significant medical complications for mother or baby.

7. Mother was in relationship with the father of this child at the time of his/her birth and is still in relationship with him.

HOW LONG WILL IT TAKE?

The survey will run for 2 weeks. It should take you about 20-30 minutes to complete.

WHAT DO I DO?

Click on the following link or copy and paste it into your browser. Before beginning the survey you will be provided with an informed consent page giving more details about your participation in the study.

[link to survey]

DO YOU KNOW OTHERS WHO MIGHT BE INTERESTED IN LEARNING MORE ABOUT THEIR 3-YEAR OLD?

The more participants there are, the more reliable and valuable the results will be. I would very much appreciate it if you would forward this invitation today to other mothers of 3-year-olds who you think might be interested in participating, and/or to bulletin boards and mailing lists you subscribe to in which mothers of young children participate.

Thank you in advance for helping me with my research. If you have more questions about my project, please feel free to e-mail me at cwinstone@sbgi.edu.

Claire L. Winstone, M.A., Ph.D.(c)
Santa Barbara Graduate Institute

WHAT MAKES YOUR 3-YEAR-OLD UNIQUE? (V-2)

As a mom, you're the expert on your child, and today your expertise can make a unique contribution to increasing our understanding of what makes 3-year-olds the way they are, while you have an opportunity to look at your child through different eyes, which can be both enlightening and helpful in day-to-day parenting.

You are invited to participate in a doctoral research study that will allow you to do just that, and later to receive a summary of the results that may provide further insights into your child and family dynamics. You may also win one of two $25.00 Amazon.com gift certificates or one of several annual subscriptions to *Pathways* family wellness magazine as an expression of appreciation for your participation.

WHO CAN PARTICIPATE?

Mothers of 3-year-olds who meet the following criteria:

1. You were over 18 at the time of giving birth to this child (Currently 36-47 months of age).

2. Your baby was born vaginally (not by cesarean) in an American hospital.

3. You did not lose a baby (miscarriage/abortion/stillbirth) immediately prior to your pregnancy with this child.

4. You did not use street drugs or alcohol following confirmation of the pregnancy.

5. Your child was not born prematurely (under 37 weeks) and/or low birth weight (i.e., less than 5 pounds 8 ounces)

6. There were no significant medical complications for you or your baby.

7. You were in relationship with the father of this child at the time of his/her birth and are still in relationship with him.

WHAT DO I DO?

If you meet the criteria above, just click on the link below or copy and paste it into your browser. Before beginning the survey you will be provided with an informed consent page giving more details about your participation in the study.

[link to survey]

HOW LONG WILL IT TAKE?

The survey will should take you about 20-30 minutes to complete. It will run for 2 weeks.

DO YOU KNOW OTHER MOMS WHO MIGHT BE INTERESTED IN LEARNING MORE ABOUT THEIR 3-YEAR OLD?

Please forward this invitation to other mothers, mailing lists and message boards: the more participants, the more reliable and valuable the results of the research.

Thank you in advance for helping me with my research. If you have more questions about my project, please feel free to e-mail me at cwinstone@sbgi.edu.

Claire L. Winstone, M.A., Ph.D.(c)

Santa Barbara Graduate Institute

Appendix G: Dissemination of Survey Invitations

E-mail Lists:

doula
rmamidwives
rmamidwives2
aTLC
toddlertime2
mother-and-baby
toddler-Activities
homeschooling_Toddlers
SCVdoulas
tinytoddlers

parentsgalore
mother-and-baby
dramamama
momsofbabiesandtoddlers
youngparentsunite
yourBabyandToddler
momshideout
mommytomommy
mommyneighborhood

Web site Forums:

About: Development forum: parenting
Mothering.com
iParenting Media
MOPS (Mothers of Preschoolers)
BabyCenter
ParentCenter
iVillage

Professional Mailing Lists:

ICARE (LA County Dept. of Mental Health)
Connie Lillas: Infant Mental Health Training list
Family Wellness First (bulletin of www.icpa.org: International Chiropractic Pediatric Association)
Mothering Magazine: This Week at Mothering.com bulletin
California First 5 Association

Web sites:

http://www.ccrcla.org/home Childcare Resource Center

www.kidswork.biz

www.Mothering.com

My gratitude and sincere apologies to anyone who forwarded the invitation to others, as requested, or placed the invitation on their Web site, who has not been identified here.

Appendix H: Responses to Survey Item on Labor

During your labor you had (select one) (these respondents selected "Other (describe)":

- epidural
- IV antibiotics for group B strep
- pitocin, & magnesium sulfate intravenously
- the IV was connected twice to deliver antibiotics
- Epidural
- heplock then IV halfway through
- dont remember
- Heplock for IV antibiotics for GBS+, but nothing else went in the line
- baby-heart-beat monitor
- epidural because it became necissary when labor stopped
- started with none, added heplock when complications started to arise, evenutally had pitocin - but no fluids
- IV w/fluids, & pitocin
- Pitocin and heplock
- Epidural
- epidural
- episiotomy
- nothing at all.
- Epidural
- IV with antibiotic for strep
- antibiotics for Strep B
- An IV with Pitocin after 15 hrs. of labor
- unmedicated natural birth
- an IV toward the end of labor to prepare for possibility of medical intervention (due to extended labor on day 3)
- pitocin
- IV antibiotics for 20 minutes
- IV with antibiotics
- the last hour I had an IV in my hand, put in while I was pushing
- iv fluids pitocin and antibiotics
- none
- IV antibiotics due to my miltral valve prolapse
- electronic fetal monitoring
- nothing
- pitocin
- antibiotic for gbs, with heplock afterward
- a band around my stomach to hold down the fetal monitor and contraction monitors

Appendix I: Responses to Survey Item on Early Feeding

During first 6 months your baby was fed (these respondents selected "Other (describe)":

- Breastfed, at 4 months started solid food against my better judgement
- breastfed, & expressed bm via bottle
- for first 2 weeks bottle and breast and the entirely on breast
- Couldn't latch on, used a paper cup 50% of the time
- Fed with combination of breast and bottle (pumped milk) when I went back to work.
- breast milk only--breast and bottle
- breast, & bottle but only had breastmilk
- nursed while at home and given pumped breastmilk while I was at work
- breastmilk via bottle at daycare after 10 weeks
- breastfed and EBM in bottle
- Exclusive breast milk, some by bottle
- Breast for 4 weeks, then bottle
- exclusive breast when I was home, breastmilk in a bottle given by her father when I worked
- breastmilk from bottle, no latch, then goats milk from bottle
- I was unable to get my baby to latch on (tied-tongue, no support) so I pumped milk and gave formula. It broke my heart.
- Breast and breast milk via bottle, solids at about 4.5 mos
- Combo breast/bottle- but BM only, no formula- only bottle when I was at work.
- Breast and pumped breast milk in a bottle
- first breast then bottle
- breast exclusively until 4 months
- primarily breastfed, supplemented with formula for 2 months due to poor weight gain
- breast and some solids at 4-6 months

Appendix J: Polyvagal Theory Diagram

Jackson's Theory of Dissolution

"The higher nervous system arrangements inhibit (or control) the lower, and thus, when the higher are suddenly rendered functionless, the lower rise in activity."

–John Hughlings Jackson (1835-1911)
Father of English Neurology
Quoted by Stephen Porges 11/01

Parasympathetic

"Voodoo Death"

Alarm

Catatonia

Disassociation

Immobility

Rest

Sympathetic

Discharge

Freeze

Fight/Flight

Alarm

Orient

Mob Action

Contact

Group Psychology

Group Action

Social

Teamwork, Group Action

Love, empathy, comfort

Communication

We play our newest, best card first, if that doesn't work (or has not worked in the past as determined by the amygdala), we try our older, second card. If that doesn't work, we play our oldest, last card. If that doesn't work we are in extreme danger of death.

Slide prepared by John Chitty, Colorado School of Energy Studies, www.energyschool.com

Diagram from *Triune Autonomic Nervous System: Experimental Applications based on Craniosacral Therapy* by J. Chitty, 2002

References

Alexander, J. M., McIntire, D. D., & Leveno, K. J. (2000). Forty weeks and beyond: Pregnancy outcomes by week of gestation. *Obstetrics & Gynecology, 96*(2), 291–294.

Alfirevic, Z., Devane, D., & Gyte, G. M. (2006). Continuous cardiotocography (CTG) as a form of electronic fetal monitoring (EFM) for fetal assessment during labour. *Cochrane Database of Systematic Reviews, 3*(CD006066).

Als, H., Tronick, E., Lester, B. M., & Brazelton, T. B. (1977). The Brazelton Neonatal Behavior Assessment Scale (BNBAS). *Journal of Abnormal Child Psychology, 5*(3), 215–231.

American College of Obstetricians and Gynecologists. (1999, November). Induction of labor. *ACOG Practice Bulletin, 10.* Washington, DC: Author. Excerpt retrieved September 1, 2002, from http://www.medem.com

American College of Obstetricians and Gynecologists. (2004, July). Vaginal birth after previous cesarean delivery. *ACOG Practice Bulletin, 54.* Washington, DC: Author. Summary retrieved December 27, 2006, from http://www.guideline.gov/ summary/summary.aspx?doc_id=6374

Appleby, L. (1998). Violent suicide and obstetric complications: The link is mental illness [Editorial]. *British Medical Journal, 317*(7169), 1333–1334.

Arms, S. (1997). *Immaculate deception II: Myth, magic and birth.* Berkeley, CA: Celestial Arts.

Bakan, P., & Peterson, K. (1994). Pregnancy and birth complications: A risk factor for schizotypy. *Journal of Personality Disorders, 8*(4), 299–306.

Bales, K. L., Abdelnabi, M., Cushing, B. S., Ottinger, M. A., & Carter, C. S. (2004). Effects of neonatal oxytocin manipulations on male reproductive potential in prairie voles. *Physiology and Behavior, 81*(3), 519–526.

Bales, K. L., & Carter, C. S. (2003a). Developmental exposure to oxytocin facilitates partner preferences in male prairie voles (*Microtus ochrogaster*). *Behavioral Neuroscience, 117*(4), 854–859.

Bales, K. L., & Carter, C. S. (2003b). Sex differences and developmental effects of oxytocin on aggression and social behavior in prairie voles (*Microtus ochrogaster*). *Hormones and Behavior, 44*(3), 178-184.

Bales, K. L., Kim, A. J., Lewis-Reese, A. D., & Carter, C. S. (2004). Both oxytocin and vasopressin may influence alloparental behavior in male prairie voles. *Hormones and Behavior, 45*(5), 354–361.

Bales, K. L., Pfeifer, L. A., & Carter, C. S. (2004). Sex differences and developmental effects of manipulations of oxytocin on alloparenting and anxiety in prairie voles. *Developmental Psychobiology, 44*(2), 123–131.

Bales, K. L., Plotsky, P. M., Young, L. J., Lim, M. M., Grotte, N., Ferrer, E., et al. (2007). Neonatal oxytocin manipulations have long-lasting, sexually dimorphic effects on vasopressin receptors. *Neuroscience, 144*(1), 38–45.

Baumgarder, D. J., Muehl, P., Fischer, M., & Pribbenow, B. (2003). Effect of labor epidural anesthesia on breast-feeding of healthy full-term newborns delivered vaginally. *The Journal of the American Board of Family Practice, 16*(1), 7–13.

Black, B. P., & McBride, W. G. (1979). Children born after elective induction of labor. *Medical Journal of Australia, 2*(7), 362–363.

Blasco, T. M. A. (2007). Prenatal and perinatal memories and imprints in preverbal children: Clinical observations using videotape examination. *Journal of Prenatal and Perinatal Psychology and Health, 22*(1), 33–55.

Block, J. (2007). *Pushed: The painful truth about childbirth and modern maternity care.* Cambridge, MA: Da Capo Lifelong Books.

Bloom, S. L., Spong, C. Y., Thom, E., Varner, M. W., Rouse., D. J., Weininger, S., et al. (2006). Fetal pulse oximetry and cesarean delivery. *New England Journal of Medicine, 355*(21), 2192–2202.

Bolte, A., Breuker, K. H., Haase, W., & Stille, J. (1976). Advantages and disadvantages of deliveries after induction of labour by convenience. *Geburtshilfe und Frauenheilkunde, 36*(3), 220–237. Abstract retrieved from MEDLINE database.

Brazelton, T. B. (1984). *Neonatal Behavioral Assessment Scale.* London: Blackwell.

Brumbaugh, C. G. (1922). The present standard of obstetrical practice in rural Pennsylvania. *Pennsylvania Medical Journal, 26,* 283–284.

Buckley, S. J. (2005). *Gentle birth, gentle mothering: The wisdom and science of gentle choices in pregnancy, birth, and parenting.* Brisbane, Australia: One Moon.

Buckley, S. J. (2007). *Hormonal physiology of childbirth.* Manuscript in preparation.

Cabrera, N., Shannon, J., & Tamis-LeMonda, C. (2007). Fathers' influence on their children's cognitive and emotional development: From toddlers to pre-K. *Applied Developmental Science, 11*(4), 208–213.

Cahill, D. J., Boylan, P. C., & O'Herlihy, C. (1992). Does oxytocin augmentation increase perinatal risk in primigravid labor? *American Journal of Obstetrics and Gynecology, 166*(3), 847-850. Abstract retrieved from MEDLINE database.

Cammu, H., Marten, G., Ruyssinck, G., & Amy, J. J. (2002). Outcome after elective labor induction in nulliparous women: A matched cohort study. *American Journal of Obstetrics and Gynecology, 186*(2), 240–244.

Carter, C. S. (1998). Neuroendocrine perspectives on social attachment and love. *Psychoneuroendocrinology, 23*(8), 779–818.

Carter, C. S., Harris, J., & Porges, S. W. (2007). *Neural and evolutionary perspectives on empathy.* Unpublished manuscript.

Cartwright, A. (1977). Mothers' experiences of induction. *British Medical Journal, 2*(6089), 745–749.

Casella, G., & Berger, R. L. (2002). *Statistical inference* (2nd ed.). Pacific Grove, CA: Thompson Learning.

Cassidy, T. (2006a). *Birth: The surprising history of how we are born.* New York: Atlantic Monthly.

Cassidy, T. (2006b). *The mommy uprising*. Retrieved December 28, 2006, from http://www.bostonmagazine.com/articles/the_mommy_uprising

Castellino, R., Takikawa, D., & Wood, S. (1997). *The caregiver's role in birth and newborn self-attachment needs.* Santa Barbara, CA: Castellino Training. (Available from Castellino Training, 1105 N. Ontare Rd., Santa Barbara, CA 93105)

Chamberlain, D. B. (1998). *The mind of your newborn baby* (3rd ed.). Berkeley, CA: North Atlantic.

Chamberlain, D. B. (1999). Obstetrics and the prenatal psyche. *Journal of Prenatal and Perinatal Psychology and Health, 14*(1/2), 97–118.

Cheek, D. (1986). Prenatal and perinatal imprints: Apparent prenatal consciousness as revealed by hypnosis. *Journal of Prenatal and Perinatal Psychology and Health, 1*(2), 97–110.

Chitty, J. (2001). *Polyvagal theory, the triune autonomic nervous system, and therapeutic applications.* Retrieved July 30, 2007, from http://www.energyschool.com/ writings

Claycomb, C. D., Ryan, J. J., Miller, L. J., & Schnakenberg-Ott, S. D. (2004). Relationships among attention deficit hyperactivity disorder, induced labor, and selected physiological and demographic variables. *Journal of Clinical Psychology, 60*(6), 689–693.

Cohen, J. (1988). *Statistical power analysis for the behavioral sciences* (2nd ed.). New York: New York University Press.

Corry, M. (2004). Recommendations from Listening to Mothers: The first national U.S. survey of women's childbearing experiences. *Birth: Issues in Perinatal Care, 31*(1), 61–65.

Crost, M., & Kaminski, M. (1998). Breast feeding at maternity hospitals in France in 1995. National perinatal survey. *Archives of Pediatrics, 5*(12), 1316–1326. Abstract retrieved from MEDLINE database.

Crowell, D. H., Sharma, S. D., Philip, A. G., Kapuniai. L. E., Waxman, S. H., & Hale, R. W. (1980). Effects of induction of labor on the neurophysiologic functioning of newborn infants. *American Journal of Obstetrics & Gynecology, 136*(1), 48–53.

Csaba, G. (1980). Phylogeny and ontogeny of hormone receptors: the selection theory of receptor formation and hormonal imprinting. *Biological reviews of the Cambridge Philosophical Society., 55*(1), 47-63.

Csaba, G. (2008). Hormonal imprinting: Phylogeny, ontogeny, diseases and possible role in present-day human evolution. *Cell Biochemistry and Function, 26*(1), 1–10.

Csaba, G., Knippel, B., Karabélyos, C., Inczefi-Gonda, A., Hantos, M., & Tekes, K. (2004). Endorphin excess at weaning durably influences sexual activity, uterine estrogen receptor's binding capacity and brain serotonin level of female rats. *Hormone and Metabolic Research, 36*(1), 39–43. Abstract retrieved from MEDLINE database.

Cushing, B. S., & Carter, C. S. (2000). Peripheral pulses of oxytocin increase partner preferences in female, but not male, prairie voles. *Hormones and Behavior, 37*(1), 40–56.

Davis-Floyd, R. (1992). *Birth as an American rite of passage.* Berkeley, CA: University of California Press.

Dawood, M. Y., Wang., C. F., Gupta, R., & Fuchs, F. (1978). Fetal contribution to oxytocin in human labor. *Obstetrics and Gynecology, 52*(2), 205–209. Abstract retrieved from MEDLINE database.

Dean, R. S., Gray, J. W., & Anderson, J. L. (1996). Underlying factor structure of perinatal events. *International Journal of Neuroscience, 84*(1–4), 55–63.

Declercq, E. R., Sakala, C., Corry, M. P., & Applebaum, S. (2006). *Listening to mothers II: Report of the second national U.S. survey of women's childbearing experiences.* New York: Childbirth Connection.

Declercq, E. R., Sakala, C., Corry, M. P., Applebaum, S., & Risher, P. (2002). *Listening to mothers: Report of the first national U.S. survey of women's childbearing experiences.* New York: Maternity Center Association.

DeGangi, G. A., Breinbauer, C., Doussard-Roosevelt, J., Porges, S., & Greenspan, S. (2000). Prediction of childhood problems at three years in children experiencing disorders of regulation during infancy. *Infant Mental Health Journal, 21*(3), 156–175.

DeLee, J. B. (1921). The prophylactic forceps operation. *American Journal of Obstetrics and Gynecology, 1,* 34–44.

DiGirolamo, A. M., Grummer-Strawn, L. M., & Fein, S. (2001). Maternity care practices: Implications for breastfeeding. *Birth, 28*(2), 94–100.

Doussard-Roosevelt, J. A., Montgomery, L. A., & Porges, S. W. (2003). Short-term stability of physiological measures in kindergarten children: Respiratory sinus arrhythmia, heart period, and cortisol. *Developmental Psychobiology, 43*(3), 230–242.

D'Souza, S. W., Lieberman, B., Cadman, J., & Richards, B. (1986). Oxytocin induction of labor: Hyponatraemia and neonatal jaundice. *European Journal of Obstetrics, Gynecology, and Reproductive Biology, 22*(5/6), 309–317.

Eisenberg, N. (1997, April). *Emotion-related regulation.* Paper presented at the biennial meeting for the Society for Research in Child Development, Washington, DC.

Eishima, K. (1992). The effects of obstetric conditions on neonatal behavior in Japanese infants. *Early Human Development, 28*(3), 253–263.

Ekman, G., Granstrom, L., & Ulmsten, U. (1986). Induction of labor with intravenous oxytocin or vaginal PGE2 suppositories. A randomized study. *Acta Obstetricia et Gynecologica Scandinavica, 65*(8), 857-859.

Emerson, W. R. (1998). Birth trauma: The psychological effects of obstetrical interventions. *Journal of Prenatal and Perinatal Psychology and Health, 13*(1), 11–44.

Enkin, M., Keirse, J. N. C., Neilson, J., Crowther, C., Duley L., Hodnett, E., et al., J. (2000). *A guide to effective care in pregnancy and childbirth.* New York: Oxford University Press.

Faraway, J. (2004). *Linear models with* R. Boca Raton, FL: Chapman & Hall.

Faraway, J. (2005). *Extending the linear model with* R: *Generalized linear, mixed effects and nonparametric regression models.* Boca Raton, FL: Chapman & Hall.

Fausett, M. B., Barth, W. H., Jr., Yoder, B. A., & Satin, A. J. (1997). Oxytocin labor stimulation of twin gestations: Effective and efficient. *Obstetrics and Gynecology 90*(2), 202–204.

Fedrick, J. (1974). Sudden unexpected death in infants in the Oxford Record Linkage area. *British Journal of Preventive & Social Medicine, 28*(3), 164–171.

Fein, D., Allen, D., Dunn, M., Feinstein, C., Green, L., Morris, R., et al. (1997). Pitocin induction and autism. *American Journal of Psychiatry, 154*(3), 438b–439b.

Fisher, R. A. (1922). On the interpretation of χ^2 from contingency tables, and the calculation of *P. Journal of the Royal Statistical Society, 85*(1), 87–94.

Flouri, E., & Buchanan, A. (2003). What predicts fathers' involvement with their children? A prospective study of intact families. *British Journal of Developmental Psychology, 21*(1), 81–97.

Friedman, E. A. (1955). Primigravid labor: A graphicostastistical analysis. *Obstetrics and Gynecology, 6*(6), 567-589.

Friedman, E. A., Sachtleben, M. R., & Wallace, A. K. (1979). Infant outcome following labor induction. *American Journal of Obstetrics and Gynecology, 133*(6), 718–722.

Fries, A. B., Ziegler, T. E., Kurian, J. R., Jacoris, S., & Pollak, S. D. (2005). Early experience in humans is associated with changes in neuropeptides critical for regulating social behavior. *Proceedings of the National Academy of Sciences of the United States of America, 102*, 17237–17240. Retrieved October 28, 2007, from http://www.pnas.org/cgi/content/full/102/47/17237

Fuchs, A. R., & Fuchs, F. (1984). Endocrinology of human parturition: A review. *British Journal of Obstetrics and Gynaecology, 91*(10), 948–967. Abstract retrieved from MEDLINE database.

Fuchs, A. R., Goeschen, K., Husslein, P., Rasmussen, A. B., & Fuchs, F. (1983). Oxytocin and initiation of human parturition: III. Plasma concentrations of oxytocin and 13, 14-dihydro-15-keto-prostaglandin F2 alpha in spontaneous and oxytocin-induced labor at term. *American Journal of Obstetrics & Gynecology, 147*(5), 497–502. Abstract retrieved from MEDLINE database.

Fuchs, A. R., Romero, R., Keefe, D., Parra, M., Oyarzun, E., & Behnke, E. (1991). Oxytocin secretion and human parturition: Pulse frequency and duration increase during spontaneous labor in women. *American Journal of Obstetrics & Gynecology, 165*(5, Pt. 1), 1515–1523.

Gale, S., Ozonoff, S., & Lainhart, J. (2003). Brief report: Pitocin induction in autistic and nonautistic individuals. *Journal of Autism and Developmental Disorders, 33*(2), 205–208.

Gawande, A. (2006, October 9). The score: How childbirth went industrial. *The New Yorker.* Retrieved October 15, 2006, from http://www.newyorker.com/archive/ 2006/10/09/061009fa_fact

Gimpl, G., & Fahrenholz, F. (2001). The oxytocin receptor system: Structure, function, and regulation. *Physiological Reviews, 81*(2), 629–683.

Glantz, J. C. (2003). Labor induction rate variation in upstate New York: What is the difference? *Birth, 30*(3), 168–174.

Glasson, E. J., Bower, C., Petterson, B., de Klerk, N., Chaney, G., & Hallmayer, J. F. (2004). Perinatal factors and the development of autism: A population study. *Archives of General Psychiatry, 61*(6), 618–627.

Goer, H. (1995). *Obstetric myths versus research realities: A guide to the medical literature.* Westport, CT: Bergin & Garvey.

Goer, H. (1999). *The thinking woman's guide to a better birth.* New York: Berkley.

Goeschen, K. (1989). Premature rupture of membranes near term: Induction of labor with endocervical prostaglandin E2 gel or intravenous oxytocin. *American Journal of Perinatology, 6*(2), 181-184.

Graham, E. M., Petersen, S. M., Christo, D. K., & Fox, H. E. (2006). Intrapartum electronic fetal heart rate monitoring and the prevention of perinatal brain injury. *Obstetrics and Gynecology, 108*(3, Pt. 1), 656–666. Abstract retrieved from MEDLINE database.

Green, L., Fein, D., Modahl, C., Feinstein, C., Waterhouse, L., & Morris, M. (2001). Oxytocin and autistic disorder: Alterations in peptide forms. *Biological Psychiatry, 50*(8), 609–613.

Gülmezoglu, A. M., Crowther, C. A., & Middleton, P. (2006). Induction of labour for improving birth outcomes for women at or beyond term. *Cochrane Database of Systematic Reviews, 4*(CD004945). Retrieved September 7, 2007, from http://www.cochrane.org/reviews/en/ab004945.html

Gutkowska, J., Jankowski, M., Mukaddam-Daher, S., & McCann, S. M. (2000). Oxytocin is a cardiovascular hormone. *Brazilian Journal of Medical and Biological Research, 33*(6), 625–633.

Haire, D. (1972). The cultural warping of childbirth. *International Childbirth Education Association News, 11*(1), 5–35.

Hamilton, B. E., Martin, J. A., & Ventura, S. J. (2007). Births: Preliminary data for 2006. *National Vital Statistics Reports, 56*(7), 1–18. Retrieved January 26, 2008, from http://www.cdc.gov/nchs/data/nvsr/nvsr56/nvsr56_07.pdf

Hannah, M. E., Hannah, W. J., Hellmann, J., Hewson, S., Milner, R., & Willan, A. (1992). Induction of labor as compared with serial antenatal monitoring in post-term pregnancy: A randomized controlled trial. *New England Journal of Medicine, 326*(24), 1587–1592.

Heilman, K. J., Bal, E., Bazhenova, O. V., & Porges, S. W. (2007). Respiratory sinus arrhythmia and tympanic membrane compliance predict spontaneous eye gaze behaviors in young children: A pilot study. *Developmental Psychobiology, 49*(5), 531–542.

Hollander, E. (1996). *Studies in oxytocin.* New York: Seaver Autism Research Center.

Hollander, E., Bartz, J., Chaplin, W., Phillips, A., Sumner, J., Soorya, L., et al. (2007). Oxytocin increases retention of social cognition in autism. *Biological Psychiatry, 61*(4), 498–503.

Hollander, E., Novotny, S., Hanratty, M., Yaffe, R., DeCaria, C. M., Aronowitz, B. R., et al. (2003). Oxytocin infusion reduces repetitive behaviors in adults with autistic and Asperger's disorders. *Neuropsychopharmacology, 28*(1), 193–198.

Holsti, O. R. (1969). *Content analysis for the social sciences and humanities.* Reading, MA: Addison Wesley.

Hosley, C. A., & Montemayor, R. (1997). Fathers and adolescents. In M. E. Lamb (Ed.), *The role of the father in child development* (pp. 162–178). New York: Wiley.

Insel, T. R. (2003). Is social attachment an addictive disorder? *Physiology and Behavior, 79*(3), 351–357.

Jacob, S., Brune, C. W., Carter, C. S., Leventhal, B. L., Lord, C., & Cook, E. H. (2007). Association of the oxytocin receptor gene (OXTR) in Caucasian children and adolescents with autism. *Neuroscience Letters, 417*(1), 6–9.

Jacobson, B., & Bygdeman, M. (1998). Obstetric care and proneness of offspring to suicide as adults: Case-control study. *British Medical Journal, 317*(7169), 1346–1349.

Jacobson, B., & Bygdeman, M. (1999). Authors defend methods used in their paper [Letter to the editor]. *British Medical Journal, 318*(7185), 737.

Jacobson, B., Eklund, G., Hamberger, L., Linnarsson, D., Sedvall, G., & Valverius, M. (1987). Perinatal origin of adult self-destructive behavior. *Acta Psychiatrica Scandinavica, 76*(4), 364–371.

Jacobson, B., Nyberg, K., Eklund, G., Bygdeman, M., & Rydberg, U. (1988). Obstetric pain medication and eventual adult amphetamine addiction in offspring. *Acta Obstetricia et Gynecologica Scandinavica, 67*(8), 677–682.

Jacobson, B., Nyberg, K., Gronbladh, L., Eklund, G., Bygdeman, M., & Rydberg, U. (1990). Opiate addiction in adult offspring through possible imprinting after obstetric treatment. *British Medical Journal, 301*(6760), 1067–1070.

Johnson, J. D., Aldrich, M., Angelus, P., Stevenson, D. K., Smith, D. W., Herschel, M. J., et al. (1984). Oxytocin and neonatal hyperbilirubinemia: Studies of bilirubin production. *American Journal of Diseases of Children, 138*(11), 1047–1050. Abstract retrieved from MEDLINE database.

Johnson, R. A., & Wichern, D. W. (2002). *Applied multivariate statistical analysis* (5th ed.). Upper Saddle River, NJ: Prentice Hall.

Jonas, W., Wiklund, I., Nissen, E., Ransjö-Arvidson, A. B., & Uvnäs-Moberg, K. (2007). Newborn skin temperature two days postpartum during breastfeeding related to different labor ward practices. *Early Human Development, 83*(1), 55–62.

Keettel, W. C., Randall, J. H., & Donnelly, M. M. (1958). The hazards of elective induction of labor. *American Journal of Obstetrics and Gynecology, 75*(3), 496–505.

Kimura, T., Takemura, M., Nomura, S., Nobunaga, T., Kubota, Y., Inoue, T., et al. (1996). Expression of oxytocin receptor in human pregnant myometrium. *Endocrinology, 137*(2), 780–785.

Kinsella, S. M., Pirlet, M., Mills, M. S., Tuckey, J. P., & Thomas, T. A. (2000). Randomized study of intravenous fluid preload before epidural analgesia during labour. *British Journal of Anaesthesia, 85*(2), 311–313. Retrieved December 9, 2007, from http://bja.oxfordjournals.org/cgi/content/full/85/2/311

Kirsch, J. K. (1997). A study of the relationship between perinatal risk factors and temperament in children. *Dissertation Abstractions International: Section B. The Sciences and Engineering, 58*(4B), 2173.

Kirsch, P., Esslinger, C., Chen, Q., Mier, D., Lis, S., Siddhanti, S., et al. (2005). Oxytocin modulates neural circuitry for social cognition and fear in humans. *Journal of Neuroscience, 25*(49), 11489–11493.

Kitzinger, S. (1975). *Some mothers' experiences of induced labour.* London: National Childbirth Trust.

Kitzinger, S. (2006). *Birth crisis.* New York: Routledge.

Kitzinger, S., Green, J., Chalmers, B., Keirse, M., Lindstrom, K., & Hemminki, E. (2006). Why do women go along with this stuff? *Birth, 33*(2), 154–158.

Klein, M. C. (2004). Quick fix culture: The cesarean-section-on-demand debate [Guest Editorial]. *Birth, 31*(3), 161–164.

Klein, M. C., Enkin, M. W., Kotaska, A., & Shields, S. G. (2007). The patient-centered (r)evolution. *Birth, 34*(3), 264–266.

Klein, M. C., Sakala, C., Simkin, P., Davis-Floyd, R., Rooks, J. P., & Pincus, J. (2006). Why do women go along with this stuff? *Birth, 33*(3), 245–250.

Kosfeld, M., Heinrichs, M., Zak, P. J., Fischbacher, U., & Fehr, E. (2005). Oxytocin increases trust in humans. *Nature, 435*(7042), 673–676.

Krippendorf, K. (2004). *Content analysis: An introduction to its methodology* (2nd ed.). Thousand Oaks, CA: Sage.

Kumaresan, P., Han, G. S., Anandarangam, P. B., & Vasicka, A. (1975). Oxytocin in maternal and fetal blood. *Obstetrics and Gynecology, 46*(3), 272–274. Abstract retrieved from MEDLINE database.

Kutner, M. H., Nachtsheim, C. J., & Neter, J. (2004). *Applied linear regression models* (4th ed.). New York: McGraw-Hill Irwin.

Leboyer, F. (1975). *Birth without violence.* New York: Knopf.

Lieberman, E., & O'Donoghue, C. (2002). Unintended effects of epidural analgesia during labor: A systematic review. *American Journal of Obstetrics and Gynecology, 186*(Suppl. 5), S31–S68. Abstract retrieved from MEDLINE database.

Lilienfeld, A. M., Pasamanick, B., & Rogers, M. (1955, May). Relationship between pregnancy experience and the development of certain neuropsychiatric disorders in childhood. *American Journal of Public Health and the Nation's Health, 45*(5, Pt. 1), 637–643.

Lippert, T. H., Mueck, A. O., Seeger, H., & Pfaff, A. (2003). Effects of oxytocin outside pregnancy. *Hormone Research, 60*(6), 262–271.

Lyerly, A. D., Mitchell, L. M., Harris, L. H., Kukla, R., Kupperman, M., & Little, M. O. (2007). Risks, values, and decision making surrounding pregnancy. *Obstetrics and Gynecology, 109*(4), 979–984.

Martin, J. A., Hamilton, B. E., Sutton, P. D., Ventura, S. J., Menacker, F., Kirmeyer, S., et al. (2007). Births: Final data for 2005. *National Vital Statistics Reports, 56*(6), 1–104.

Matsuzawa, J., Matsui, M., Konishi, T., Noguchi, K., Gur, R. C., Bilker, W., et al. (2001). Age-related volumetric changes of brain gray and white matter in healthy infants and children. *Cerebral Cortex, 11*(4), 335–342.

McBride, W. G., Lyle, J. G., Black, B., Brown, C., & Thomas, D. B. (1977). A study of five year old children born after elective induction of labor. *Medical Journal of Australia, 2*(14), 456–459.

McCarty, W. A. (2002a). Keys to healing and preventing foundational trauma: What babies are teaching us. *Bridges, 13*(4), 8–12.

McCarty, W. A. (2002b). The power of beliefs: What babies are teaching us. *Journal of Prenatal and Perinatal Psychology and Health, 16*(4), 341–360.

McCraty, R., Atkinson, A., & Tomasino, D. (2001). *Science of the heart: Exploring the role of the heart in human performance.* Boulder Creek, CA: HeartMath Research Center, Institute of HeartMath.

McKee, L., Roland, E., Coffelt, N., Olson, A., Forehand, R., Massari, C., et al. (2007, May). Harsh discipline and child problem behaviors: The roles of positive parenting and gender. *Journal of Family Violence, 22*(4), 187–196.

Menticoglou, S., & Hall, P. F. (2002). Routine induction of labor at 41 weeks gestation: Nonsensus consensus. *British Journal of Obstetrics and Gynaecology, 109*(5), 485–491.

Milsom, I., Ladfors, L., Thiringer, K., Niklasson, A., Odeback, A., & Thornberg, E. (2002). Influence of maternal, obstetric and fetal risk factors on the prevalence of birth asphyxia at term in a Swedish urban population. *Acta Obstetricia et Gynecologica Scandinavica, 81*(10), 909–917.

Mittendorf, R., Williams, M. A., Berkey, C. S., & Cotter, P. F. (1990). The length of uncomplicated human gestation. *Obstetrics and Gynecology, 75*(6), 929–932.

Modahl, C., Green, L., Fein, D., Morris, M., Waterhouse, L., Feinstein, C., et al. (1998). Plasma oxytocin levels in autistic children. *Biological Psychiatry, 43*(4), 270–277.

Monarch Pharmaceuticals. (2004). *Pitocin: Prescribing information.* Bristol, TN: Author.

Murphy-Lawless, J. (1998). *Reading birth and death: A history of obstetric thinking.* Bloomington, IN: Indiana University Press.

Myers, E. R., Blumrick, R., Christian, A. L., Datta, S., Gray, R. N., Kolimaga, J. T., et al. (2002, March). Management of prolonged pregnancy: Summary. *Evidence Report/Technology Assessment, 53* (AHRQ Publication No. 02-E012). Rockville, MD: Agency for Healthcare Research and Quality.

Nagata, I., Kato, K., Makimura, N., Uesato, T., Seki, K., & Kikuchi, Y. (1983). Comparison of plasma oxytocin levels during spontaneous labor and labor induced by amniotomy, prostaglandin F2 alpha, and prostaglandin E2. *American Journal of Obstetrics and Gynecology, 147*(3), 259–267.

Neugebauer, R., & Reuss, M. L. (1998). Association of maternal, antenatal and perinatal complications with suicide in adolescence and young adulthood. *Acta Psychiatrica Scandinavica, 97*(6), 412–418.

NICHD Early Child Care Research Network. (2004). Affect dysregulation in the mother-child relationship in the toddler years: Antecedents and consequences. *Development and Psychopathology, 16*(1), 43–68.

Nissen, E., Lilja, G., Widstrom, A. M., & Uvnäs-Moberg, K. (1995). Elevation of oxytocin levels early post partum in women. *Acta Obstetricia et Gynecologica Scandinavica, 74*(7), 530–533.

Niswander, K. R., & Patterson, R. J. (1963, August). Hazards of elective induction of labor. *Obstetrics and Gynecology, 22*(2), 228–233.

Niswander, K. R., Patterson, R. J., & Randall, C. L. (1960, April). Elective induction of labor. *American Journal of Obstetrics and Gynecology, 79*(4), 797–800.

Niswander, K. R., Turoff, B. B., & Romans, J. (1966). Developmental status of children delivered through elective induction of labor: Results of a 4-year follow-up study. *Obstetrics and Gynecology, 27*(1), 15–20.

Nyberg, K. (2000). Long-term effects of labor analgesia [Letter to the editor]. *Journal of Obstetric, Gynecologic, & Neonatal Nursing, 29*(3), 226.

Nyberg, K., Allebeck, P., Eklund, G., & Jacobson, B. (1992). Socio-economic versus obstetric risk factors for drug addiction in offspring. *British Journal of Addiction, 87*(12), 1669–1676.

Nyberg, K., Allebeck, P., Eklund, G., & Jacobson, B. (1993). Obstetric medication versus residential area as perinatal risk factors for subsequent adult drug addiction in offspring. *Paediatric and Perinatal Epidemiology, 7*(1), 23–32.

Nyberg, K., Buka, S. L., & Lipsitt, L. P. (2000). Perinatal medication as a potential risk factor for adult drug abuse in a North American cohort. *Epidemiology, 11*(6), 715–716.

O'Driscoll, K., Jackson, R. J., & Gallagher, J. T. (1969). Prevention of prolonged labour. *British Medical Journal, 2*(5655), 477–480.

O'Dwyer, J. (1997). Schizophrenia in people with intellectual disability: The role of pregnancy and birth complications. *Journal of Intellectual Disability Research, 41*(3), 238–251. Abstract retrieved from MEDLINE database.

Odent, M. (1999). *The scientification of love.* London: Free Association.

Odent, M. (2001). *Is breast best? Beyond the immediate impassioned responses.* London: Primal Health Research Center.

Odent, M. (2002). *The farmer and the obstetrician.* London: Free Association.

O'Herlihy, C. (1993). Active management: A continuing benefit in nulliparous labor. *Birth, 20*(2), 95-97.

Ounsted, M. K., Hendrick, A. M., Mutch, L. M. M., Calder, A. A., & Good, F. J. (1978). Induction of labour by different methods in primiparous women: I. Some perinatal and postnatal problems. *Early Human Development, 2*(3), 227–239. Abstract retrieved from MEDLINE database.

Out, J. J., Vierhout, M. E., Verhage, F., Duivenvoorden, H. J., & Wallenburg, H. C. (1985). Elective induction of labor: A prospective clinical study: II. Psychological effects. *Journal of Perinatal Medicine, 13*(4), 163–170.

Out, J. J., Vierhout, M. E., Verhage, F., Duivenvoorden, H. J., & Wallenburg, H. C. (1986). Characteristics and motives of women choosing elective induction of labour. *Journal of Psychosomatic Research, 30*(3), 375–380. Abstract retrieved from MEDLINE database.

Palmer, S. R., Avery, A., & Taylor, R. (1979). The influence of obstetric procedures and social and cultural factors on breast-feeding rates at discharge from hospital. *Journal of Epidemiology and Community Health, 33*(4), 248–252.

Panthuraamphorn, C. (1994). How to maximize human potential at birth. *Journal of Prenatal and Perinatal Psychology and Health, 9*(2), 117–126.

Pates, J. A., & Satin, A. J. (2005). Active management of labor. *Obstetrics and Gynecology Clinics of North America, 32*(2), 221–230.

Patton, M. Q. (2002). *Qualitative research and evaluation methods* (3rd ed.). Thousand Oaks, CA: Sage.

Phaneuf, S., Asbóth, G., Carrasco, M. P., Liñares, B. R., Kimura, T., Harris, A., et al. (1998). Desensitization of oxytocin receptors in human myometrium. *Human Reproduction Update, 4*(5), 625–633.

Phaneuf, S., Rodríguez Liñares, B., TambyRaja, R. L., Mackenzie, I. Z., & López Bernal, A. (2000). Loss of myometrial oxytocin receptors during oxytocin-induced and oxytocin-augmented labour. *Journal of Reproduction and Fertility, 120*(1), 91–97.

Phares, V. (1996). *Fathers and developmental psychopathology.* New York: Wiley.

Porges, S. W. (1995). Orienting in a defensive world: Mammalian modifications of our evolutionary heritage. A polyvagal theory. *Psychophysiology, 32*(4), 301–318.

Porges, S. W. (2001). The polyvagal theory: Phylogenetic substrates of a social nervous system. *International Journal of Psychophysiology, 42*(2), 123–146.

Porges, S. W. (2003). Social engagement and attachment: A phylogenetic perspective. *Annals of the New York Academy of Sciences, 1008*(1), 31–47.

Porges, S. W. (2004). Neuroception: A subconscious system for detecting threats and safety. *Zero to Three, 24*(5), 19–24.

Porges, S. W. (2007). The polyvagal perspective. *Biological Psychology, 74*(2), 116–143.

Prechtl, H. F. R. (1977). *The neurological examination of the full-term newborn infant: A manual for clinical use from the Department of Developmental Neurology* (2nd ed.). Cambridge, MA: Cambridge University Press.

Raine, A., Brennan, P., & Mednick, S. A. (1994). Birth complications combined with early maternal rejection at age 1 year predispose to violent crime at age 18 years. *Archives of General Psychiatry, 51*(12), 984–988.

Raine, A., Brennan, P., & Mednick, S. A. (1997). Interactions between birth complications and early maternal rejection in predisposing individuals to adult violence: Specificity to early-onset violence. *American Journal of Psychiatry, 154*(9), 1265–1271.

Ramsey, P. S., Ramin, K. D., & Ramin, S. M. (2000). Labor induction. *Current Opinion in Obstetrics & Gynecology, 12*(6), 463–473.

Rank, O. (1929). *The trauma of birth.* New York: Harcourt Brace.

Ray, S., & Mandel, B. (1987). *Birth and relationships.* Berkeley, CA: Celestial Arts.

Rayburn, W. F., & Zhang, J. (2002). Rising rates of labor induction: Present concerns and future strategies. *Obstetrics and Gynecology, 100*(1), 164–167.

Rhoades, D. A., Latza, U., & Mueller, B.A. (1999). Risk factors and outcomes associated with nuchal cord: A population-based study. *Journal of Reproductive Medicine, 44*(1), 39–45. Abstract retrieved from MEDLINE database.

Rojansky, N., Reubinoff, B., Tanos, V., Shushan, A., & Weinstein, D. (1997). High risk pregnancy outcome following induction of labour. *European Journal of Obstetrics, Gynecology, and Reproductive Biology, 72*(2), 153-158.

Rowe-Murray, H. J., & Fisher, J. R. W. (2001). Operative intervention in delivery is associated with compromised early mother-infant interaction. *British Journal of Obstetrics and Gynaeacology, 108*(10), 1068–1075.

Russell, J. A., Douglas, A. J., & Ingram, C. D. (2001). Brain preparations for maternity: Adaptive changes in behavioral and neuroendocrine systems during pregnancy and lactation. An overview. *Progress in Brain Research, 133*(2), 1–38.

Russell, J. A., Leng, G., & Douglas, A. J. (2003). The magnocellular oxytocin system, the fount of maternity: Adaptations in pregnancy. *Frontiers in Neuroendocrinology, 24*(1), 27–61.

Rutter, M., Tizard, J., & Whitmore, K. (Eds.). (1970). *Education, health and behaviour.* London: Longmans.

Sakala, C. (2006). Carol Sakala's letter from North America: An uncontrolled experiment: Elective delivery predominates in the United States. *Birth, 33*(4), 332–335.

Salk, L., Lipsitt, L., Sturner, W., Reilly, B., & Levat, R. (1985). Relationship of maternal and perinatal conditions to eventual adolescent suicide. *Lancet, 1*(8429), 624–627.

Save the Children. (2006). *State of the world's mothers 2006: Saving the lives of mothers and newborns.* Retrieved December 3, 2006, from www.savethechildren.org/ publications/mothers/2006/SOWM_2006_final.pdf

Schore, A. N. (2005). Back to basics: Attachment, affect regulation, and the developing right brain: Linking developmental neuroscience to pediatrics. *Pediatrics in Review, 26*(6), 204–217.

Simpson, K. R., & Atterbury, J. (2003). Trends and issues in labor induction in the United States: Implications for clinical practice. *Journal of Obstetric, Gynecologic, and Neonatal Nursing, 32*(6), 767–779.

Singhi, S., & Singh, M. (1979). Pathogenesis of oxytocin-induced neonatal hyperbilirubinaemia. *Archives of Disease in Childhood, 54*(5), 400–402. Abstract retrieved from MEDLINE database.

Smith, L. J. (2007). Impact of birthing practices on the breastfeeding dyad. *Journal of Midwifery and Women's Health, 52*(6), 621–630.

Sorensen, H. T., Rothman, K. J., Gillman, M. W., Steffensen, F. H., Fischer, P., & Sabroe, S. (1999). Historical cohort study of in utero exposure to uterotonic drugs and cognitive function in young adult life. *British Medical Journal, 318*(7181), 433–434.

Takeda, S., Kuwabara, Y., & Mizuno, M. (1985). Effects of pregnancy and labor on oxytocin levels in human plasma and cerebrospinal fluid. *Endocrinologia Japonica, 32*(6), 875–880.

Tamis-LeMonda, C., Shannon, J., Cabrera, N., & Lamb, M. (2004, November). Fathers and mothers at play with their 2- and 3-year-olds: Contributions to language and cognitive development. *Child Development, 75*(6), 1806–1820.

Thompson, R. A. (1994). Emotion regulation: A theme in search of a definition. *Monographs for the Society of Research in Child Development, 59*(2/3), 25–52.

Torvaldsen, S., Roberts, C. L., Simpson, J. M., Thompson, J. F., & Elwood, D.A. (2006). Intrapartum epidural analgesia and breastfeeding: A prospective cohort study. *International Breastfeeding Journal, 1,* 24–26. Retrieved from http://www.internationalbreastfeedingjournal.com/content/1/1/24

U.S. Department of Health and Human Services, Health Resources and Services Administration, Maternal and Child Health Bureau. (2004). *Child health USA 2007.* Rockville, MD: Author.

Uvnäs-Moberg, K. (2003). *The oxytocin factor.* Cambridge, MA: Da Capo Press.

Verny, T. R., & Weintraub, P. (2002). *Tomorrow's baby: The art and science of parenting from conception through infancy.* New York: Simon & Schuster.

Vierhout, M. E., Out, J. J., & Wallenburg, H. C. S. (1985). Elective induction of labor: A prospective clinical study: I. Obstetric and neonatal effects. *Journal of Perinatal Medicine, 13*(2), 155–162.

Volmanen, P., Valanne, J., & Alahuhta, S. (2004). Breast-feeding problems after epidural analgesia for labour: A retrospective cohort study of pain, obstetrical procedures and breast-feeding practices. *International Journal of Obstetric Anesthesia, 13*(1), 25–29.

Wagner, M. (1994). *Pursuing the birth machine: The search for appropriate birth technology.* Campertown, Australia: Ace Graphics.

Wagner, M. (2001). Fish can't see water: The need to humanize birth. *International Journal of Gynaecology and Obstetrics, 75*(Suppl. 1), S25–S37. Retrieved November 23, 2006, from http://www.acegraphics.com.au/articles/wagner03.html

Wagner, M. (2006). *Born in the USA: How a broken maternity system must be fixed to put women and children first.* Los Angeles: University of California Press.

Wahl, R. U. (2004). Could oxytocin administration during labor contribute to autism and related behavioral disorders? A look at the literature. *Medical Hypotheses, 63*(3), 456–460.

Withuhn, T. F., Kramer, K. M., & Cushing, B. S. (2003). Early exposure to oxytocin affects the age of vaginal opening and first estrus in female rats. *Physiology and Behavior, 80*(1), 135–138. Abstract retrieved from MEDLINE database.

World Health Organization. (1985). Appropriate technology for birth. *Lancet, 2*(8452), 436–437.

World Health Organization. (2005). *The world health report: 2005: Make every mother and child count.* Geneva, Switzerland: Author. Retrieved December 30, 2006, from http://www.who.int/whr/2005/en/

Wu, S., Jia, M., Ruan, Y., Liu, J., Guo, Y., Shuang, M., et al. (2005). Positive association of the oxytocin receptor gene (OXTR) with autism in the Chinese Han population. *Biological Psychiatry, 58*(1), 74–77.

Zappitelli, M., Pinto, T., & Grizenko, N. (2001). Pre-, peri-, and postnatal trauma in subjects with attention-deficit hyperactivity disorder. *Canadian Journal of Psychiatry, 46*(6), 542–548.

Zeanah, C. H., Jr. (Ed.). (2000). *Handbook of infant mental health* (2nd ed.). New York: Guilford.

Zhang, J., Yancey, M. K., & Henderson, C. E. (2002). U.S. national trends in labor induction, 1989–1998. *Journal of Reproductive Medicine, 47*(2), 120–124. Abstract retrieved from MEDLINE database.

Zuppa, A. A., Vignetti, M., Romagnoli, C., & Tortorolo, G. (1984). Assistance procedures in the perinatal period that condition breast feeding at the time of discharge from the hospital. *Pediatria Medica E Chirurgica, 6*, 367–372. Abstract retrieved from MEDLINE database.

www.ingramcontent.com/pod-product-compliance
Lightning Source LLC
Chambersburg PA
CBHW081146280526
45787CB00008B/3242